# METROPOLITAN RAILWAY
# ROLLING STOCK

*A Met goods train, hauled by an F class 0–6–2, probably c.1915-1920, and including a Met cattle wagon.*     L&GRP

*A view of Neasden Works from the south end, with, in the fore-ground, a pair of Single Bolster (i.e. Rail/Timber) wagons newly repainted into LPTB livery.*

# METROPOLITAN RAILWAY ROLLING STOCK

by JAMES R. SNOWDON

*Another panoramic view of Neasden Works from the south end, taken in the mid-1930s and showing, from the left, the works, with a large number of Metropolitan goods wagons outside, the saw mills and wood store and, centre to right, behind the car shed, a Bogie stock trailer set.*

A. CRUIKSHANK COLLECTION

# INTRODUCTION

ON 1st July 1933 the Metropolitan Railway ceased to exist as a separate railway company and all its property and operations became absorbed into the newly formed London Passenger Transport Board. London Transport, as the Board quickly became known, was formed to operate the capital's bus, tram and underground railway services as a publicly owned service rather than relying on the former owning companies to provide a service.

For most of the underground railways, there was little change. They were all, apart from the Metropolitan, already under the same management and there was a high degree of standardisation in equipment, operation and livery. Only the Metropolitan was the odd man out. It was about to undergo a culture shock. It was about to be dragged, kicking and screaming into the twentieth century. More of this later.

The Metropolitan Railway had its roots firmly in the 19th century. It began operations in January 1863, using locomotives and carriages provided by the Great Western Railway as part of the joint arrangements under which the railway's construction had been financed. As we shall see, relations between the two companies soon soured, leading to the Great Western's abrupt withdrawal from the operation. The Metropolitan, although managing to borrow other stock to tide things over, was forced to acquire its own rolling stock. Unlike many other railways of its size, the Metropolitan took a very active part in the design, and, at times, construction of its own rolling stock. Its engineers were strong supporters of standardisation, as a result of which there is, in all of its

own rolling stock, a very strong sense of continuity over the seventy years of the railway's independent existence.

In many ways, the Metropolitan was the odd man out amongst London's urban railways in that it served a territory far more diverse than that of its long-time rival, the Metropolitan District Railway, or of the later underground railways, all of which would, in modern terms, have been classed as rapid transit systems, carrying solely passenger traffic. The Met, as it is often known, although its roots lay in urban London, soon grew into a miniature main-line railway, serving a sizeable area of countryside to the north-west of London, extending out into the depths of Buckinghamshire. As a result, it developed not only passenger services, both suburban and long-distance, but also a thriving goods traffic, for which it developed a wide range of wagons.

The study which follows charts the development of the Metropolitan's rolling stock from its beginnings as a truly independent railway in 1863, through to its absorption into the London Passenger Transport Board in 1933, when, swamped by the interests of the Underground group, its independent character was effectively stifled. It was not long before its non-passenger interests were handed over, along with much of the freight stock and the locomotive fleet, to the control of the London & North Eastern Railway, with whom, as successors to the Great Central Railway, the Metropolitan co-existed.

*Neasden carriage shed in the mid-1930s, with the bogie tool van in fresh LPTB livery sharing space with Dreadnought stock still in full Metropolitan livery.*

1

*The outer reaches of the Metropolitan at the turn of the century, with Neasden-built E class 0—4—4T hauling a typical 5½-coach set of 8-wheel stock, the '½' being an ex-Twin Stock carriage. Coupled inside the set, the second vehicle, was one of the milk vans rebuilt from another Twin Stock carriage.*

# CHAPTER ONE
# THE EARLY CARRIAGES

WHEN the Metropolitan Railway first opened for service in 1863, the following stock and locomotives were provided by the Great Western Railway under the joint arrangements by which the railway had been funded. Although they were, like the Metropolitan's original line between Paddington and Farringdon, built to the GWR's broad gauge standards, they were, even for the GW, something of a novelty in a time when four- and six-wheeled stock was normal; they were massive carriages some 38 feet long, running on eight wheels, Doubtless as a result of their size, they have become commonly known as the 'Long Charlies'. A particular feature of their construction was the underframe, in that the four axles were not mounted in bogies but held by hornguides directly from the frame. The flexibility required to negotiate curves was obtained by allowing the axleboxes to move laterally in the hornguides. Lateral control was effected by connecting the springs to the underframe with long pendulum links.

Unfortunately, the relations between the two companies soon turned sour, with the result that the Great Western withdrew its stock in August 1863. The Metropolitan had been aware that all was not well from at least March and had ordered locomotives from Beyer Peacock (the famous 4-4-0 'Met. Tanks') and carriages from the Ashbury Carriage and Iron Company. The carriages, 34 in number, were delivered by 1st October 1863 and replaced a selection which had been borrowed from the Great Northern and London & North Western Railways to keep things going in the interim.

It would seem that the GW carriages had been reasonably satisfactory in their design for the Metropolitan carriages bore a strong resemblance to them. Not surprisingly, the Metropolitan's were built to the narrow (standard) gauge dimensions. There have been suggestions that these carriages were simply narrow gauge copies of the GW vehicles; indeed, Robert H. Burnett, who became the Metropolitan's Locomotive Superintendent in 1864, said as much in 1895 when writing articles for *The Engineer* in celebration of the railway's Diamond Jubilee. Nonetheless, whilst there was a strong resemblance between the two, there were fundamental differences in the length and the compartment dimensions, of which there were only two sizes instead of the Great Western's three.

The carriages, all 39ft 6in long and 8ft 3in wide, were built in three basic types with either six 1st class, eight 2nd/3rd class or three 1st and four 2nd/3rd class compartments. The compartment dimensions were such that three 1st class took up the same length as four 3rd class. As built, handbrakes, of Newall's pattern, were provided on all of the 2nd class and some of the 3rd class carriages, with the guard being accommodated in the end compartment. No separate luggage compartment was provided, although, to compensate for this, the guard's compartment was provided with a double door to assist in the loading of bulky items. To do this the quarterlight panel immediately to the right of the door proper was arranged to hinge.

The first class compartments with accommodation for eight passengers on well-upholstered seats covered in blue carriage cloth, fixed armrests, curtained windows and a carpeted floor, were luxurious. By comparison, the lower classes were accommodated in compartments provided only with hard bench seats; third class had to suffer bare woodwork, whilst those in second class were given the dubious comfort of a thin seat squab covered in green American cloth and a matching shoulder pad.

The underframes for these carriages, like those of their broad gauge predecessors, were constructed from angle-iron sections, with horn plates to restrain the axles longitudinally. Unusually, the frame was some 12in shorter over the headstock faces than the body, largely as a result of the headstock angles being fitted flange outwards. This arrangement facilitated a degree of close coupling using normal length side buffers and screw shackles. Side chains were provided as usual to guard against the effects of breakage of the screw coupling. The wheels, which were of 3ft 6in or 7¼in nominal diameter, were initially set at 5ft 9in–16ft 0in–5ft 9in centres, the outer distances being changed on later batches to 6ft 0in. The axleboxes were not provided with the usual slots for the horn guides but were flat-sided; instead, angle-iron horn blocks were provided so that the boxes were free to move laterally but were restrained in the fore and aft direction, thus allowing the wheelbase to adapt to negotiate curves. Because of the lateral movements, only the inner axles were provided with brake blocks, irrespective of the type of brake fitted.

Between 1863 and 1868, 142 of these 8-wheel 'rigid' carriages were delivered to the Metropolitan Railway as follows:

| Year | Builder | Numbers | Class | Total |
|------|---------|---------|-------|-------|
| 1863 | Ashbury | 1–34 | various | 34 |
| 1864 | Oldbury | 35–40 | 1st | 6 |
| 1865 | Oldbury | 41–60 | various | 20 |
| 1866 | Oldbury | 61–72 | various | 12 |
| 1866 | Oldbury | 73–82 | 3rd | 10 |
| | | 83–86 | 2nd | 4 |
| | | 87–90 | 1st | 4 |
| | | 91–92 | 1st/2nd | 2 |
| 1868 | Ashbury | 93–142 | various | 50 |
| | | | | 142 |

Robert Burnett, when he succeeded to the position of Locomotive Superintendent in 1864, was clearly not overly satisfied with the suspension arrangements on the early batches, so on the last twenty ordered in 1866 from Oldbury (Nos. 73–92), radial axleboxes were fitted to the outer axles, doubtless to alleviate the effects of flange grinding which must have afflicted the previous arrangement.

Unfortunately, the radial axleboxes proved to be too expensive and unreliable, in that they tended to bind, with the result that, for the 1868 Ashbury batch, a revised design was used. The outer axles were carried in a form of pony

# METROPOLITAN RAILWAY 8-WHEELED COACHES – 2nd & 3rd CLASS

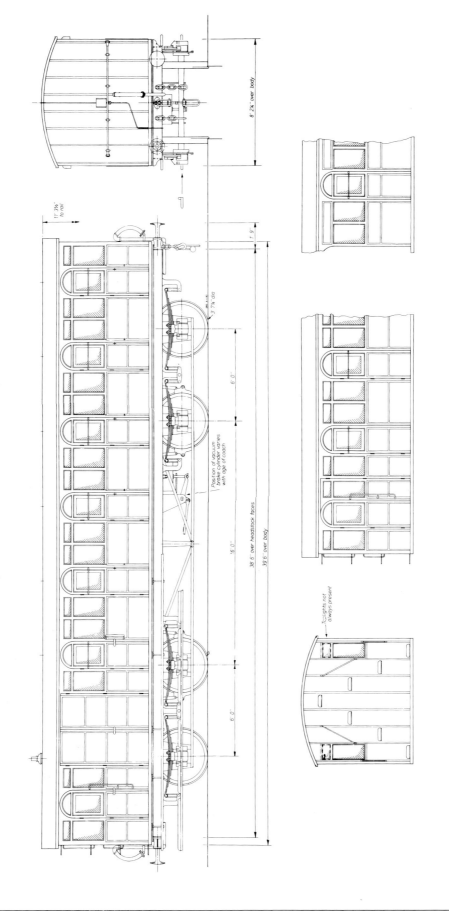

8' 2¼" over body

11' 3¾" to rail

11' 9"

3' 7¾" dia

6' 0"

16' 0"

6' 0"

38' 6" over headstock faces

39' 6" over body

Position of vacuum brake cylinder varies with age of coach

Tc_lights not always present

Main drawing - Long Brake 3rd
Subsidiary drawings - Short brake compartment (some 3rd class & all 2nd class coaches)
            - Altered panelling and glazing on coaches refurbished c.1908-9

NOTE :-
1 Due to a virtually complete lack of drawings, complete accuracy cannot be guaranteed
   in respect of the underframe
2 Lighting - originally low-pressure gas using collapsible roof-mounted reservoirs
   Subsequently high pressure gas with underframe mounted tanks. Some coaches
   finally equipped with electric lighting
3 For 8-compartment 3rd class coach, substitute standard compartments for guards/
   luggage accommodation

truck which swung about a pivot situated over the inner axle. From this pivot, two arms were spread, each attached to the axlebox, which, although placed between the horn plates, were not guided by them. To control the lateral movement of the axle, the bearing springs were restrained by pendulum links as before, although these were of greater length to allow the necessary lateral freedom to the axle.

This latter design, perhaps unwittingly, infringed a patent held by W. Bridges Adams who, after a great deal of acrimonious correspondence, instigated legal action against the Metropolitan Railway. The matter was eventually settled in 1871 with an out-of-court settlement of £585 in favour of Mr Adams.

By this time the Metropolitan had received further batches of carriages:

| Year | Builder | Numbers | Class | Total |
|------|---------|---------|-------|-------|
| 1869 | Oldbury? | 143–144 | 1st & 2nd | 2 |
| 1869 | Oldbury | 145–148 | 3rd | 4 |
|      |         | 149–157 | 2nd | 9 |
|      |         | 158–168 | 1st | 11 |
| 1870 | Ashbury | 169–171 | 1st | 3 |
|      |         | 172–174 | 2nd | 3 |
|      |         | 175–177 | 1st/2nd | 3 |
|      |         | 178–180 | 1st/3rd | 3 |

*'A' class No. 2 in the early 1900s with a Main Line train for Rickmansworth. The train, headed by one of the Passenger Brake Vans, was a standard 5-coach set, all 8-wheel stock except for an ex Twin Stock Third third from the rear of the train.*

A. CRUIKSHANK COLLECTION

*1884 Cravens-built Third Brake 251. As will be noted from the amount of daylight, there were no partitions between pairs of seating bays. The break in the waist panelling at the left-hand end marks the additional door provided to the guard's compartment.*

# METROPOLITAN RAILWAY 8-WHEELED COACHES

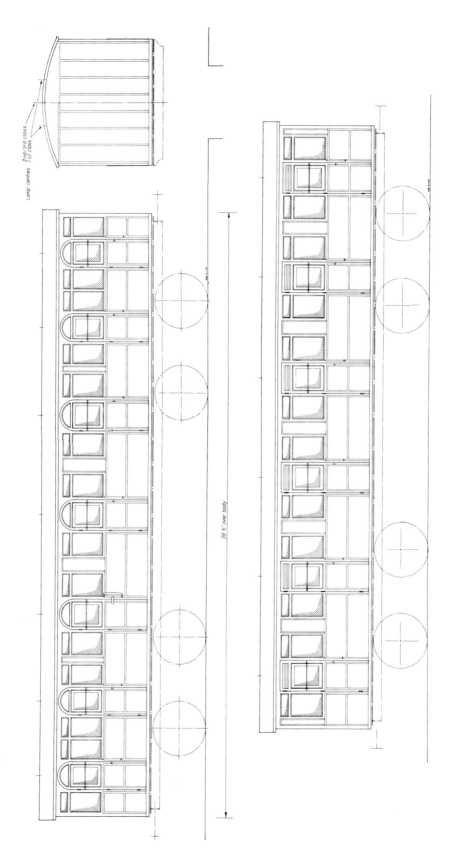

2nd/3rd class
1st class

Lamp centres

39' 6" over body

Upper drawing - 1st/2nd or 3rd class composite carriage
Lower drawing - 1st class carriage, showing square topped
doors used up to 1868 (Carriages 1-92)

For underframe and end details, refer to drawing of 3rd class
brake carriage. End view shows panelling arrangements
found on some early examples of these carriages

*1884 Brown Marshall-built Brake Third 295 at Quainton Road, serving out its last days on the Brill branch.* H. C. CASSERLEY

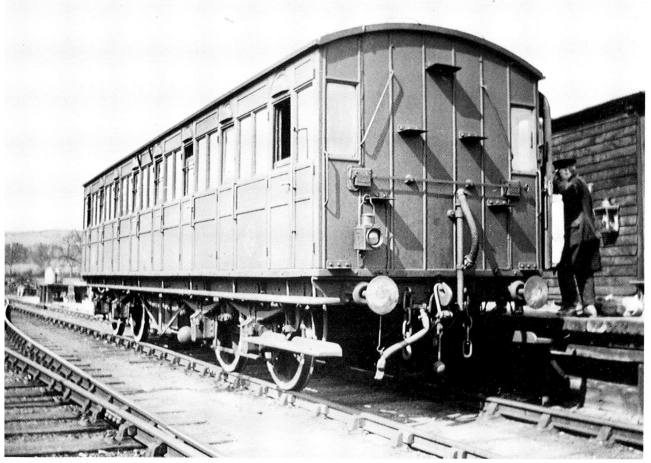

*Another 8-wheel Brake Third, at Brill, in its final form with electric lighting.*

*This view of a down Verney Jct train near Northwood in 1898, shows a C class 0–4–4 Tank, No. 68, hauling one of the Birmingham-built Milk Vans (Met Nos. 1-4), followed by standard 5-coach set, i.e. five rigid 8-wheel coaches with a single 4-wheeled ex 'Twin set' carriage as the penultimate vehicle.*                                                                     L & GRP

The twelve vehicles built by Ashbury in 1870 (Nos. 169–180) were standard 8-wheelers, presumably without the offending radial axles. The remainder were a unique batch of 4-wheeled carriages. These were numbered 143–168 and were semi-permanently coupled in pairs, earning for themselves the name 'twin carriages'.

The twin carriages and the two batches of Ashbury vehicles built 1868–70 were provided for services on the newly opened St John's Wood extension, the opening of the Circle as far as South Kensington, and the District Railway, which was opened to Blackfriars in 1870 and which was worked, until 1871, by the Metropolitan. When the District got its own rolling stock, the Metropolitan ended up with a substantial amount of spare stock. This was stabled in sidings at Moorgate, Barbican and Farringdon until it was absorbed by extensions in the mid- and late-1870s.

It is interesting to note that the memory of the first extension of the Metropolitan from the 'main' line at Baker Street to St John's Wood is still alive today. Trainmen still refer to the lines north of Baker Street as 'the Wood line', 'the Branch' or 'the Extension' in spite of London Transport's titling of the working timetable for the line 'Metropolitan Main'. In this work 'extension' has been used as the normal term.

No new rigids were built until 1879. There then followed several batches until the last in 1884:

| Year | Builder | Numbers | Class | Total |
|------|---------|---------|-------|-------|
| 1879 | Ashbury | 181–185 | 2nd | 5 |
|      |         | 186–195 | 3rd | 10 |
| 1880 | Ashbury | 196–201 | 3rd | 6 |
|      |         | 202–204 | 1st | 3 |
|      |         | 205–207 | 2nd | 3 |
|      |         | 208–210 | cpo. | 3 |
| 1881 | Ashbury | 211–216 | 3rd | 6 |
| 1883 | Brown M | 217–236 | 3rd | 20 |
|      |         | 237–238 | 2nd | 2 |
|      |         | 239–240 | 1st | 2 |
|      |         | 241 | cpo. | 1 |
| 1884 | Cravens | 242–244 | cpo. | 3 |
|      |         | 245–260 | 3rd | 16 |
| 1884 | Gloucester | 261–276 | 3rd | 16 |
| 1884 | Cravens | 277–284 | 1st | 8 |
| 1884 | Brown M | 285–301 | 2nd | 17 |
|      |         |         |      | 121 |

All of these vehicles were basically to the same design as the earlier batches. The classes as listed here are as accurate as can be determined, bearing in mind that some carriages were later converted to different types. Some of them were built as brake vehicles.

There were detail design changes over the years. The famous round-topped Metropolitan hinged door, which became a hallmark of the rolling stock, was not provided on the early 'rigids'. It first appeared on the 1868 Ashbury batch (Nos. 93–142). Until the mid-1870s, illumination was effected by means of glass enclosed gas jets set in the roof, two per compartment, set either side of the roof-mounted gas reservoir. This took the form of a collapsible rubber bag contained within a box on the roof, rather like an unglazed clerestory. These were recharged with town gas obtained via standpipes at various terminal stations. Because the gas was not compressed, each charge only lasted for some three hours, with the result that later batches of second and third class carriages were only fitted with one lamp per compartment, set on alternating sides of the gas reservoir, combined with a reduction in the height of the partitions. By 1873, consideration was actively being given to improving the lot of the passenger, with the result that early in 1873, one train on the then St John's Railway was equipped with Silber's petroleum lamps. These had also been tried on the North London Railway, where one lamp had subsequently exploded for no apparent reason. This prospect was not to the Met's liking and resulted in the abandonment of the system. Nonetheless, experimentation continued and in 1876 Julius Pintsch's high-pressure gas lamp was adopted for all stock. This burned an oil gas which could be stored in cylinders below the underframe at a pressure of 90 psi, thus allowing the roof-mounted equipment to be removed and the lamps centralised. The exact location of the gas cylinders is not known, other than that two were provided on first class carriages, set longitudinally behind the solebars under the inner compartments.

In response to the increased demands for luggage and parcels carriage, a new design of brake third appeared on the 1879–84 stock. A luggage compartment with full-width double doors was provided adjacent to that for the guard. Whether or not these two compartments were in communication with each other is not known.

For just over the first decade of the Metropolitan's existence, the only brakes available to stop the trains were those on the engine and in the several brake carriages in the train. This situation was evidently not satisfactory and, in the mid-1870s, the Metropolitan made history by being the first company to fully equip its rolling stock with the Smith vacuum brake. Despite its benefits, this brake was seriously deficient in that it was non-automatic and would not act in the event of a breakaway. Following the Armagh accident of 1889, the Smith brake was replaced by the Automatic Vacuum brake but not before the Metropolitan had been forced to do so under a Board of Trade order issued in November 1890. The work was completed in 1893. No change was made however, to the non-provision of any form of passenger alarm signal since the regulations only required the installation of such a system if there was more than 20 miles between stops. The Metropolitan was therefore exempt.

# THE 4-WHEELED CARRIAGES

Twice during the 19th century the Metropolitan tried 4-wheeled carriages. The first attempt came, as we have seen above, during Robert Burnett's tenure as Locomotive Superintendent. Although the 8-wheeled carriages were evidently adequate in service, they were obviously not entirely to the satisfaction of Mr Burnett. They were certainly considered over-heavy and, judging by the development of axleboxes and pony trucks, not too good at negotiating sharp curves. The result was that, in 1869, a 'twin carriage' appeared, supplied, it is believed, by the Railway Carriage Company. It comprised two 20ft 4-wheeled carriages coupled by means of a combined buffer and bar coupling, with an overall length of 43ft 8in over buffers. The two carriages, a 3-compartment 1st class and a 4-compartment 2nd class, were essentially half-length versions of the 8-wheelers, furnished to the same standards. Their riding at anything more than moderate speeds must have been distinctly debatable, since not only was their 11ft 0in wheelbase relatively short for their length, but their axleboxes, which appear to have been identical to those on the 8-wheelers, lacked any form of lateral restraint, other than the little provided by the influence of the spring links. This first pair must have been considered worthwhile as, in April 1869, twelve more pairs were ordered from the Oldbury Carriage Company. They comprised 11 first class, 9 second class and 4 third class vehicles. No records have survived as to how the carriages were paired or which of the second or third class vehicles were equipped with handbrakes. A set of drawings which appeared in

*Engineering* shows two of the lower class carriages coupled, one being equipped with handbrakes.

Although the first pair is said to have entered service on the Gloucester Road to West Brompton shuttle service between 1869 and 1870, the remainder seem to have dominated the St John's Wood services. Because of its comparative isolation from the 'Main Line' (the Circle), the stock on this line formed a convenient testing ground for such innovations as Clark's, and later, Smith's brakes, as well as various lighting systems.

For reasons which are now unknown, but may well be connected with their undoubtedly poor riding characteristics, the 'twins' do not seem to have been considered a complete success. No more were built, and in 1879, with the extension of the St John's Wood branch to Willesden and onwards, the thirteen sets were split up, conventional buffers and drawgear being fitted at the one-time inner ends, and dispersed to run singly in sets of 8-wheel stock, where they were coupled 'inside' the set. An exception was a set of five carriages which went in 1894 to work the Aylesbury–Buckingham service. None survived the arrival of the electric trains in 1905, following which they were all broken up.

Only six of the first class carriages appear to have been used in this manner, the remainder being left to stand idle until, in 1892–3, they were modified to become passenger brake vans. This involved stripping out the interior and the sides of the centre compartment, large double doors being fitted in their place to allow the loading of, principally, milk

# METROPOLITAN RAILWAY TWIN-CARRIAGE STOCK

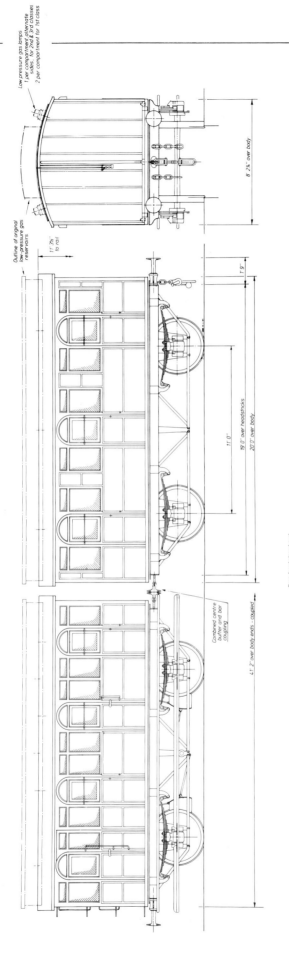

Low pressure gas lamps
1 per compartment, alternate
sides for 2nd & 3rd classes
2 per compartment for 1st class

Outline of original
low-pressure gas
reservoirs

8′ 2¼″ over body

11′ 3¾″
to rail

1′ 9″

11′ 0″

19′ 0″ over headstocks

20′ 0″ over body

Combined centre
buffer and bar
coupling

41′ 2″ over body ends - coupled

Windows without
toplights, this end

Door fixed closed and
fittings removed

20′ 0″ over body

Upper drawing - 3rd class brake + 1st class carriages
Lower drawing - Body arrangement of Brake Vans
converted from 1st class carriages

Built by the Oldbury Carriage Co. 1869

Numbered - 143, 158, 168    1st class
144, 149, 157    2nd class
145-148    3rd class

Notes :-

1   Lighting as built, this used coal gas stored at low pressure
in collapsible bellows contained within the
clerestory on the roof. Converted c.1875 to the
Pintsch system, from which time the roof reservoirs
were removed.

2   c.1879 some or all of the carriages were fitted with standard
buffing & drawgear at both ends for use as single
vehicles in trains of 8-wheel stock.

3   6  1st class carriages converted 1892-3 to Brake vans for use
with milk traffic. Renumbered 1-6. Replaced 1900.

4   Brakes hand only on some 2nd & 3rd class carriages as built.
Clark's & Smith's brakes tried variously until 1892,
when Automatic Vacuum Brake fitted. Cylinder
arrangement as per 8-wheel stock, acting on shoes
outboard of wheels

in churns. At the same time, automatic vacuum brakes were fitted, unusually, with only four brake shoes working on the outer side of the wheels. The maximum permitted load was only three tons, a figure probably dictated by their relatively lightweight construction. This, together with their lively riding characteristics, restricted their usefulness; they were regarded as a liability if placed at the rear of a train. As a result, they only ran until 1900, when they were replaced by new purpose-built vans.

# LATER DEVELOPMENTS (Renamed RIGID REBUILDS?)

Until the arrival of the 4-wheeled 'Jubilee' stock in 1887, the Metropolitan was entirely dependent on the slab-sided 4- & 8-wheeled carriages already described. There were 301 of these, over half of which were by then over twenty years old and probably showing their age, especially in comparison with stock on other railways. There were also prospects of extending services to Aylesbury and beyond and, for such journeys, the 'Jubilee' stock had already proved disappointing; the thought of travelling in an 8-wheeler (particularly third class!) for such distances would have been forbidding and may well have been considered untenable by the management. This may have been the motivation behind the rebodying, over the period 1895–1897, of five 8-wheeled carriages dating from the late 1860s.

Externally, these new bodies differed in that they were 6in longer, at 40ft, with turned-under sides and ends. Their visual appearance changed with the use of unequally-divided waist panels in place of the previously traditional equal division, as well as the omission of toplights. Internally, the changes were more marked, particularly for the second and third class passengers; the cramped and barely upholstered 4ft 10in compartment of the original design was replaced by one some 5ft 6in between partitions, with decent padding. At this stage, gas lighting was retained, distributed on the basis of two lamps per compartment for first class, one for second and third class.

Of the five carriages thus converted, two were turned out as first class brakes, one first class and two second or third class, the latter having seven compartments instead of the six (or 5 + guard) of the first class vehicles. A curious feature was that the two first class brakes were fitted with square topped doors; apart from the saloon carriage, such doors had been superseded in 1867 by the round-topped variety, which were carried by the remaining three rebodied carriages. Their subsequent perambulations are, by and large, a complete mystery. It is known that the two brake firsts normally worked with the two Rothschild saloons as a self-contained train. Virtually nothing is known of the other three carriages, other than that they appear to have run as isolated vehicles in trains of unrebuilt 8-wheel stock. Other than that, the first and one of the thirds (or seconds) appeared in the inaugural train on the Uxbridge branch, together with the two saloons and the brake firsts. From some notes on a surviving copy of the body drawing, it would appear that the two brake firsts at some time were demoted to composites, only the centre two compartments retaining their original status, before being downgraded completely some time prior to 1925, by which time they and one of the third class carriages (No. 72) were running as a 3-coach set on the Chesham branch, which duty they shared with a set of 'Dreadnought' stock. By this time, electric lighting had displaced the original gas equipment. Some time after this, the two brakes migrated to the Brill branch, where they resided until the line's closure in 1935. One, No. 41, is known to have spent its last days in full London Transport 'Metropolitan Line' livery. The other three carriages seem to have disappeared completely by then, leaving virtually no trace of their existence.

Although only five carriages were thus treated, it is evident that they formed the stepping stone to the design of the Bogie stock, which were identical apart from minor changes in dimensions and their use of proper bogie underframes.

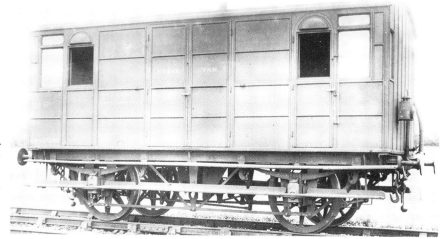

*From first class to milk traffic, an ex Twin First, converted by the removal of the interior and with new side framing and doors to the centre compartment. Curiously, the left-hand door had been left in place, but screwed closed and with its fittings removed.*

**METROPOLITAN RAILWAY 8-WHEELED CARRIAGES – 1897 REBODIED CARRIAGES**

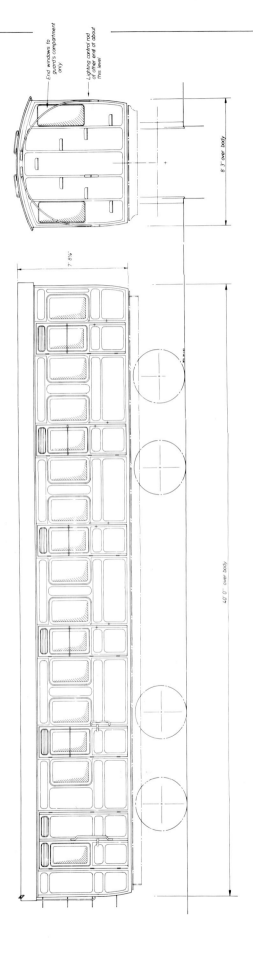

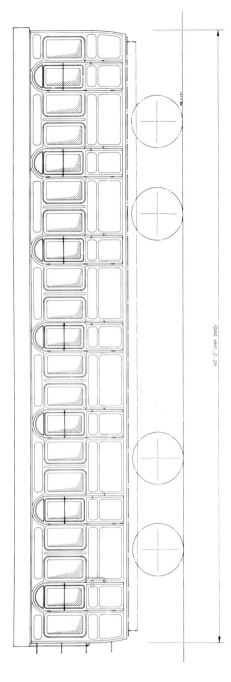

End windows to guard's compartment only

Lighting control rod at other end and at about this level

8' 3" over body

7' 8¼"

40' 0" over body

40' 0" over body

Upper drawing   1st class brake carriage nos 41 & 45
Lower drawing   3rd class carriage nos 72 & 89

For 1st class carriage no 44, replace guard's accommodation
by standard 1st class compartment and substitute round-
for square-topped doors

For underframe detail refer to drawings of 3rd class
carriage as built

*The Brill branch train in its last days, with rebuilt Brake First 41 repainted into LPTB livery, inscribed 'Metropolitan Line'.*

*One of the two Brake First coaches built immediately prior to the Bogie stock on the frames of older 8-wheel vehicles and used, initially, with the Rothschild saloons.*

H. F. WHEELLER

After the electrification in 1904, a number of 8-wheel carriages were retained for excursion and peak time use, latterly being refurbished in an attempt to improve their spartan comforts. Outwardly these vehicles, as seen here, lost their toplights and lower panelling, the latter being replaced by the uneven arrangement shown.

# POST ELECTRIFICATION DEVELOPMENT

*Willesden Green Junction c.1905 with an unidentifiable Westinghouse locomotive heading a 6-coach set of 8-wheel stock toward Baker Street.*

With the electrification of the urban part of the Metropolitan system in 1905–6, most of the steam-hauled carriages, the majority of which were of the 8-wheeled type, became redundant. Over one hundred went for scrap, whilst at least 22 were sold for use on light railways in France. The Metropolitan retained 76, 30 being made up into 6-coach sets for standby use and as seasonal excursion stock. Little is known of their subsequent history, other than that in 1911, following the arrival of the first 'Dreadnought' stock, one set was sold to a Mr R. Frazer, who seems to have been active at the time as a supplier of second-hand coaching stock to various minor railways. It is to be presumed that the other remaining sets followed soon after, as the 1912 batches of Dreadnought stock were delivered.

The remaining 46 carriages were placed into storage, where they remained until 1909 when the District Railway withdrew from the operation of the Inner Circle, leaving the Metropolitan to provide all the rolling stock required. To relieve the rolling stock shortage which resulted from this, 18 of the stored carriages were selected for refurbishment by Neasden Works and formed into 6-coach sets to be electrically hauled on the inner suburban services from 1909. For this purpose they were thoroughly overhauled, losing the toplights and gaining a more conventional panelling layout in the process, as well as being fitted with electric lighting and heating, for which purpose they were also fitted with shoe gear and 600V cabling, though this could not be used for traction.

As far as is known, the 48 carriages involved were made up in sets as follows, though there is no certainty in regard to how fixed these were in practice.

**Steam sets**

| SB/3 | 3 | 1 | Compo | 3 | LB/3 |
|------|------|------|-------|------|------|
| 300 | 223 | 280 | 209 | 217 | 249 |
| 236 | 294 | 240 | 208 | 220 | 226 |
| 295 | 194 | 239 | 210 | 187 | 268 |
| 213* | 292 | 279 | 278 | 285 | 273 |
| 269 | 301 | 283 | 264 | 237 | 252 |

*Long brake 3rd

**Electric sets**

| LB/3 | 3 | 1 | 1 | 3 | LB/3 |
|------|------|------|------|------|------|
| 199 | 298 | 282 | 277 | 289 | 214 |
| 266 | 288 | 274 | 204 | 287 | 263 |
| 261 | 271 | 203 | 202 | 270 | 251 |

# THE FINAL YEARS

As has already been noted, many of the 8-wheeled carriages, as well as a number of the new Jubilee stock carriages, found their way onto other minor railways, where they gave good service for many more years. The earliest departures were those sold immediately after electrification, it being known that, in 1906, seven second class carriages dating from 1883–4 were sold to the Societé des Chemins de fer Economiques, through British agents, for £60 apiece. Nine more followed later that year and in 1908, a further six were sold to 'a French Railway Company'.

The arrival of the Dreadnought stock in 1910–12 spelled the end for the five steam sets, at least three being sold to a Mr Frazer, from whom the Burry Port & Gwendraeth Valley Railway purchased 12 carriages; these lasted until the mid-1920s, being inherited by the Great Western Railway. In 1914, a further seven assorted carriages went to the Rhymney Railway whilst seventeen were sold to the Isle of Wight Railway, where, suitably re-equipped with Westinghouse air brakes and electric lighting, they ran until the late 1920s before being withdrawn. Even then, they

escaped being broken up, the bodies of twelve ending up as beach huts at St Helens, where they remain, albeit somewhat decrepit, to this day.

Of the remainder, eleven, including the five rebodied carriages used to set the pattern for the later Bogie stock, were retained for various purposes by the Metropolitan, some surviving to be inherited by London Transport. The Brill branch provided work for some of these until its closure in 1935, whilst four others were fitted with brushes and scrapers to keep the conductor rails clear of ice and snow in winter. Exactly when they were scrapped is not known, but it was before about 1937.

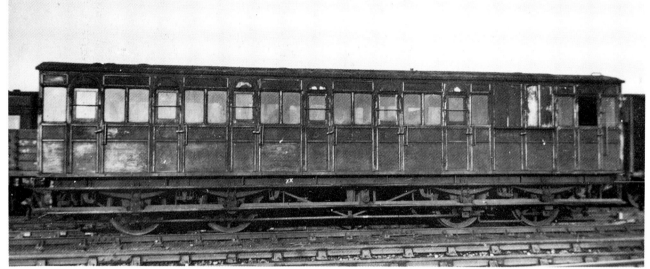

*An unidentifiable Brake Third in what must have been the last days of its life, judging by its run-down condition. Nonetheless, it still appears sound and will have repaid the Metropolitan's investment many times over.*

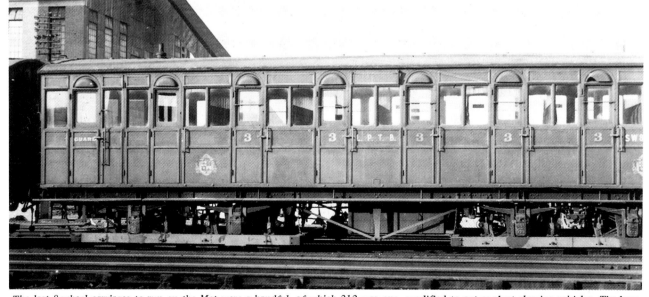

*The last 8-wheel carriages to run on the Met were a handful, of which 212 was one, modified to act as sleet clearing vehicles. The long shoebeams each carried four wire brushes, held down on the conductor rail surfaces in an attempt to prevent ice from building up, thereby obstructing the current flow. This photograph, taken in late 1937, shows 212, now renumbered in the LT SWXX series, and carrying the LPTB's initials alongside the Met's coat of arms.*
A. CRUIKSHANK COLLECTION

*An example of an 8-wheel Composite, rebuilt by the Met with unequal panelling, no toplights and now seeing out its last years under Southern Railway ownership on the Isle of Wight. Carrying SR number 6344, this vehicle was photographed at Brading in March 1929.*

H. F. WHEELLER

'B' class No. 59 on the way to Rickmansworth in the 1890s with a close-coupled 8-coach train of Jubilee stock.

# CHAPTER TWO
# THE JUBILEE STOCK

THE inability of the 8-wheeled carriages to negotiate sharp curves was brought to a head again in 1884, when modifications to the track layout at Mansion House in connection with the completion of the Inner Circle resulted in the sharpening of some already very tight curves, resulting in a series of minor derailments. During the ensuing enquiry, a critical item of evidence was that given by a District Railway ganger who had witnessed the wheels of the Met's 8-wheeled carriages lifting clear of the rails and falling back as the trains stopped and started. Not surprisingly, the inspecting officer, Major General Hutchinson, recommended in his report that the Met should devise an improved arrangement for future rolling stock.

The opportunity for change came in 1887, when new rolling stock was required to cope with the extension from Pinner to Rickmansworth. Although the logical development would have been to use bogies, by then becoming well established on other railways' main line stock, the 4- (and 6-) wheeled carriage was still accepted as normal for lesser duties. Given this, as well as, one suspects, the greater first cost of bogie carriages, the Metropolitan reverted to the use of short-wheelbase 4-wheeled carriages. Their arrival co-incided with Queen Victoria's Silver Jubilee, resulting in these carriages promptly becoming referred to as the 'Jubilee' stock.

The design of these carriages marked a complete break with the staid uprightness of the 8-wheel carriages and their 4-wheeled derivatives. For the first time, the sides and ends were curved in below the waist, whilst the standardised length of 27ft 6in accommodated either 4 first class compartments, or 5 second or third class. Both second and third class brake vans were provided, the latter having two compartments replaced by a single large compartment for the guard and for other luggage or parcels; in third class brakes, the guard was housed in an ordinary sized compartment. In both cases, additional seating was provided in the guard's compartment for use during the peak periods. One novel feature, not adopted by the other main line railways until decades later, was that the glazing was fitted from the inside of the body, rather than from without, thus considerably easing the task of replacement. Although this feature was retained on the later batches of Jubilee stock, it was not perpetuated on subsequent new designs, suggesting that there may have been difficulties, probably in keeping the rainwater from rotting the timber framing at the bottom of the windows. The lower panelling on these carriages was significantly deeper than on the 8-wheelers, resulting in a rather high waist line, and correspondingly shorter windows. The top lights, which had become a typical Met feature, were retained in a deeper form to assist in maintaining decent lighting levels within the compartments.

As has been noted earlier, one of the principal reasons for the reversion to a 4-wheeled design, especially after the virtual failure of the 'twin carriages', was the need to have stock

*An unidentifiable view, probably at Neasden, of two Metropolitan trains. The one noteworthy feature, at left, is an ex-Twin stock Third, close-up pictures of which are rare.*

# METROPOLITAN RAILWAY JUBILEE STOCK COACHES

Main drawing - Third class brake
For ordinary third class carriage
replace guard's compartment by
normal compartment as per other
end of carriage

Lower right - Second class brake

Lower left - Brake end of second class brake
after conversion to saloon

Wheelbase - originally 14' 0" on all carriages,
altered after delivery on carriages
allocated to Main Line service

Coupling arrangements - originally by means of a
combined radial buffer and coupler
of unknown type within sets. Altered
to form shown on Main Line sets

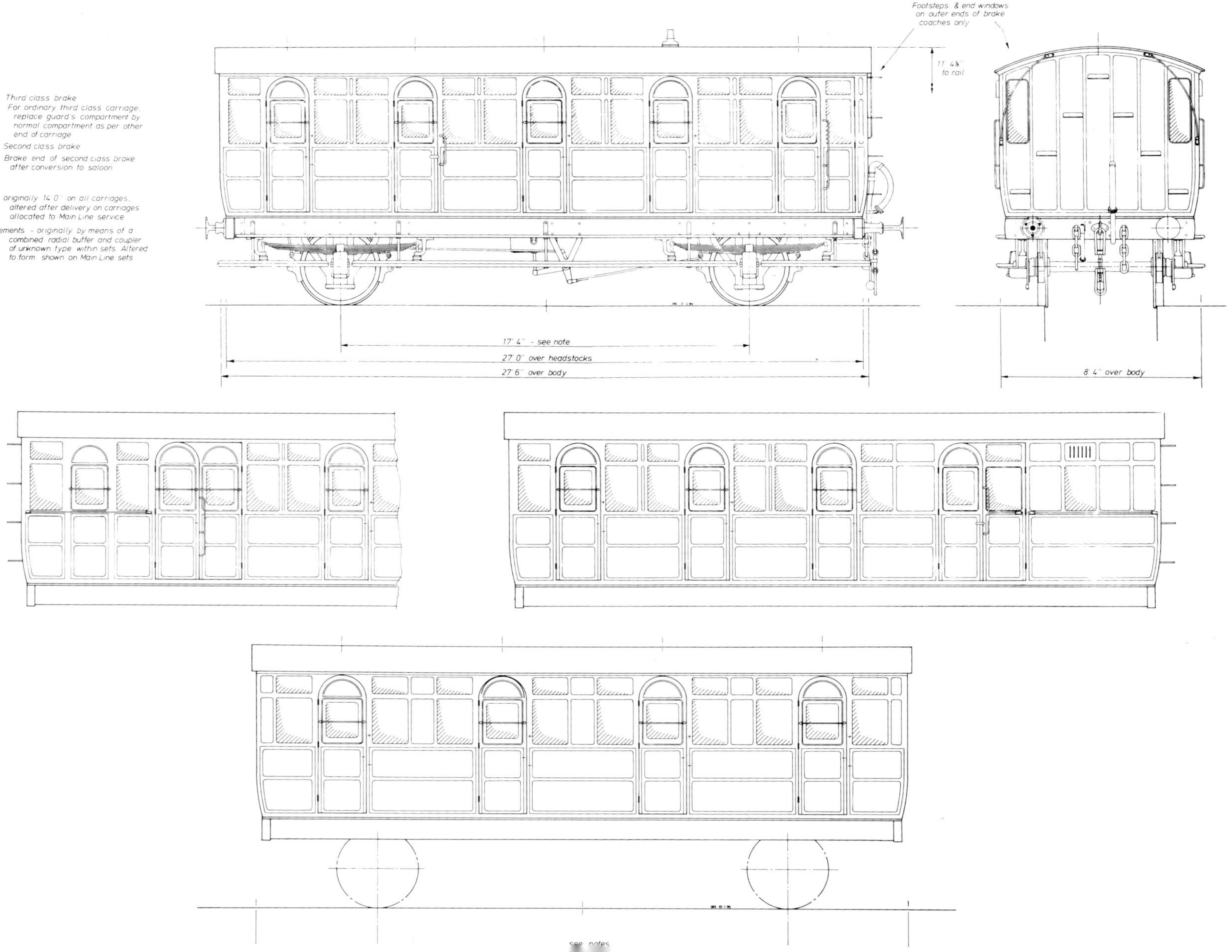

Footsteps & end windows
on outer ends of brake
coaches only

8' 4" over body

17' 4" to rail

17' 4" - see note

27' 0" over headstocks

27' 6" over body

8' 4" over body

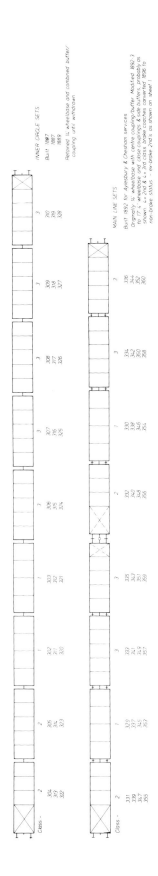

which could negotiate tight curves with greater safety than could the 8-wheeled stock. This resulted in their having a wheelbase of only 14ft 0in, unusually short for a carriage of their size, as well as the provision of a radially pivoted combined buffer and coupling of a type then employed on the New York Elevated Railway to facilitate operation on the tight curves; only the outer ends of the brake carriages were fitted with conventional side buffers and drawgear. A consequence of the latter was that, in a further break from previous practice, this new stock was formed into block trains of nine vehicles. Timber was, for the first time on the Met, employed for the underframe construction, being used throughout with the addition of iron flitch plates running the full length of the outer face of the solebars.

Initially, three complete trains were supplied by Craven Bros. of Sheffield, the prototype in 1887, followed by two more in 1889, each made up as B2.2.1.1.3.3.3.3.B3 for service on the Inner Circle, displacing older 8-wheeled stock to Main Line workings. Vacuum brakes of the simple, i.e. non-automatic, type were provided on each carriage, these being replaced from 1891–93 by automatic vacuum brakes. Pintsch's high-pressure oil-gas lighting was provided throughout.

To provide stock for the new extension to Aylesbury, a further 32 carriages to the same designs were ordered, again from Cravens, being put into service in 1892. As it was intended that the trains should divide at Chalfont Road to serve both Aylesbury and Chesham, the carriages of this order were formed in sets of four, made up as B3.3.1.B2, each set having long buffers at the outer ends, combined drawbars and buffers being provided within the set as previously.

Unfortunately, the relatively short wheelbase of these carriages did not make for stable running at higher speeds, nor did the radial couplings, unlike conventional buffers, help to steady the resultant oscillations. While this would not have been evident at the moderate speeds achievable on the Inner Circle's sinuous tracks, it was patently intolerable when they were operated on the Extension services. All eight sets of the 1892 batch were returned to Cravens for modification under the terms of their guarantee. This resulted in two major changes being made to improve their riding; firstly, the wheelbase was lengthened to 17ft 4in, the maximum possible without major modifications being required to the underframe, and secondly, the replacement of the radial drawgear by a more conventional arrangement using short side buffers to retain the close coupling. Not only was all this work undertaken at Cravens' own expense, but the Met also managed to extract from them a further settlement of £1,000 in compensation for the loss of traffic which had resulted from the poor performance of these carriages.

The three Inner Circle 9-coach sets were not modified, evidently being considered satisfactory at the lower speeds encountered on that service, with the result that the Jubilee stock fleet was split into two completely separate and non-interchangeable groups.

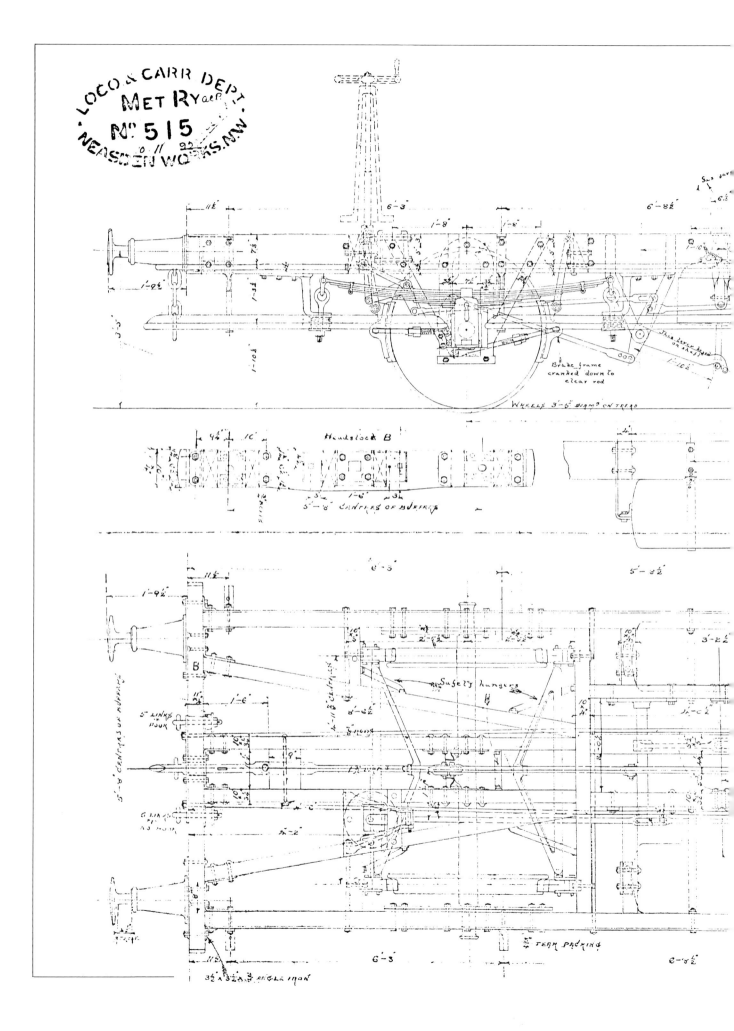

# METROPOLITAN RAILWAY.
## UNDERFRAME FOR SECOND CLASS BRAKE CARRIACE

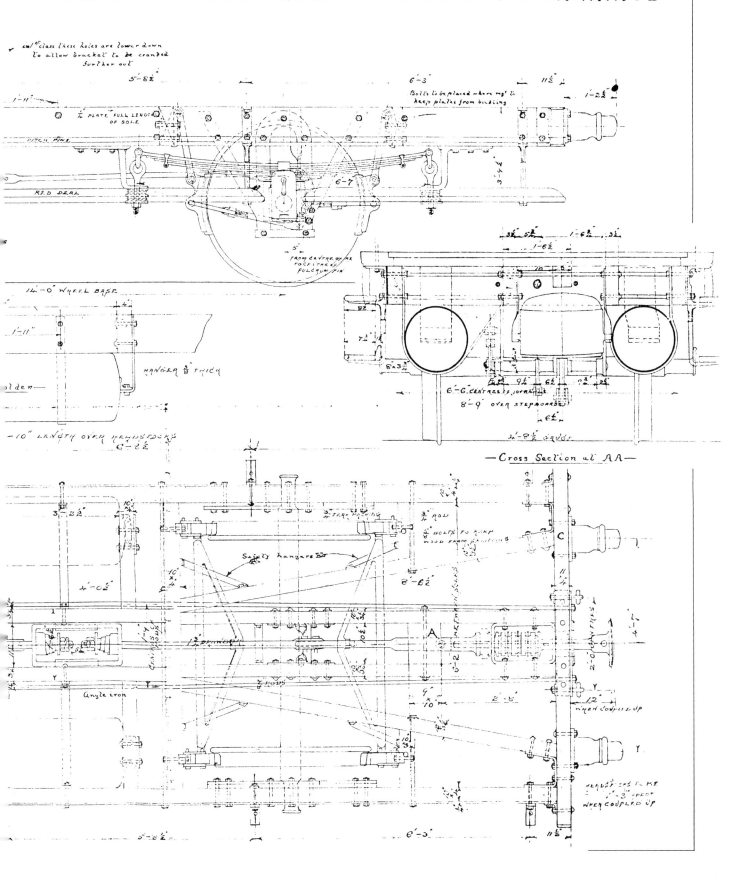

Cross Section at AA

*Another Jubilee carriage, First Class No. 321, after modernisation and installation of electric lighting. It will be noted that only smokers needed ventilation!*
LT COLLECTION

*First Class Jubilee carriage 346 in its original condition, with quarter- and top-lights to each compartment, and gas lighting. The glazing on these vehicles was unusual in that it was fitted from the inside, making the usual window mouldings unnecessary.*    L. T. COLLECTION

One other feature that rapidly became evident by its absence was the lack of an efficient heating system. Like all of the Metropolitan's stock until then, the only form of heating was that provided by footwarmers; this was inadequate for the Main Line, resulting in the installation of Laycock's steam heating apparatus on the Aylesbury sets in 1894. The Circle sets remained unmodified.

The practice of dividing the trains at Chalfont was abandoned in 1896, resulting in the two inner brake carriages in each train becoming redundant. Four of the third class brakes were rebuilt as first/third composites, the guard's compartment being converted into a small first (?) class saloon seating 14 passengers. This entailed reframing the van end of the body, allowing a droplight and quarterlights to be fitted in place of the largely blind panelling with which they had originally been fitted. Curiously, the double doors were retained, suggesting that their use was not entirely confined to passenger duties. Dummy panelling was also provided below the droplight, giving the impression of its being a door, an effect completed by the fitment of a semi-circular ventilator bonnet. The reasons for this arrangement of panelling are obscure; combined with the retention of the double doors, it gave that end of the carriage a distinctly hotchpotch appearance. At the same time, four of the second class brakes were reconstructed as full 5-compartment second class carriages by the expedient of removing the hand brake and guard's equipment. Appropriate modifications to the buffing gear allowed the trains to be reformed as B2.2.1.1.1/3.3.3.B3, the second and third class brake carriages exchanging class at the same time, possibly reflecting the decline in second class traffic which was ultimately to lead to its abandonment some eight years later.

The electrification of the Circle in 1905 resulted in the withdrawal of the entire Jubilee stock fleet, with 32 carriages being disposed of there and then. Of these, 6 of the Inner Circle carriages went to the Mid-Suffolk Light Railway, being modified along the way by G.R. Turner to run as 3-coach sets, whilst the Weston, Clevedon & Portishead Railway acquired 7 of the Main Line carriages. A further 10 went to the Nidd Valley Railway, leaving 9 to be scrapped. The remaining 27 carriages, of both types, were retained by the Met as reserve stock.

The shortage of rolling stock during 1908 prompted a scheme to form two 5-coach trains similar in form to the

*Whilst E class No. 77 might have been the focus of the photographer's attention, this has not prevented Jubilee stock Third Brake 331 from being recorded for posterity, showing to good effect the detail of the fully-lined livery.*

Bogie stock conversions. This would have involved mounting the bodies in pairs on new steel underframes, with BTH 200hp motors. At a total length for each carriage of 54–55ft, it may be presumed that, unlike the Bogie stock motor coaches, the traction equipment would have been carried below the floor. The converted trains would have accommodated 80 first class and 320 third class passengers, but the cost was considered unjustifiable and the scheme came to nought. Instead, the 27 carriages were modernised, this including external repanelling in the same style as the Bogie stock, and formed into three trains which were put back into service, hauled by electric locomotives, in February 1909. It is to be presumed that some or all of the ex-Inner Circle coaches were also fitted with revised buffing and drawgear arrangements at this time in order to provide some operating flexibility. Electric lighting and heating was provided as part of the refurbishment, 18ft long shoebeams being fitted on the end carriages to carry the shoegear necessary to provide power for these circuits.

Along with the similarly modernised sets of 8-wheel carriages, these Jubilee stock trains survived in service until 1912, when they were finally withdrawn. Most were sold off, eight going to the Llanelly and Mynydd Mawr Railway and nine to the Bute Works Supply Co. in Cardiff; the remaining ten were considered unsaleable and were to be broken up, but three later found their way to the Rhymney Railway in

September 1914. Two others survived as grounded bodies, one of which, a first class carriage, is now in the LT Museum collection.

The Jubilee stock was numbered in sets, corresponding to the original train formations, as below. The numbering order is not random, but puts the different classes of carriage in ascending order within each set, the first class taking the lowest number. This is slightly modified with the Main Line sets, which although of 4 coaches each, were numbered as if of 8-coach formation, i.e. in the pairs in which they were delivered.

### Inner Circle 9-coach sets:

| Built | B2 | 2 | 1 | 1 | 3 | 3 | 3 | 3 | B3 |
|---|---|---|---|---|---|---|---|---|---|
| 1887 | 304 | 305 | 302 | 303 | 306 | 307 | 308 | 309 | 310 |
| 1889 | 313 | 314 | 311 | 312 | 315 | 316 | 317 | 318 | 319 |
| 1889 | 322 | 323 | 320 | 321 | 324 | 325 | 326 | 327 | 328 |

### 1892 Main Line 4-coach sets:

| B2 | 1 | 3 | B3 |
|---|---|---|---|
| 331 | 329 | 333 | 335 |
| 332 | 330 | 334 | 336 |
| 339 | 337 | 341 | 343 |
| 340 | 338 | 342 | 344 |
| 347 | 345 | 349 | 351 |
| 348 | 346 | 350 | 352 |
| 355 | 353 | 357 | 359 |
| 356 | 354 | 358 | 360 |

*One of the seven Jubilee stock carriages, a Brake Third, as modified by the WC&PR, converted to semi-open configuration with all but two of the doors screwed shut, and additional steps provided to allow boarding from ground level. This picture was taken at Clevedon on 25th June 1938.*
COLLECTION R. S. CARPENTER

# CHAPTER THREE

# MODERNISATION
# THE BOGIE STOCK

*A Metropolitan Main Line train at the turn of the 20th century, formed of a 6-coach set of Bogie stock, headed by a Passenger Brake van and hauled by an E class 0–4–4.* L&GRP

THE later 1890s constituted a period of great change for the Metropolitan; Sir Edward Watkin, who had for many years controlled the destiny of the Met, as well as the GC and SEC Railways, had been succeeded in 1894 as Chairman by John Bell and within five years the Board had been reconstructed. The departure of the autocratic Watkins was probably instrumental in T.F. Clark, who had replaced J.J. Hanbury in 1893, coming forward with a recommendation that the new stock required in 1898 for the Main Line should be carried on bogies. These had, during the Watkin era, been considered as unjustifiable on account of their extra weight and cost, but the higher speeds being attained on the Main Line were pushing the riding qualities of the existing 4- and 8-wheeled carriages to their limits, whilst the fact that bogie carriages were now universal on the other main line railways in Britain could no longer be ignored.

Tenders for these new carriages were sought from both Cravens Bros. and Ashbury, the latter company, by a promise of earlier delivery, winning an order for four 6-coach close-coupled sets which were put into service in 1898 and officially referred to as the 'Bogie Stock'. (The present day reference to them as 'Ashbury Stock' is a complete misnomer, especially as at that time, there were already 114 much older carriages in service built by that concern.)

The body design of these carriages was derived directly from the five 8-wheeled carriages which had been rebodied in 1897, and which in their turn were a development of the earlier Jubilee stock design. In appearance, they were not readily distinguishable from other contemporary carriages other than by the rounded door tops, which were to remain a feature of Metropolitan (and Great Eastern) design practice until the end.

Whilst they were only slightly longer, at 39ft 6in, than the original 8-wheel carriages of 30 years earlier, they represented a significant advance in passenger standards. They were the first of the company's stock to be fitted from new with electric lighting, although evidence of gas lamps on the original body drawings suggests that this was a late change; two 8-candlepower incandescent lamps were fitted in each compartment, supplied by two sets of accumulators and an axle driven dynamo on each coach. Laycock's steam heating apparatus was fitted from new, as was the automatic vacuum brake, two cylinders being provided, one for each bogie. No provision was made for any form of passenger alarm system, even after an attempted murder in 1909 and a subsequent Board of Trade recommendation. One block-set was experimentally fitted with an alarm in 1902, but it was not until the arrival of the Dreadnought stock in 1910 that this was adopted at all by the Metropolitan.

The underframes represented a complete departure from previous Met practice in being carried on two bogies, each of 7ft wheelbase with pressed steel frames to Fox's Patent and fitted at 25ft centres. After the excursion into timber for the Jubilee stock, underframe construction reverted to the use of rolled steel sections, braced below the solebars by a simple queenpost and truss rod arrangement. As with the previous Jubilee stock, full buffers and screw coupling were

# METROPOLITAN RAILWAY 'BOGIE STOCK' 2nd or 3rd CLASS BRAKE CARRIAGE

11' 4"
3' 4⅝" dia
7' 0"
25' 0" Centres
10"
38' 10" over headstocks
1' 9½"
39' 6" over body
8' 3" over body

Applied only to vehicles built at Neasden
Dummy panel let into corner post. Used on full second & third class coaches
7¼"
2' 9⅛"
2' 4⅜"
7¼"
18"
2⅞"
7' 3"
1' 11"
1' 3⅜"
1' 10½"
Second & Third class
1' 5⅜"
2' 0"
First class
10' 0⅜"
7' 6⅝"
7' 3"
1' 11"
8' 3"
3"

METROPOLITAN RAILWAY
Bogie Stock - cross section & compartment elevations for first and second/third class

Mouldings are 1½" × ⅝" in section
Curve radii are 2" except where required to fit non-standard panels

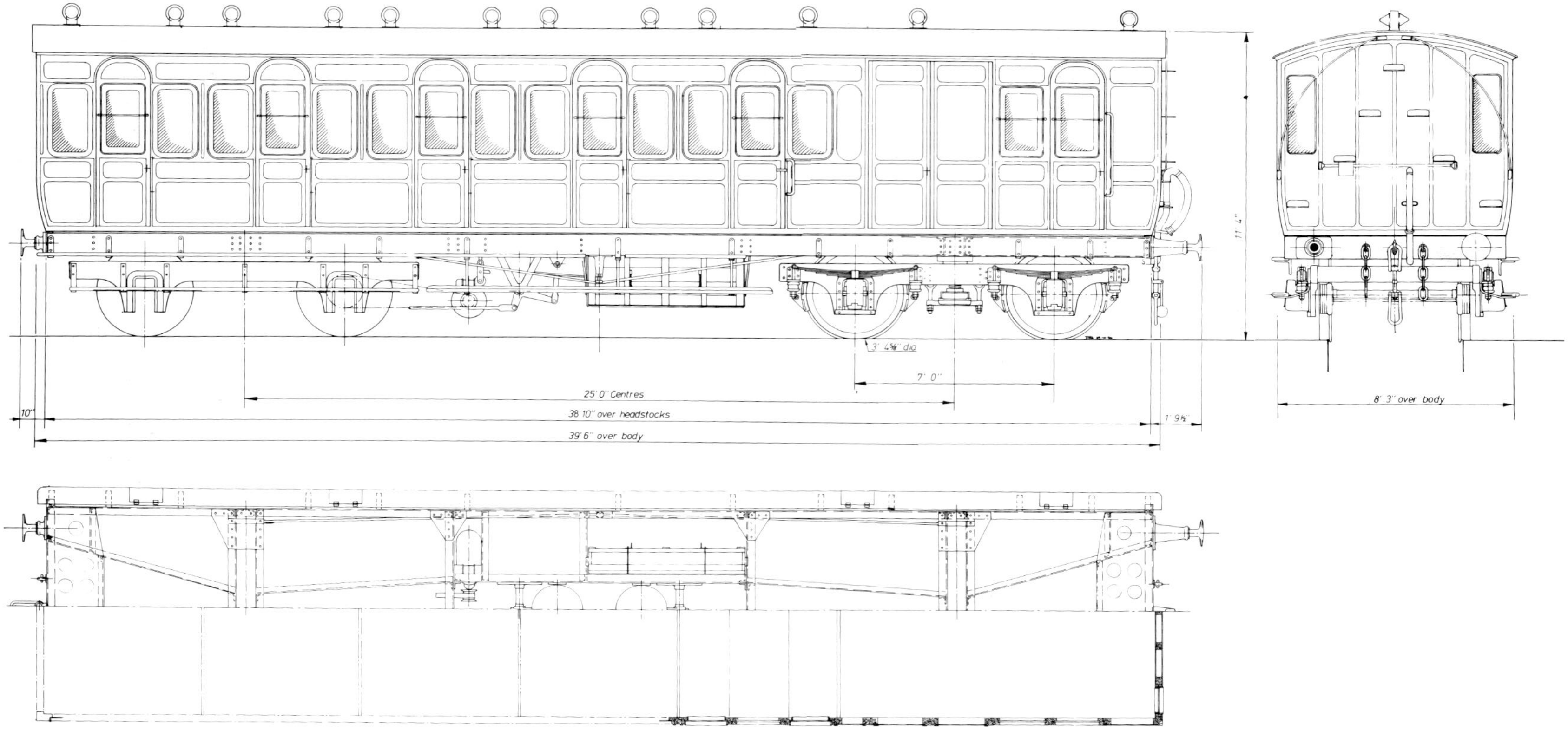

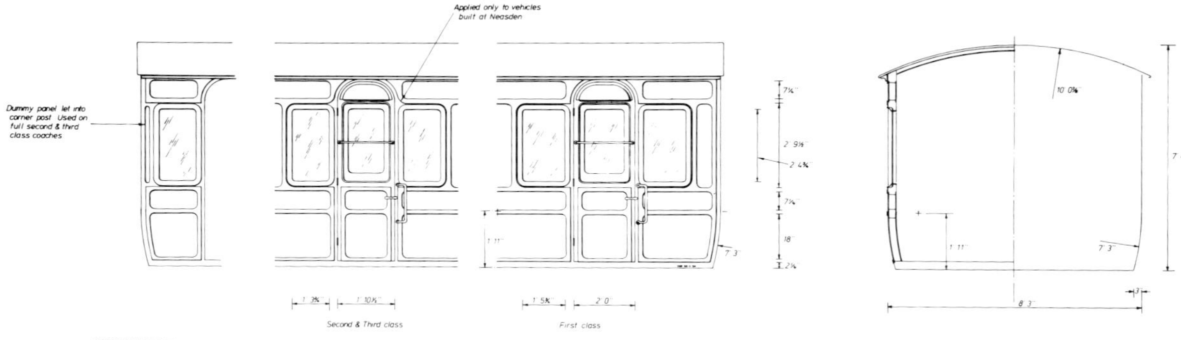

| Builders | Br 2nd | Br 3rd |
|---|---|---|
| Ashbury - 1898 | 373 | 381 |
| | 374 | 382 |
| | 375 | 383 |
| | 376 | 384 |
| Met Rly - 1900 | 395 | 385 |
| Cravens - 1900 | 396 | 386 |
| | 397 | 387 |
| Ashbury - 1900 | 398 | 388 |
| | 399 | 389 |

Modifications -
384, 387 converted to driving trailers 1905
then to BW 150 hp Motor cars 1908
380, 392 fitted with automatic coupler one end
& converted to full 3rd 1905
376, 388, 397, 398 converted to BTH motor cars 1907
373, 381 converted to full 3rd 1907
Remainder ——"——"—— 1920-4

*Bogie stock Third Class Brake, as originally built, taken probably c.1905 at Neasden.*                    LURS COLLECTION

fitted to the outer ends of the brake carriages only; the inner ends and all the remaining carriages were fitted with short buffers, set at the normal centres, and coupled by means of links pinned directly to the drawbars in place of the hook. Because of the standardisation of dimensions, it was relatively simple to convert a carriage to have normal drawgear, a feature which was later employed to advantage when the Pullman cars were first incorporated into two Bogie stock train sets.

Initially, four complete train sets of 6 coaches each were delivered, each being formed as B2.2.1.1/3.3.B3 and seating 90 first, 120 second and 150 third class passengers each. The full second and third class carriages had seven compartments each, measuring 5ft 6in between the partitions, with the brake carriages exchanging two compartments for the guard's accommodation, whilst the first class carriages were provided with six compartments measuring 6ft 5in. The curiosity was the composite, where, because of the standardisation of the body length, the six compartments which could be accommodated were roomier than their counterparts elsewhere in the train. The three thirds were, at 5ft 10½in, larger than the seconds, whilst the firsts, at 7ft 0in, were palatial and much sought after for their additional legroom.

Internally, following established practice, the third class compartments were upholstered in rep, with papier-mâché ceiling panels decorated in a floral design. Wood fittings were in polished teak, with oak-grained panelling, whilst fibre matting covered the floor. Second class passengers enjoyed crimson velvet seats with buttoned backs, corner elbow rests and linoleum flooring, relieved by the addition of a monogrammed rug. The ceiling panels, again of papier-mâché, were decorated with a gilt cornice, whilst mahogany

had supplanted teak for the internal fittings. Those privileged enough to enjoy first class travel were accommodated on silk lace and cord finished rose-coloured Baghdad moquette; woodwork, of polished walnut and sycamore, was gilt-edged. All compartments had pull-down blinds and a pair of roof vents and all were lined with noise-deadening felt. In the lower classes, each compartment was arranged to accommodate ten passengers, seated five-a-side; first class was arranged for four-a-side seating, although this could be stretched to five-a-side at peak times if the retractable arm rests were lifted.

The success of these first two sets, combined with a continuing need for new rolling stock, resulted in the acquisition of a further four sets in 1899. In a break from tradition, it was agreed that only two of these sets would be contract built, by Ashbury's; the remaining two were to be built by Neasden Works, the first, and almost the only, time in its history that the Metropolitan actually built passenger stock. In the event, Neasden's workload was such that only one train could be constructed. To make up the deficit, John Bell, acting on his own initiative, ordered not one, but two further trains from Cravens, only subsequently justifying and getting approval for his actions from the Board.

There were, in addition to the nine-set trains, two other carriages which fall into the Bogie stock fleet. These had originally been built by Brown Marshall as part of the joint Met/MDR experimental train built in 1899 for use between Earls Court and High Street, Kensington. In addition to the two motor cars, this incorporated four trailer carriages essentially to the same design as the Bogie stock. Following the termination of this trial in November 1900, the six carriages, being the joint property of both railway companies, were put up for disposal. The Metropolitan's portion, com-

METROPOLITAN RAILWAY 'BOGIE STOCK' 2nd or 3rd CLASS CARRIAGE

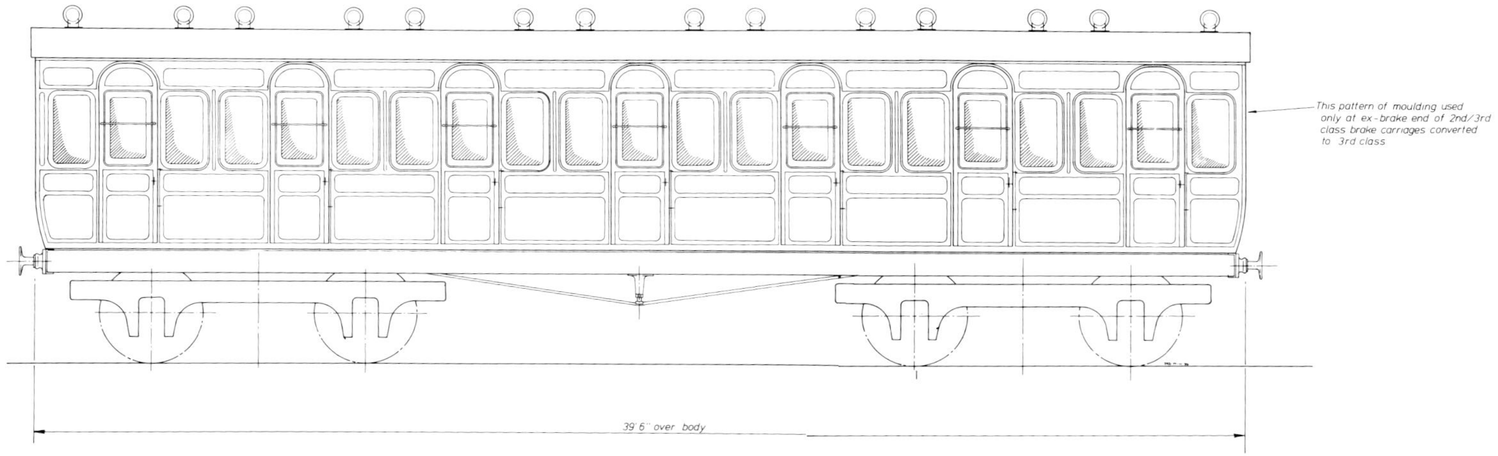

This pattern of moulding used only at ex-brake end of 2nd/3rd class brake carriages converted to 3rd class

| 2nd | 3rd class | Builder | | 476 | | Brown Marshall 1899 | Originally part of Metropolitan & Met District Rlys experimental electric train Air braked until transfer to Met Rly stock in 1903 |
|-----|-----------|---------|---|-----|---|---------------------|---|
| 369 | 377 | Ashbury | 1898 | | | | |
| 370 | 378 | | | 374, 375, 362, 383, 385, 386, 395, 396 & 399 | | | Converted from Brake 3rd Fitted initially with long buffers and screw couplings at ex-brake end Later fitted with automatic coupler in place of screw coupling |
| 371 | 379 | | | | | | |
| 372 | 380 | Met Rly | 1900 | | | | |
| 400 | 390 | | | 373 & 381 | | | As above but short buffers both ends |
| 401 | 391 | Cravens | 1900 | | | | |
| 402 | 392 | | | | | | |
| 403 | 393 | Ashbury | 1900 | | | | |
| 404 | 394 | | | | | | |

39' 6" over body

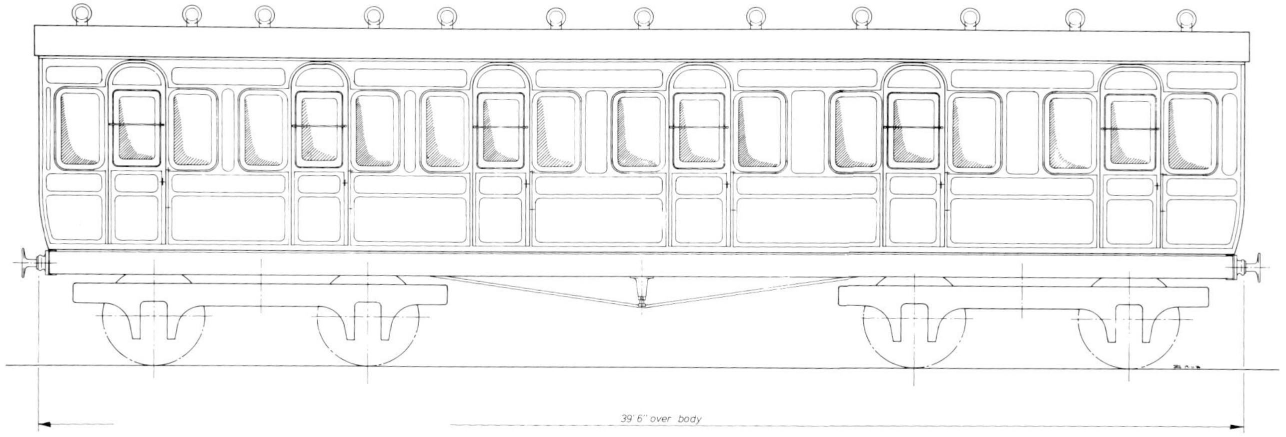

METROPOLITAN RAILWAY 'BOGIE STOCK' 1st & 3rd CLASS COMPOSITE CARRIAGE

39' 6" over body

| | Built | | |
|---|-------|---|---|
| 365-368 | Ashbury | 1898 | |
| 410 | Met Rly | 1900 | |
| 411-412 | Cravens | 1900 | |
| 413-414 | Ashbury | 1900 | |

# METROPOLITAN RAILWAY 'BOGIE STOCK' 1st CLASS CARRIAGE

| | Built | |
|---|---|---|
| 361-364 | Ashbury | 1898 |
| 405 | Met Rly | 1900 |
| 406-407 | Cravens | 1900 |
| 408-409 | Ashbury | 1900 |
| 415 | Brown Marshall 1899 as part of joint Metropolitan - Met District experimental electric train Taken into Metropolitan stock 1903 | |

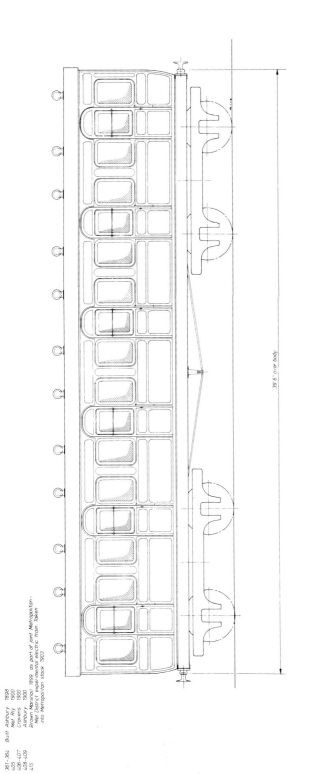

39'6" over body

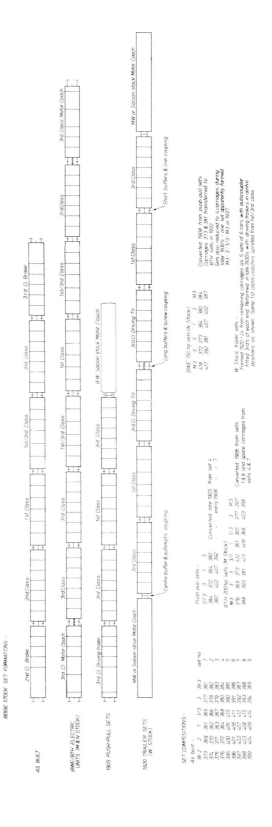

BOGIE STOCK SET FORMATIONS -

**AS BUILT**
2nd Cl Brake · 2nd Class · 1st Class · 1st/3rd Class · 3rd Class · 3rd Cl Brake

**BWE/BTH ELECTRIC UNITS (M & N STOCK)**
3rd Cl Motor Coach · 3rd Class · 1st/3rd Class · 1st Class · 3rd Class · 1st/3rd Class · 3rd Class · 3rd Class Motor Coach

**1905 PUSH-PULL SETS**
3rd Cl Driving trailer · 3rd Class · 1st Class · 1st/3rd Class · MW or Saloon stock Motor Coach

Centre buffer & automatic coupling

**1920 TRAILER SETS (W STOCK)**
MW or Saloon stock Motor Coach · 3rd Class · 1st Class · 1st Class · 3rd Cl Driving Tlr · 3rd Cl Driving Tlr · 3rd Class · MW or Saloon stock Motor Coach

Long buffers & screw coupling

Short buffers & link coupling

Converted 1908 from push-pull sets
Carriages 373 & 381 transferred to BTH sets in 1932
Sets also reduced to 4 carriages during later 1930s - one set apparently formed M3 - 3 - 1/3 - M3 in 1937

W Stock trailer sets -
Formed 1920-24 from remaining carriages as 5 sets of 6 cars with autocoupler fitted 3rd's at each end. Reformed in late 1930s with driving trailers in centre positions as shown. Some 1st class coaches uprated from 1st/3rd class.

Converted 1906 from sets 1 & 8 and spare carriages from sets 4 & 7

Converted late 1905 from set 4 - early 1906 - 7

## SET COMPOSITIONS -

**As built -**

| set no | Br 2 | 2 | 1 | 1/3 | 3 | Br 3 |
|---|---|---|---|---|---|---|
| 1 | 373 | 369 | 361 | 365 | 377 | 381 |
| 2 | 374 | 370 | 362 | 366 | 378 | 382 |
| 3 | 375 | 371 | 363 | 367 | 379 | 383 |
| 4 | 376 | 372 | 364 | 368 | 380 | 384 |
| 5 | 395 | | | | | 385 |
| 6 | 396 | 401 | 406 | 411 | 391 | 386 |
| 7 | 397 | 402 | 407 | 412 | 392 | 387 |
| 8 | 398 | 403 | 408 | 413 | 393 | 388 |
| 9 | 399 | 404 | 409 | 414 | 394 | 389 |

**Push-pull sets -**

| DT3 | 3 | 1 | 3 |
|---|---|---|---|
| 384 | 402 | 407 | 392 |
| 387 | | | |

**BTH 200hp sets (M Stock)**

| M3 | 3 | 1/3 | 3 | M3 |
|---|---|---|---|---|
| 376 | 369 | 373 | 412 | |
| 368 | 393 | 381 | 413 | 408 398 |

**BWE 150 hp sets (N Stock)**

| M3 | 3 | 3 | M3 |
|---|---|---|---|
| 418 | 372 | 379 | 364 380 384 |
| 417 | 392 | 381 | 407 402 387 |

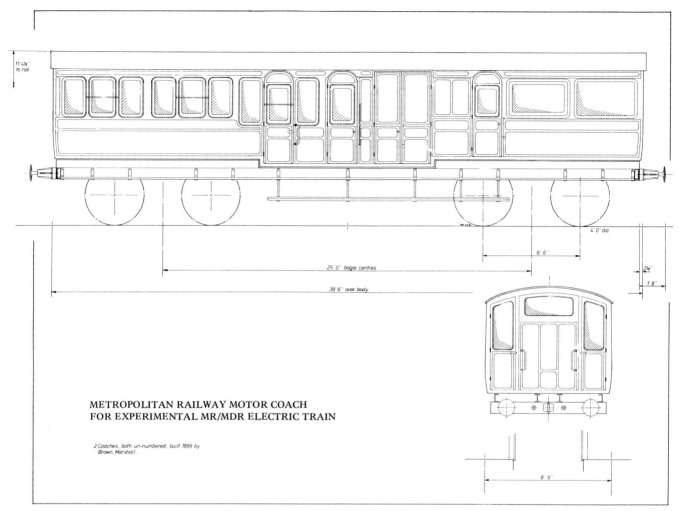

METROPOLITAN RAILWAY MOTOR COACH
FOR EXPERIMENTAL MR/MDR ELECTRIC TRAIN

2 Coaches, both un-numbered, built 1899 by
Brown, Marshall.

prising one of the motor cars and two trailer cars, one first class, the other second class, was transferred to Neasden on 27th March 1903, where they were converted for steam operation, i.e. fitted with the vacuum brake and the necessary lighting equipment, and assimilated into the general Bogie stock fleet, with which they were virtually identical. The first class carriage, now numbered 415, was put into one of the Bogie stock trains, displacing 363, which, with the second class carriage, numbered 416, was formed for a time into a train with the rebuilt rigid 8-wheeled coaches dating from 1897. The fate of the motor coach is unknown, although there is a possibility that its underframe, modified, later formed the basis of the 1910-built bogie tool van which features so prominently in photographs of the Metropolitan's breakdown train.

Until 1910, these sets were the mainstay of the through services to Chesham, Aylesbury and Verney Junction, being displaced only by the progressive introduction of the Dreadnought stock and the conversion of two sets to work with, and later as, electric stock. At least one set, probably two, was reformed after the arrival of the Pullman cars in 1910, the first class carriage being removed, and the

drawgear on the adjoining carriages being modified to the long type to accept the Pullman car's standard drawgear. Later, when the Pullmans were reformed into Dreadnought stock trains, a Bogie stock carriage was, for a time, used to replace one of the Dreadnoughts adjoining the Pullman, presumably to counter the greater length of the latter.

Although displaced from front line duties by the Dreadnoughts, they found a new lease of life on the Metropolitan's inner suburban duties, either as complete electric trains or, later, as trailer sets to be run between pairs of saloon stock motor cars or, by the late 1920s, the early MW stock motor coaches.

were delivered.

| Date | Builder | B/2 | 2nd | 1st | 1/3 | 3rd | 3/B |
|------|---------|-----|-----|-----|-----|-----|-----|
| 1898 | Ashbury | 373 | 369 | 361 | 365 | 377 | 381 |
|      |         | 374 | 370 | 362 | 366 | 378 | 382 |
|      |         | 375 | 371 | 363 | 367 | 379 | 383 |
|      |         | 376 | 372 | 364 | 368 | 380 | 384 |
| 1900 | Neasden | 395 | 400 | 405 | 410 | 390 | 385 |
|      | Cravens | 396 | 401 | 406 | 411 | 391 | 386 |
|      |         | 397 | 402 | 407 | 412 | 392 | 387 |
|      | Ashbury | 398 | 403 | 408 | 413 | 393 | 388 |
|      |         | 399 | 404 | 409 | 414 | 394 | 389 |

*A Bogie stock Brake Third, coupled to Third Class carriage, photographed c.1905.*            A. CRUIKSHANK COLLECTION

# LATER DEVELOPMENTS — ELECTRIFICATION

With the change to electric traction on the Harrow and Uxbridge services, a very large part of the Metropolitan's locomotive-hauled stock fleet was rendered surplus to requirements. Roundly two-thirds of the rigid stock fleet, together with all of the ex-Twin carriages and about half of the Jubilee stock were withdrawn and disposed of, the remainder being put into store for use on excursion services and as a strategic reserve. Only the Bogie stock remained in front-line duty, covering the remaining services north of Harrow, for which the nine 6-coach sets were more than adequate.

At the same time, however, passenger demand, spurred on by the improvements in the service brought about by electrification, was rising to the point where the available electric stock fleet was becoming insufficient. At the same time, there was more hauled stock, specifically Bogie stock, than was required for the long-distance services. The solution was obvious and, in July 1905, a proposal was put forward to create two four-coach sets of Bogie stock, formed B3-3-1-3, each of which could be coupled between two Saloon stock motor cars, or worked in push-pull mode by a single motor car. Additionally, they were arranged to be capable of steam haulage for services north of Harrow, where, presumably, the electric motor car would be detached. To achieve this, considerable alterations were necessary, particularly to the two outer vehicles, the outer ends of which had to be fitted with the centre buffers and automatic couplers required to couple to the motor cars, whilst Westinghouse air brakes had to be fitted alongside the existing vacuum equipment. The screw couplings and side buffers had also to be retained at each end to allow locomo-

tives to be coupled. The brake third was also altered considerably, being converted to a driving trailer, large end windows being fitted, whilst internally the necessary driving and brake controllers were installed. Shoegear was provided on the Driving Trailer to allow the controller to be fed, whilst it was certainly planned, if not carried out, that the heating and lighting would be converted to electric operation.

Very soon after these two sets had entered service, a more ambitious scheme was put forward and adopted for the conversion of further Bogie stock vehicles to create two complete 8-coach electric trains. The erstwhile third class brakes were converted into motor coaches, new bogies (with BTH GE69 200hp motors) being fitted, whilst considerable alterations were made to the bodies, where the number of passenger compartments was reduced to four in order to allow the electrical equipment to be housed in a new equipment compartment behind the driving cab. The guard was removed to the rear cab, but, because of difficulties with short platforms as well as the cramped environment, it was not long before the adjacent passenger compartment was appropriated and converted for the guard's use. Traction voltage lighting and heating replaced the original equipment, whilst below the floor, the existing vacuum brakes were removed and replaced by Westinghouse air brakes, standard on all the Metropolitan's other electric stock. Unusually, the original link couplings and short buffers were retained between the trailer coaches, but the two motor coaches were coupled by standard screw couplings, with normal buffers. In the event, the two trains were at first made up to only 7-coach length, the two missing vehicles being delayed by their conversion to full third class vehicles.

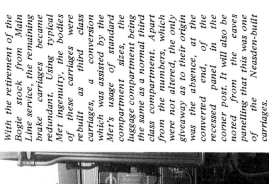

With the retirement of the Bogie stock from Main Line service, the remaining brake carriages became redundant. Using typical Met ingenuity, the bodies of these carriages were rebuilt as third class carriages, a conversion which was assisted by the Met's usage of standard compartment sizes, the luggage compartment being the same as a normal third class compartment. Apart from the numbers, which were not altered, the only giveaway as to their origin was the absence, at the converted end, of the recessed panel in the corner post. It will also be noted from the eaves panelling that this was one of the Neasden-built carriages.

LONDON UNDERGROUND

Bogie stock 1st class carriage 408 after modification in 1907/8 to run between the converted motor coaches which formed the M&N stock trains. This entailed the replacement of the vacuum brake by Westinghouse equipment and the installation of 600V heating and lighting circuits.
LONDON UNDERGROUND

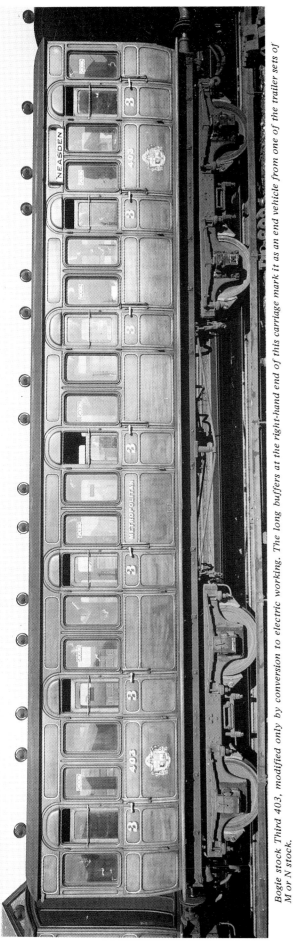

Bogie stock Third 403, modified only by conversion to electric working. The long buffers at the right-hand end of this carriage mark it as an end vehicle from one of the trailer sets of M or N stock.

A number of Bogie stock brake carriages were rebuilt over the period 1905-7 as motor coaches, half with Westinghouse equipment, the rest with BTH equipment. The control equipment was housed behind the driver, in what had been the luggage and guard's compartments, as well as one of the passenger compartments. The guard took over another compartment, until he was later consigned to the rear cab in order to provide more passenger capacity.
LONDON
UNDERGROUND

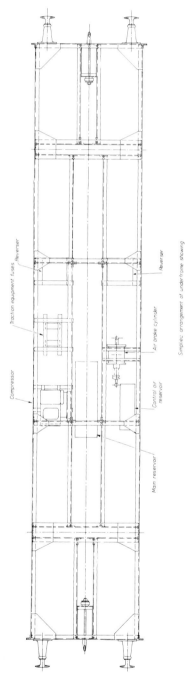

## METROPOLITAN RAILWAY BOGIE STOCK 3rd CLASS MOTOR COACH
## CONVERTED FROM 2nd or 3rd CLASS BRAKE CARRIAGES

Outline of driver's side door on BTH coaches

Upper stepboard on all bogie stock coaches moved to this position at unknown date after conversion to electric working

8' 3" over body

Shoebeam removed to show bogie detail.

See note

1' 0"

25' 0" Centres

38'10" over headstocks

39' 6" over body

11' .7"

Traction equipment fuses    Reverser

Reverser

Compressor

Air brake cylinder

Control air reservoir

Main reservoir

Simplified arrangement of under frame showing layout of structural members and major equipment on BTH equipped cars

Nos 376 ,386 ,397 & 398 converted 1907  BTH equipment
384 & 387 converted 1908 from Driving Trailers  BWE equipment
417 & 418 converted 1908 from motor coaches built for 1889
experiments at Wembley Park  BWE equipment

Note - BTH equipped coaches fitted with ME type bogies   3' 2" dia wheels
BWE                MC                                                          3' 0"

*An N class train passing through Willesden Green towards Baker Street.*                                    L & GRP

The 1907 agreement, under which the Metropolitan took over the operation of the complete Circle service, put a considerable strain on the fleet, as a result of which the decision was taken to upgrade the two 4-coach trailer sets to self-contained 6-coach electric trains, designated as N stock. The two driving trailers were converted to motor cars, thus releasing the BTH motor cars for service elsewhere, whilst the other two motor coaches were converted from the two 'new' motor coaches were converted from the vehicles built for the Wembley Park electrification experiments.

The four electric train sets thus created, were not all alike, two being Westinghouse equipped, with 150hp motors, whilst the other two were equipped with BTH control gear driving 200hp traction motors. The fundamental differences in control between the two types of equipments and the different numbers of train lines meant that the motor coaches had to be kept as matched pairs; the trailer cars were all equipped with BTH type 10-core train lines and so could be coupled between either type of motor coach.

The first of the 1906 converted trains, designated as M stock, was put into operation in July 1906 on the Uxbridge service, running as a 7-coach formation. An additional third class carriage was added in 1907, once the programme for lengthening the inner area platforms had been completed. Nonetheless, some of the platforms were still rather short for the 330ft length of these trains, with the result that the

guard, who had been relegated to the back cab, was not in the platform. This, together with the lack of facilities available in the cab, resulted in one of the passenger compartments being appropriated for the guard's use, with a connection being provided between it and the adjacent luggage compartment.

The four trains thus created were generally used on the Inner suburban services, where they remained until the Stanmore branch was opened in 1932. At this time the two Westinghouse equipped sets were reduced to four vehicles only for use of this branch.

The progressive introduction of the Dreadnought stock over the period 1912–19 displaced the remaining locomotive-hauled Bogie stock completely from front-line service. However, the continuing need for more electric trains was to lead to their being converted in the early 1920s into five block sets of trailer cars to be worked between Saloon stock motor cars or, later, the prototype MW stock motor coaches. As in the earlier conversions, the coaches were fitted with BTH-type 10-core through control cables and Westinghouse air brakes in place of their original vacuum equipment. Additionally, whilst the original close-coupling arrangements were retained within the sets, the outer vehicles of each set had to be modified to take the centre buffer and automatic coupler required to work with the Saloon and MW stock motor coaches. To allow the train to be split into

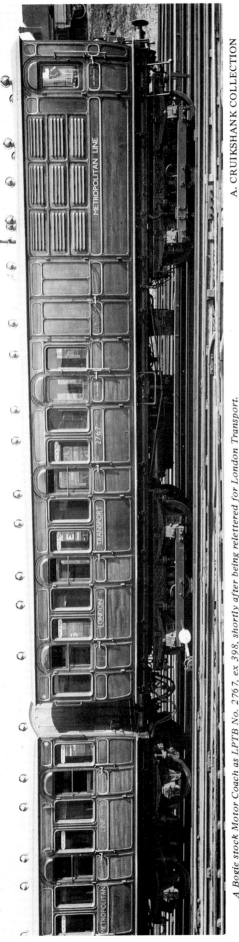

*A Bogie stock Motor Coach as LPTB No. 2767, ex 398, shortly after being relettered for London Transport.*

A. CRUIKSHANK COLLECTION

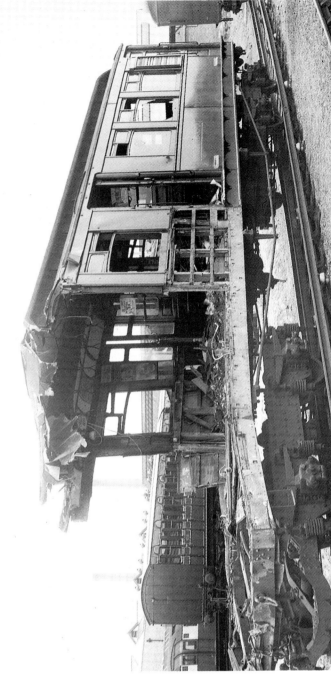

*Seen in the background of a photograph of an accident-damaged District car is Bogie stock coach 9758, ex Met 370. Of greatest interest is that, judging by the relative shades of grey, this coach was painted in LT red, with black mouldings, picked out with yellow or straw lining. Although a number of photographs show Bogie stock in LT 'Metropolitan Line' livery with lined-out panels, this is the only one which appears to have been painted red rather than varnished teak.* AUTHOR'S COLLECTION

two halves, to allow more economical operation during the off-peak periods, the two third class coaches in the centre of each train were modified to Driving Trailers, the end compartment being appropriated to accommodate the driving controls, new windows cut into the vehicle end and, unusually for the electric stock, standard buffers and screw couplings fitted.

The arrival of the various batches of the MW stock in 1929 and 1931 rendered these Bogie stock sets redundant, as a consequence of which they were withdrawn from service pending scrapping. Six vehicles were destined to have a future life as 3-coach push-pull sets for use on the Chesham

branch, where they were steam hauled. For this, they were re-equipped with vacuum brakes, although not in the original arrangement, and the necessary control gear to enable the steam locomotive to be remotely controlled. The two sets thus created were put into service in 1941 and remained on the branch service until September 1960, when the electrification of the Metropolitan to Amersham and Chesham was completed and they were replaced by the purpose-built A60 stock. Of the six coaches, four survived to be acquired by the Bluebell Railway, where they remain, whilst one was retained by London Transport for preservation.

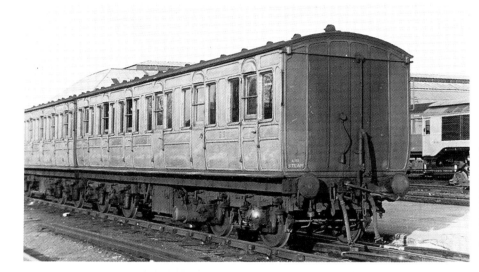

*Bogie stock Third Composite, as returned to steam working, with vacuum brakes and push-pull fittings for use in one of the two Chesham branch sets. The number, 515, was that allocated by LT, not its original Met number (Met 515 was an MW stock trailer coach).* H. LUFF

*Bogie stock Driving Trailer Third, reconverted to steam working, seen at Chalfont on 4th May 1954. This 3-coach set consisted of Met coach Nos. 518, 515 and 513.* H. F. WHEELLER

*An unidentified H class locomotive hauling a 6-coach train of Dreadnought stock, some time in the 1920s or early 1930s.*

A. CRUIKSHANK COLLECTION

# CHAPTER FOUR
# THE DREADNOUGHT STOCK

THE arrival in 1899 of the Great Central in London was to result in considerable problems for the Metropolitan. Before long, the superior comforts of the GCR trains were resulting in a drift of passengers away from Baker Street, which the Metropolitan, by then deeply absorbed in the process of electrifying its suburban network, was unable to counter effectively. The problems were compounded when, in 1907, the Metropolitan took over the working of the entire Inner Circle service, bringing about a dire shortage of rolling stock, particularly motor cars. The consequent withdrawal of the saloon stock trains from the St John's Wood services led to trains of renovated 8-wheel carriages being returned to service on the Main Line, together with two sets of saloon stock trailers.

By 1910, even the Bogie stock, by then only 12 years old, was being outclassed by the new rolling stock coming into service on the Great Central trains. Thus, when new carriages were required to allow the extension of the peak time Aylesbury services to the City, something new was needed.

Neasden drawing office set to work to improve upon the Bogie stock and, by early 1910, had produced tentative arrangement drawings for a new class of compartment stock. Two designs appeared, both based upon the dimensions of the saloon stock, of which there was an over-large surplus at the time as a result of the changes to the operation of Inner Circle services. They were full-bodied carriages 51ft 5in long and 8ft 6in wide, with semi-elliptical roofs, Accommodation was provided for either 9 third class or 8 first class compartments. It is to be noted that, even at this stage, it was clearly intended that only the bodies were to be new, the underframes being drawn from surplus saloon stock trailer cars.

This, however, was not to be the definitive design. That the general concept was satisfactory is evidenced by the relatively small differences between these initial designs and the final version. Changes were made in two areas, the width, which was increased to 8ft 9in, and the size of the first class compartments, resulting in there being seven, instead of eight, compartments in the first class coaches.

The first carriages to the new design were not in fact for locomotive haulage, being the two composite motor cars ordered in 1910 to allow the Harrow–Uxbridge shuttle services to be operated more economically. Only the bodies of these two cars were new, being mounted on the underframes from saloon stock motor cars previously withdrawn from service following major damage. The choice of a compartment, rather than saloon, type body for these cars may originate in a desire to use them as prototypes for the forthcoming new main line stock, possibly influenced by the fact that the standard saloon stock car body would have required significant changes to be made in its door layout in order to accommodate both the first and third class passengers without encroaching upon the driving cabs.

Evidently, the new design was to everyone's satisfaction, for later that year an order was placed with the Metropolitan C&W for ten carriages to the new design, the underframes and bogies to be recovered from ten 1905 stock first class trailer cars which had been rendered surplus to requirements by the changes which had occurred in the operation of the Inner Circle services during the previous two years. The 'new' carriages were to be formed into two 5-coach trains, each consisting of two first class coaches and a third class coach between a pair of third class brake coaches. Unlike the previous Bogie stock trains, each carriage was fitted with conventional screw couplings and side buffers at both ends.

In comparison with earlier Metropolitan locomotive-hauled coaching stock, these new carriages were enormous; not only were they longer by 12 feet than the Bogie stock, but they were wider and, more obviously, roomier as a result of the adoption of the high semi-elliptical roof profile. Like the similarly massive 70ft coaches which had not long before appeared on the Great Western, they soon became known, albeit unofficially, as the Dreadnought stock, doubtless following the lead set by the Royal Navy in naming its new battleships. Officially, the Met only ever referred to them as Main Line stock.

In addition to the provision of the new bodies, considerable work was required on the underframe in order to allow for locomotive haulage. Although the underframe structure and bogies were retained, new self-contained buffers and screw couplings replaced the centre buffer and automatic coupling, whilst two 18in vacuum brake cylinders were substituted for the original Westinghouse equipment. A passenger alarm system, first tried experimentally on a Bogie stock train in 1902, was fitted from the beginning, making these the first Met coaches in ordinary service to incorporate the facility. For this, a chain (the communication cord) running inside the cantrail through each compartment, was connected by rodding to a valve on the coach end which, when operated, admitted air to the brake pipe, thus destroying the vacuum and applying the brakes. Tell-tale flaps attached to the ends of the rods on the carriage end were provided to allow the train crew to locate the affected carriage.

In view of the considerable departure which this stock represented from earlier designs, it is perhaps surprising to find that gas, rather than electric, lighting was provided, despite the fact that the running costs of this system had increased substantially with the mass withdrawal of the older steam stock following electrification, and that the bogie stock, by then 12 years old, had been electrically lit from new. However, the electrical lighting of carriages, other than in electric trains, was still in its infancy, so that the reversion to gas may reflect continuing development problems with the batteries and charging dynamos, possibly allied to difficulties arising from the relatively low operating speeds of trains

*A 3rd class compartment in an MW stock coach (although it could just as easily be a Dreadnought) in the 1933-35 period. The map shows the Brill branch, but, interestingly, not the Uxbridge branch.*

AUTHOR'S COLLECTION

south of Baker Street. Nonetheless, the illumination arrangements were an improvement on the earlier stocks, in that the open flame burners had given way to Wellsbach incandescent mantles, considerably improving the quality and quantity of light provided. As ever, first class passengers were treated to more light than their third class companions.

A peculiarity of these first ten Dreadnought coaches was that the underframe, which used outward-facing angle-irons for longitudes, was wider over the solebars than the bottom of the new bodies. To cover the projecting solebars, a substantial quarter-round moulding was fitted along the whole length of the bottom edge of the body. Later Dreadnought stock carriages were built on new purpose-designed underframes whose in-turned channel section solebars did not project outside the body, thus making the rebuilt coaches instantly identifiable.

Internally, the arrangement of the third class seating followed the precedent set by the two electric Dreadnought cars, groups of two or three seating bays being without full-height partitions and connected by a centre gangway to form semi-open saloons. First class carriages retained the normal arrangement of individual compartments.

These two trains were evidently thought successful, for the Dreadnought design was to become the standard for all subsequent compartment stock. Three further batches, amounting to 92 coaches of varying types were ordered in 1912, 1919 and 1923, following which the design was developed into the MV & MW electric multiple unit stock, production of which ran to 72 trailer and 60 motor coaches.

The introduction of the Dreadnoughts to the City services was not without difficulty, being marked by increasing complaints of delays not only to the through services but also to the other services sharing the Inner Circle tracks. Following investigations, it was concluded that the cause of the problem was the low tractive effort and hence poor acceleration of the electric locomotives, compounded by their short collector shoe span being insufficient to avoid interruption at crossings, particularly in and around Baker Street. To avoid damage to the electrical equipment, it was necessary to shut off and coast across the gap before re-applying power, thus further worsening the loss of performance; whilst this situation had existed ever since the introduction of the locomotives, two factors were combining to render it intolerable. Not only was a 5-coach train of Dreadnought stock some 20 tons heavier than the 6-coach Bogie stock trains it replaced, but traffic levels on the Main and Circle Lines were increasing. To overcome these problems, one train was experimentally equipped in 1915 with a through 600 volt train line, connected to shoegear on the outermost bogies of the train and coupled by a jumper cable to the locomotive. Although this was successful in allowing the locomotive to remain under power whilst traversing crossings, thus improving acceleration and reducing wear and tear on the drawgear, no further work was done until the end of 1916. By then, the growing threat of air raids on London had caused a blackout to be imposed, a measure

*The interior of an MW stock 1st class compartment, complete with carpet and door locks bearing the 'Live in Metroland' legend engraved on the inner face of the casing. The style was virtually unchanged from the first Dreadnought carriages of 1910, some twenty years earlier, and looks quite palatial, especially compared with its modern-day successors.* AUTHOR'S COLLECTION

which the Metropolitan's locomotives, in particular, were blithely ignoring. Complaints from the War Office in this regard finally stung the Met into taking action, with the result that 600V bus lines were fitted to all of the locomotive-hauled stock, including the Pullman cars and other non-passenger vehicles, such as milk vans, horse-boxes and passenger brake vans, which were commonly attached to the Main Line trains. The later 1919 and 1923 batches of Dreadnought stock were similarly equipped during construction.

Over the course of the first two decades of the twentieth century, the growing number of serious fires which had followed from railway accidents led to increasing pressure from the Board of Trade to replace gas with electric lighting, by then established as a viable means of providing illumination. By the end of the First War, only 43 of the Metropolitan's carriages used gas for lighting, a factor which was already making the cost of gas production unattractive; given this, the external pressures against the continuing use of gas were sufficient to persuade the Board to order the conversion in 1918 of the remaining stock using the Stone's system. Future stock, in fact limited to the subsequent 1919 and 1923 Dreadnought stock batches, was to be equipped with electric lighting from new. Unlike the other main line railways, the Metropolitan did not generally adopt through control of the

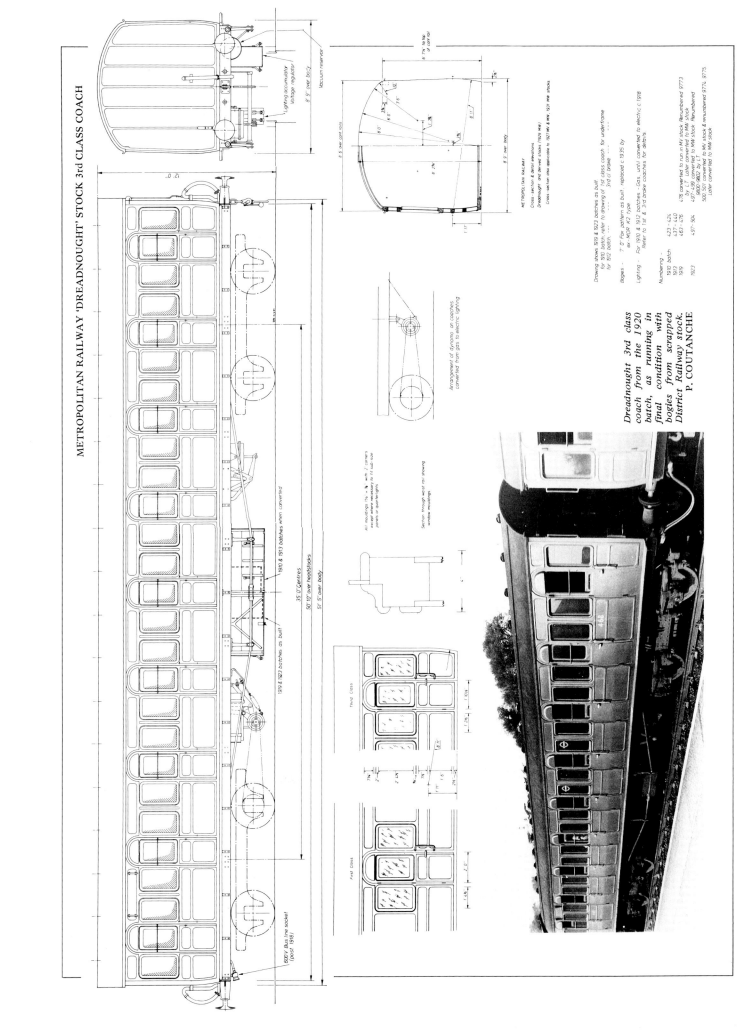

METROPOLITAN RAILWAY 'DREADNOUGHT' STOCK 3rd CLASS COACH

*Dreadnought 3rd class coach from the 1920 batch, as running in final condition with bogies from scrapped District Railway stock.*
*P. COUTANCHE*

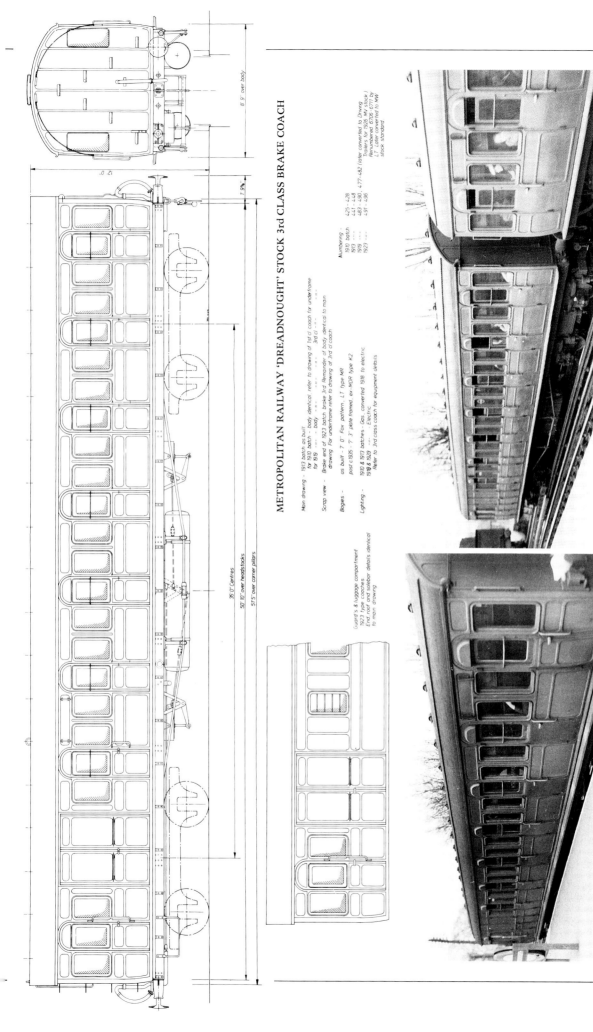

## METROPOLITAN RAILWAY 'DREADNOUGHT' STOCK 3rd CLASS BRAKE COACH

Main drawing - 1913 batch as built
           for 1910 batch - body identical refer to drawing of 1st cl coach for underframe
           for 1919 -"- - body -"-     -"-    3rd cl -"-

Scrap view - Brake end of 1923 batch brake 3rd. Remainder of body identical to main
           drawing. For underframe refer to drawing of 3rd cl coach

Bogies - as built - 7'0" Fox pattern. LT type MR
        post c1925 - 7'3" plate framed, ex-MDR type K2

Lighting - 1910 & 1913 batches - Gas converted 1918 to electric
         1919 & 1923 -"-       - Electric
         Refer to 3rd class coach for equipment details

Numbering -
1910 batch    425 - 428
1913  -"-     441 - 448
1919  -"-     483 - 490   477 - 482 (later converted to Driving
1923  -"-     491 - 496           Trailers for 1926 MV stock)
                         Renumbered 6726-6711 by
                         LT. Later converted to MW
                         stock standard

Guard's & luggage compartment
1923 type coaches
End, roof and solebar details identical
to main drawing

12' 0"
1' 9¾"
35' 0" Centres
50' 10" over headstocks
57' 5" over corner pillars
8' 9" over body

**Left:** *An original Dreadnought Brake 3rd 426 from the 1910 batch, built on redundant frames from 1905 stock trailer cars. The underframes from these were slightly wider than the bogies, hence the quarter-round moulding along the bottom edge, unique to the original vehicles. Above: 1912-built Dreadnought Brake 3rd 443.*

P. COUTANCHE

# METROPOLITAN RAILWAY 'DREADNOUGHT' STOCK 1st CLASS COACH

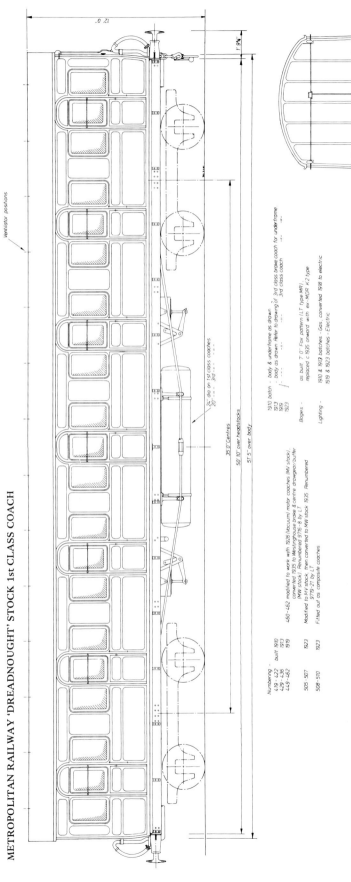

Ventilator positions

12' 0"

1' 9"

24" dia on 1st class coaches
20" — 3rd — — —

35' 0" Centres

50' 10" over headstocks

51' 5" over body

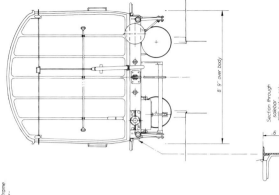

Section through
solebar
1910 batch only

8' 9" over body

*Dreadnought 1st 459, built in 1920, in final con-dition running on ex-District Railway K2 bogies and demoted to 3rd class.*    P. COUTANCHE

Numbering -    built    1910
419 - 422           1910
429 - 436           1913
449 - 462           1919

505 - 507           1923

508 - 510           1923

460 - 462 modified to work with 1926 (vacuum) motor coaches (MV stock),
           converted 1935 to Westinghouse brake & centre drawgear/buffer
           (MW stock). Renumbered 9716-8 by LT
Modified to MV stock, then converted to MW stock 1935. Renumbered
           9719-21 by LT
Fitted out as composite coaches

1910 batch - body & underframe as drawn
1913 - body as drawn. Refer to drawing of 3rd class brake coach for underframe
1919 - — — — — — — — 3rd class coach
1923 - — — — — — — — —

Bogies -    as built 7' 0" Fox pattern (LT type MR)
           replaced c.1935 onward with ex-MDR K2 type

Lighting -  1910 & 1913 batches - Gas, converted 1918 to electric
           1919 & 1923 batches - Electric

lighting, mainly because the difficulties which would arise during the changeover period, since the existing manually-operated gas control valves could not readily be modified. Instead the push-bar system was retained, the gas valve being replaced by an electric switch box, a feature which remained standard until the final batch of MW stock in 1931, although the trains of Bogie stock which had been converted to electric working had been fitted with a form of through control.

One feature that was totally lacking on either of the two types of electric locomotives acquired at the time of the main line electrification was any provision for carriage heating. Consequently, once trains left their steam locomotives behind at Wembley, or later Harrow, the passengers had to survive on what warmth remained. On those trains which ran only as far as Baker Street, the consequent lack of heating may have been tolerable. However, there were many trains which, having worked through to the City, spent the middle part of the day stabled, where they could not be heated at all; a return journey in winter cannot have been at all comfortable. The installation of through 600V power

bus-lines in 1916 on the loco-hauled stock paved the way for further development, but it was not until 1921 that this situation was resolved by the installation in each carriage of twelve 100 volt 350 watt heaters, connected in two strings of six across the power train line.

In the case of the Dreadnought stock, where each carriage had either seven or nine compartments, the division of heating elements was, perforce, somewhat uneven; the chances of a reasonably warm journey home were distinctly better in the first class, or third class brake, carriages than in the full thirds, where only three of the nine compartments boasted more than one heater. Such provision proved to be neither adequate nor acceptable, with the result that in 1926 the matter was raised again, when it was decided to fit three heaters to each compartment. In practice, the result was that the first class coaches were fitted with an extra six heaters, whilst the third class coaches received an extra twelve, thus making the latter better heated than the first class!

A unique feature of the original Dreadnought stock was the way in which groups of two and three third class compartments were linked together by a centre gangway to form

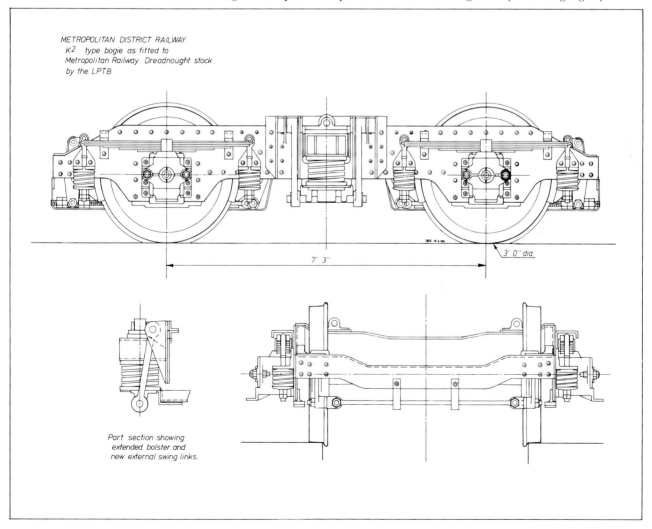

METROPOLITAN DISTRICT RAILWAY
K2 type bogie as fitted to
Metropolitan Railway Dreadnought stock
by the LPTB

7' 3"

3' 0" dia

Part section showing
extended bolster and
new external swing links

# METROPOLITAN RAILWAY 'DREADNOUGHT' STOCK COMPOSITE MOTOR CAR

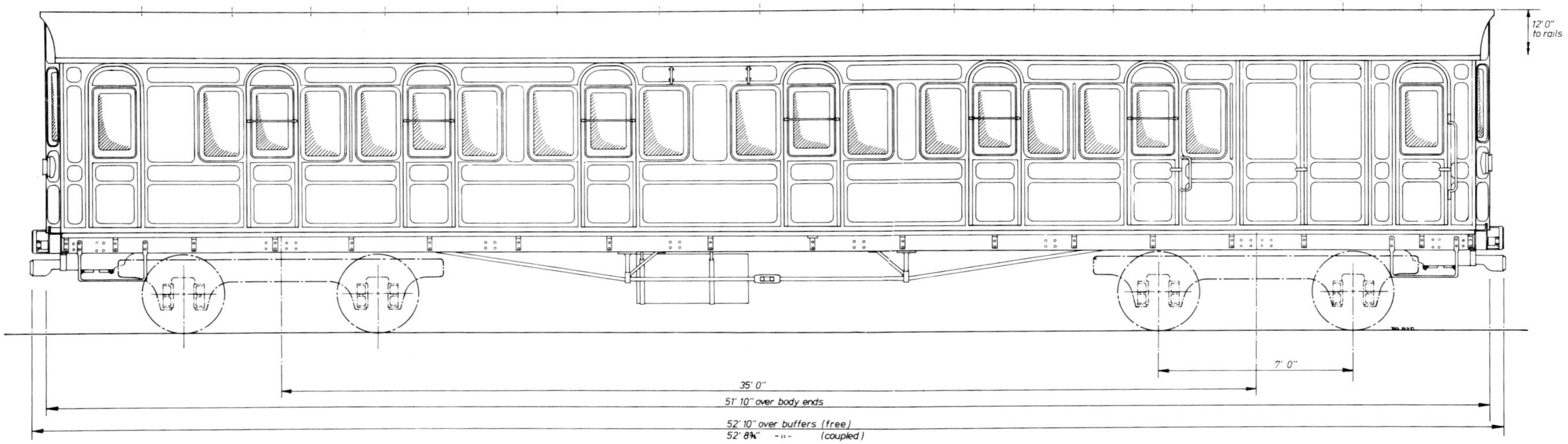

12' 0"
to rails

7' 0"

35' 0"

51' 10" over body ends

52' 10" over buffers (free)

52' 8¾" - " - (coupled)

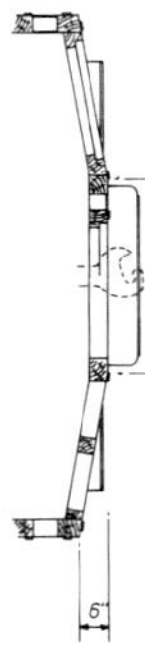

8' 9" over body

Sectional plan of body end
above and below windows

3' 3"

6"

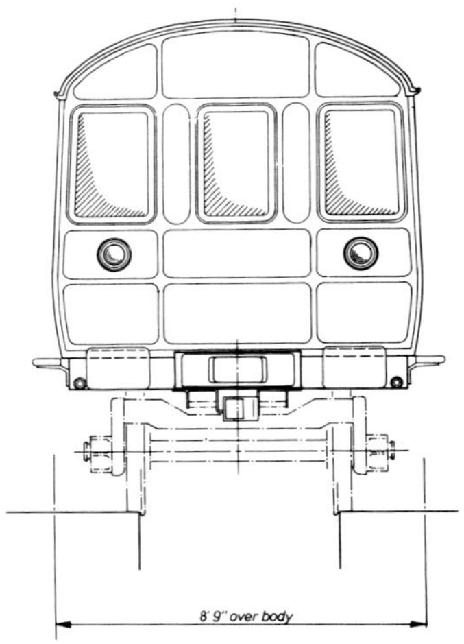

Nos. 46 (LT 2768) rebuilt 1910 using underframe & equipment
from collision damaged BTH motor car MB & MC type bogies
69 (LT 2769) similarly rebuilt 1910 from fire damaged
BWE motor car. Original 200 hp GE 69 motors
replaced with 150 hp GE 76 type MD type bogies

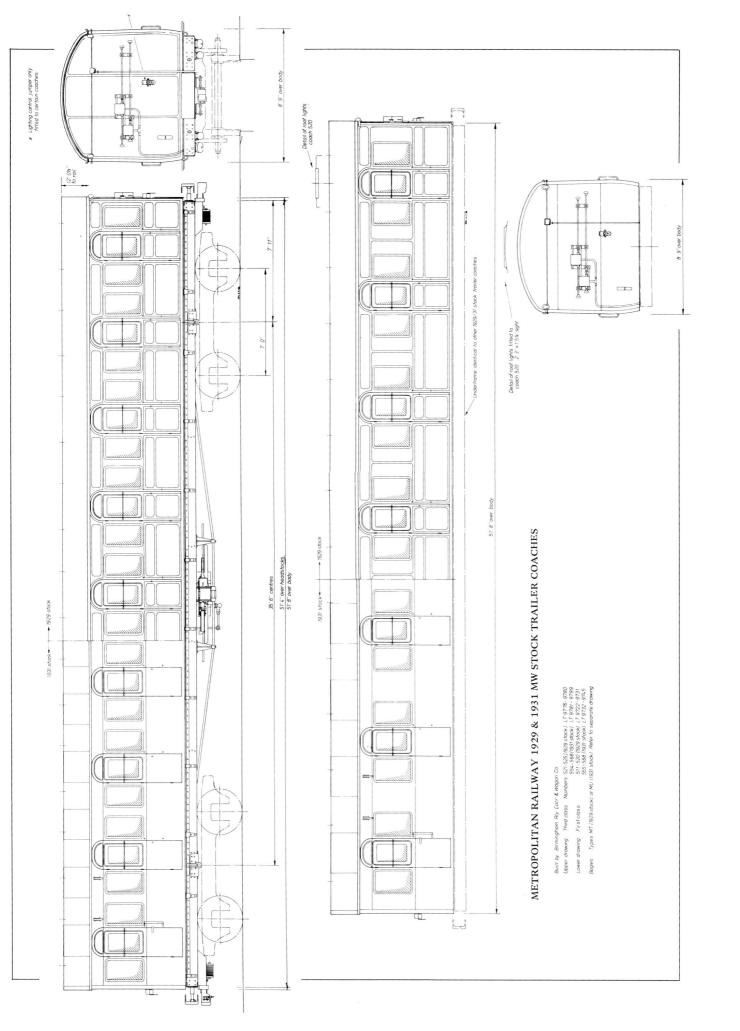

# METROPOLITAN RAILWAY 1929 & 1931 MW STOCK TRAILER COACHES

x Lighting control jumper only fitted to certain coaches

12' 0½" to rail

8' 9" over body

7' 11"

7' 0"

35' 6" centres

51' 4" over headstocks

51' 8" over body

1929 stock

1931 stock

Detail of roof lights coach 520

Underframe identical to other 1929/31 stock trailer coaches

Detail of roof lights fitted to coach 520   2' 3" x 1⅝" sight

51' 8" over body

1929 stock

1931 stock

8' 9" over body

Built by  Birmingham Rly Carr & Wagon Co
Upper drawing  Third class   Numbers  521-525 (1929 stock)  LT 9776-9780
                                    554-568 (1931 stock)  LT 9781-9799
Lower drawing  First class            511-520 (1929 stock)  LT 9722-9731
                                    555-568 (1931 stock)  LT 9732-9745
Bogies  Types MT (1929 stock) or MU (1931 stock)  Refer to separate drawing

The heyday of the Metropolitan train, with five Dreadnoughts, two of which were 1st class, flanking one of the two Pullman cars, pictured in the 1920s.

A. CRUIKSHANK COLLECTION

Dreadnought Brake Third No. 491, one of the batch built in 1923 with enlarged brake compartments.

A. CRUIKSHANK COLLECTION

*H class 4–4–4T No. 109, at Chalfont on 21st May 1934 with a typical 6-coach train of Dreadnought stock with (leading) an example of a 1923 stock Brake Third.* H. F. WHEELLER

small semi-saloons, a feature intended to facilitate a more even distribution of passengers. However, although this was perpetuated in the subsequent 1912 and 1919 batches, it carried the penalty of reducing the overall capacity of the coach by up to 12 seats. By 1923, with the growth of longer distance commuting, the missing seats were more valuable an asset than the gangway, resulting in the abandonment of this feature. The 1923 and 1925 batches of Dreadnought stock, as well as all the subsequent compartment electric stock reverted to the normal arrangement of individual compartments, whilst the earlier carriages were progressively modified from 1930 onwards. Only the two electric Dreadnought shuttle cars were to retain their semi-open third class layout.

At the time of their debut, the two Dreadnought stock trains consisted of five carriages, made up as B3-3-1-1-B3, providing roughly the same numbers of seats as the 6-coach Bogie stock trains, although the proportion of first class accommodation was increased. The 1912 sets were constituted similarly, remaining so until the early 1920s when they were augmented by the addition of a second third class carriage to cope with the growing traffic resulting from the development of the Metropolitan estates (Metroland) along the line north of Harrow. By 1927, even six coaches were not always enough, necessitating a further increase to 7-coach train lengths, a move largely made possible by the arrival of the first Main Line electric sets for the Watford electrification. Seven coach sets remained the rule until after the LPTB takeover, when a 6-coach train formation was stan-

dardised, although the need for economy had resulted in 1932 on the splitting of these trains into 3- and 4-coach sets for off-peak operation.

| 419–422 | I | 1910 | 2 trains B3-3-1-1-B3 |
| 423–424 | 3 | 1910 | |
| 425–428 | B3 | 1910 | |
| | | | |
| 429–436 | I | 1912 | 4 trains B3-3-1-1-B3 |
| 437–440 | 3 | 1912 | |
| 441–448 | B3 | 1912 | |
| | | | |
| 449–462 | I | 1919 | 7 trains B3-3-3-1-1-B3 |
| 463–476 | 3 | 1919 | |
| 477–490 | B3 | 1919 | |
| | | | |
| 491–496 | B3(L) | 1923 | 3 trains B3-3-1-1/3-B3L |
| 497–504 | 3 | 1923 | |
| 505–507 | I | 1923 | |
| 508–510 | I/3 | 1923 | |

The entire fleet of Dreadnought stock coaches survived to be inherited by the LPTB in July 1933, although by then 18 of them were no longer locomotive-hauled, having been adapted to run with the six 1927 MW stock motor coaches built for the then recently electrified Watford and Rickmansworth services.

Under the LPTB's 1935 new works programme, which envisaged the electrification of the Main Line as far as Amersham, it was intended that many more of the remaining Dreadnought stock coaches — known by the LPTB as 'Steam Stock' — would be similarly converted to run with new MW stock motor coaches, a move which could have

*1st class Dreadnought carriage No. 431 in the mid-1950s, running on modified District K2 bogies fitted by LPTB in place of the Fox patent 7ft 0in bogie utilised hitherto.*
AUTHOR'S COLLECTION

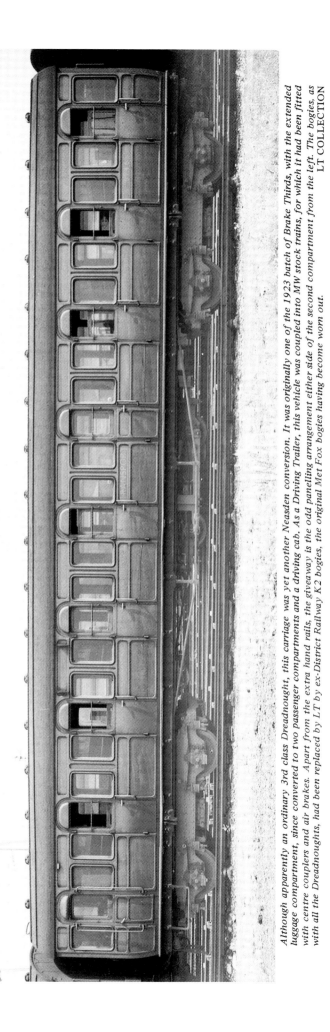

*Although apparently an ordinary 3rd class Dreadnought, this carriage was yet another Neasden conversion. It was originally one of the 1923 batch of Brake Thirds, with the extended luggage compartment, since converted to two passenger compartments and a driving cab. As a Driving Trailer, this vehicle was coupled into MW stock trains, for which it had been fitted with centre couplers and air brakes. Apart from the extra hand rails, the giveaway is the odd panelling arrangement either side of the second compartment from the left. The bogies, as with all the Dreadnoughts, had been replaced by LT by ex-District Railway K2 bogies, the original Met Fox bogies having become worn out.*
LT COLLECTION

*H class 4—4—4T at Chorleywood in the late 1920s with a typical 5-coach train of Dreadnought stock.*          LENS OF SUTTON

resulted in considerable economies. Blocks of electric stock numbers were even allocated for their conversion, but in the event, the whole project was never undertaken; the events that were later to culminate in World War II deferred the further electrification of the Metropolitan until the end of the 1950s, whilst the continuing need for electric multiple unit stock was to result in the building of the 1929/31 MW stock fleet, themselves descended directly from the Dreadnought stock.

By the late 1940s, the pressed steel bogies with which these carriages had been fitted were increasingly suffering from cracked frames, the incidence of serious defects eventually reaching a level which made it necessary to replace many of the bogies completely. At the same time, the scrapping of ex-District Railway cars was making available a considerable number of K2 type plate-framed bogies in good condition and capable of further service. The result was that, apart from Nos. 424 and 447, both of which had been withdrawn from service in December 1939, the entire Dreadnought fleet was refitted with the K2 bogies, which they retained until they themselves were displaced in 1960–61 by the arrival of the London Transport A60 stock and the cessation of the locomotive-hauled Baker Street–Aylesbury service.

Of the 87 Dreadnought stock carriages originally built, three were saved for preservation, being retired to the Keighley and Worth Valley Railway, where they remain. The remainder were all sold off as scrap. Of the three preserved, the third class brake is notable in being one of the original 1910 rebuilds.

*The outer end of a Dreadnought Brake Third, with all the clutter of lighting controls, piping and traction jumper cables.*

*The interior of the same Pullman car, looking towards the pantry, and, in this case, the barman.*

# CHAPTER FIVE

# THE PULLMAN CARS

Mayflower *as built showing the original number and cream livery, seen from the non pantry side.*     AUTHOR'S COLLECTION

WHEN the Great Central opened its new London Extension, it actively sought to poach the lucrative first class traffic from the Metropolitan, whose route it shared from Quainton Road into London. As part of this strategy, the GCR Board had agreed on 22nd October 1909 to accept an offer made by the Pullman Car Company to provide their line with Pullman services for a period of 15 years. No contract ever materialised from this decision, however, because on 28th January 1910 the GCR Board changed its mind and decided to build their own luxury stock for these services. The Metropolitan, then absorbed in the process of electrifying its inner suburban lines, was understandably alarmed by this prospect and took the decision that it, too, should run Pullman cars in competition. Negotiations were entered into with the Pullman Car Company, culminating in the acceptance in March 1909 of a 30-year agreement for the provision of two new first class cars for use on the longer distance services. This also provided that if after their first year of operation receipts were insufficient to meet the railway's expenses, the Pullman company would, at their discretion, either make good the loss or terminate the arrangement. Further, if under the provisions of its 1906 joint working agreement with the GCR, the Metropolitan ceased to operate services north of Harrow, the arrangement would also be terminated insofar as it concerned such services.

The two cars were built by the Birmingham Railway Carriage & Wagon Co. Ltd. along with ten others for the South Eastern & Chatham Railway (in which William Watkin also had an interest). Like the SE&CR cars, the two Met Pullmans were 51ft long over the saloon, 57ft 6in over the vestibules. Thereafter, although their external appearance was very much in the Pullman style, with matchboarded lower sides, the two Metropolitan cars differed radically in being narrower and lower in order to fit the restricted Metropolitan loading gauge, particularly in the Finchley

Road–Baker Street tunnels, through which a standard car would not have passed. As a consequence they were only 8ft 5in wide and 12ft 4in high, distinctly smaller in cross-section than normal cars. The bogies, although outwardly of standard Pullman pattern for the period, differed in being of shorter than normal wheelbase and having 3ft 4in nominal diameter wheels. The usual Pullman Buckeye coupler and sprung gangway would not have been appropriate for these cars, which were instead provided with screw couplings and side buffers; as no other Metropolitan coaches were equipped with through gangways, these were never fitted, although provision was made for them, the centre vestibule doors being sealed.

Internally, each car was divided into two saloons and a coupé compartment, each seating 8, 7 and 4 passengers respectively on loose leather-upholstered armchairs. Silk damask window blinds were provided, surmounted by ormolu baggage racks, whilst plate glass partitions were provided to separate the two saloons. The two cars differed in that one was panelled in fiddleback mahogany inlaid with satinwood, with green upholstery and carpets to match; the other was panelled in oak inlaid with holly with predominantly crimson upholstery and carpets. Lighting was by electricity, the customary table-top lamps being provided on each of the glass-topped tables, which were also equipped with bell pushes with which to summon the attendant. A small buffet counter and pantry were provided at one end of the car in order to serve light refreshments, gas being retained to supply the cooking equipment. The other end of the car was taken up with a lavatory.

In keeping with Pullman practice, the two cars, being first class, were named, in this case *Mayflower* and *Galatea*. The choice of names was, however, unusual in that they were not female, as was normal, but after the contenders for the 1886 Americas Cup. Why this choice was made remains totally obscure, although it does appear to have been made by the

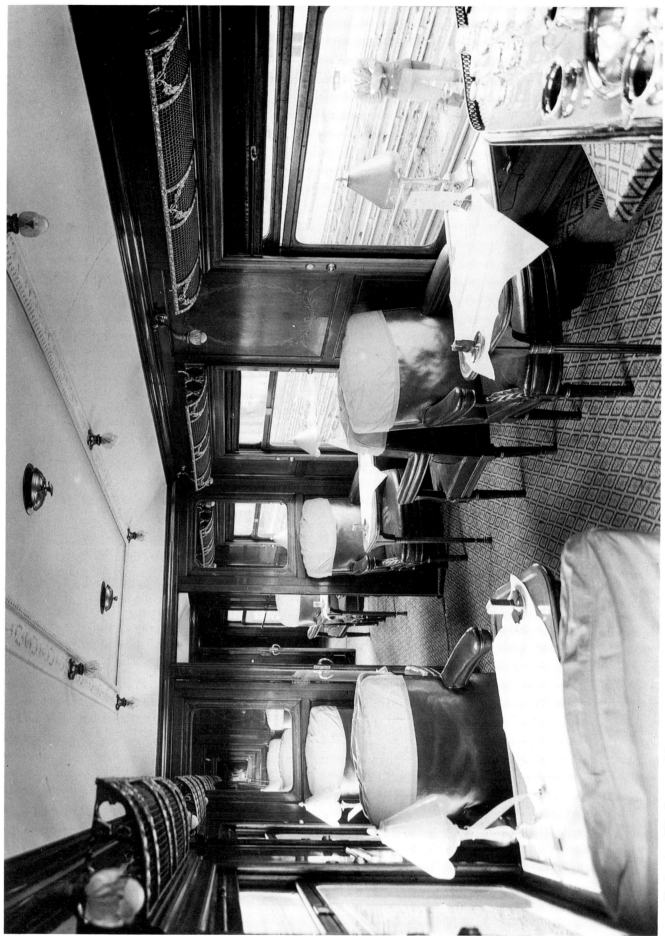

*The interior of Mayflower or Galatea looking from the pantry end.*

Pullman Company rather than being a whim of the Metropolitan directors. The two cars were finished in the traditional Pullman livery of umber and cream, which they carried until 1922. Not surprisingly, the cream upperworks had proved to be difficult to keep clean in the smoky confines of the Metropolitan tunnels. With varnished teak being the standard livery of the rest of the Metropolitan fleet, it is perhaps no surprise that this was also suggested for the Pullman cars. Their owners were not overly impressed by this proposal, preferring instead the dark crimson lake which they had employed for some years on the SE&CR cars. The outcome was that the cars reappeared in crimson lake, which finish they retained until they were finally withdrawn in 1939.

Because these cars were longer than anything previously run on the Metropolitan, apart from the rebuilt Rothschild saloon, it was considered highly desirable to check the gauge of, in particular, the tunnels in the Baker Street area and on the Circle where these cars could be run. Accordingly, a gauging car was constructed from the underframe of the fire-damaged saloon-stock motor car 46, wooden extensions being provided over the headstocks to simulate the additional end overhang of the Pullman, whilst one of the bogies was re-mounted on a temporary bolster to allow for the greater bogie centre distance. Operation of this revealed that the cars could be safely run on the Metropolitan, although one of the crossovers at Aldgate had to be realigned in order to minimise the risk of buffer-locking, particularly with the old 'rigid' stock.

Their inaugural trip took place on 27th May, 1910, when they were used to convey a party of railway officers and guests from both the Met and the Underground companies, as well as representatives from the press, from Liverpool Street to Aylesbury and back. The train was formed from the two Pullmans, on the only occasion they would ever be seen together, between which was the Rothschild Saloon, and completed at either end by a Bogie stock Third Class brake, the latter being provided, presumably, solely for the purpose of conveying the guard.

Ordinary service commenced on 1st June, 1910, when two of the Bogie stock Main Line sets were reformed with a Pullman car in place of the first/third class composite coach, necessitating the fitment of full-length buffers and screw drawgear to the ends of the two adjoining vehicles. With these two sets a daily service of four up and five down trains was provided, running variously between Baker Street, Liverpool Street and Aldgate and Aylesbury, Verney Junction and Chesham. First class fares were charged, with the usual Pullman supplement, in this case 6d for journeys anywhere between Aldgate and Rickmansworth and 1 shilling for journeys beyond the latter. The outbreak of World War I heralded a sharp drop in patronage, causing the supplementary fare to be reduced to 6d, irrespective of distance travelled, in an effort to maintain traffic. This, together with a reduction in the refreshment rates, was suc-

cessful and was to last from its introduction on 1st January 1915 until the cessation of hostilities in 1918.

Their association with the Bogie stock was shortlived, the arrival of the first Dreadnought stock in September 1910 causing the former to be progressively relegated to lesser duties and ultimately conversion to electric stock. Thus the two cars were remarshalled into trains of Dreadnought stock, where the latter's possession of conventional drawgear allowed them to be inserted and removed from sets as required by demand, normally displacing one of the first class cars.

Although the two cars were based at Neasden, they were often stabled at outlying stations overnight, ready for the first up service of the following morning, except at weekends. One was regularly stabled at Verney Junction, ready for attachment to the first up through service in the morning. Sir Harry Verney, a Metropolitan Board member from January 1920, would normally be the first passenger of the day, joining the train at Granborough Road; most business for the cars originated from the Amersham and Chorleywood area.

Periodically each of the two cars had to be withdrawn for overhaul, requiring the provision of an alternative vehicle if standards were to be maintained. As the usual recourse of substituting another Pullman car was impossible, due to the restrictions imposed by the Metropolitan's loading gauge, the only alternative was to use the Rothschild Saloon, suitably modified by the addition of catering facilities; staff continued to be provided by the Pullman Car Company.

One of the two Pullmans, together with the saloon, participated in the inaugural train on the Watford branch, the two vehicles being formed into a train otherwise composed of 1929 MW stock. As this latter stock was Westinghouse braked and equipped only with centre couplers and buffers, considerable ingenuity must have been required to accommodate the Pullman and the Saloon, both of which had side buffers and vacuum brakes. Whilst the adjoining MW trailer coaches could quite readily have been modified to carry side buffers, in view of the Dreadnought design origins, there is no evidence to suggest that air brake equipment was fitted to the Pullman or the Saloon. It is not impossible that the two vehicles ran unbraked, with the front and rear parts of the train connected by a temporary through brake pipe.

The Pullman services, which continued to be a feature of the Metropolitan Line after the formation of the LPTB in 1933, eventually succumbed, like so many other things, to the outbreak of the Second World War. The last service ran on Saturday, 7th October, 1939, after which the two cars found their way to the LPTB's Acton Works, where they languished in the open until early in 1941 when they were taken to Hampton Court (Southern Railway). Here they were separated from their bogies and taken by road to nearby Hinchley Wood, where they served as an office-cum-store for a local wood merchant until 1948, when they were scrapped.

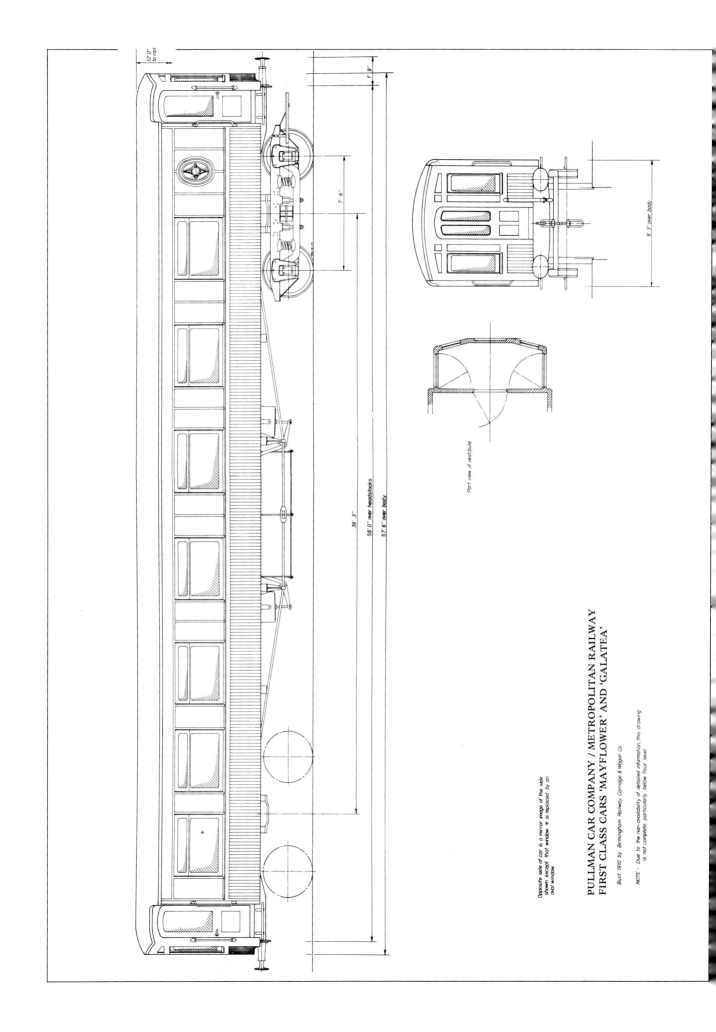

12' 0" to rail

1' 9"

7' 6"

39' 3"

56' 0" over headstocks

57' 6" over body

8' 3" over body

Part view of vestibule

Opposite side of car is a mirror image of the side shown except that window # is replaced by an oval window

**PULLMAN CAR COMPANY / METROPOLITAN RAILWAY FIRST CLASS CARS 'MAYFLOWER' AND 'GALATEA'**

Built 1910 by Birmingham Railway Carriage & Wagon Co

NOTE:- Due to the non-availability of detailed information, this drawing is not complete, particularly below floor level.

LONDON UNDERGROUND

Galatea c.1935 (?) in the later crimson livery, seen from the pantry side.

It is only on close inspection that this photograph reveals that it shows more than just two Metropolitan trains in the Buckinghamshire countryside. The train on the right was the Rothschild special, formed of both of the special saloons, then in their unrebuilt 6-wheel form, flanked by the two rebodied 8-wheel 1st class brake carriages. The train on the left is almost as remarkable for, although formed of 8-wheel stock, the second vehicle was one of the two rebodied 3rd class carriages. The original photograph is undated, as well as anonymous, but the livery of the 1st class sections of the left-hand train, as well as its haulage by an open-cabbed 4–4–0 suggests that the late 1890s is likely.

# CHAPTER SIX
# METROPOLITAN RAILWAY SALOON COACHES

WHEN, in 1892, the Metropolitan's northern expansion reached Aylesbury, the new station at Wendover was to provide Alfred Rothschild, whose country seat was at Halton, with a more convenient access to the City than had hitherto been possible from Tring, on the London & North-Western Railway. For a time, it seems that he was content to reserve a first class compartment, but this arrangement cannot have been entirely to his satisfaction, for in June 1895, tenders were sought by the Metropolitan for the construction of one or two saloon carriages specifically intended for his use, resulting in a contract being awarded to Brown, Marshall for two vehicles at £660 each.

These saloons, the only two to run on the Metropolitan, were unique in having 6-wheeled underframes, carrying bodies 32ft long and 8ft 3in wide. Internally, these saloons were not unlike the many other family saloons which graced the fleets of most of the other main-line railways, having a large saloon flanked by, at one end, a luggage compartment, and, at the other end, a compartment for personal staff. Connecting the latter, which measured 6ft 1in between partitions and was furnished to first class standards, and the main saloon, was a short corridor, on opposite sides of which were a lavatory and wash-room.

The saloon itself was equipped with two settees fixed along either side, a matching pair of built-in armchairs at the far (non-toilet) end and, probably, a central drop-leaf table, polished panelling and a decorated lincrusta ceiling completing the interior decor. Lighting was provided by Pintsch gas lamps, whilst Laycock's steam heating equipment was almost certainly provided, it having already become standard on the contemporary Jubilee stock.

At the time of their construction, these two carriages were unique on the Metropolitan Railway in being fitted with a passenger alarm, in this case Spagnoletti's electrical system rather than the more usual mechanical system acting directly on the brake pipe. The Spagnoletti system did not comply with the requirements of the Board of Trade for passenger alarm equipment, then obligatory on all trains travelling more than 20 miles between stops. Since Wendover is 33½ miles from Baker Street, Rothschild's usual destination, an additional, unadvertised, stop was made at Rickmansworth in order to achieve legality. A proposal was made in 1901 to fit the standard direct-acting alarm system, which would have rendered the intermediate stop superfluous, but this was, in the event, never acted upon.

In service, the two saloons ran as a pair, coupled between the two first class brake carriages (Nos. 41 & 45) which had been built at this time on the frames of two eight-wheeled carriages dating from c.1863. Although originally set aside for the use of the Rothschild family, the two saloons were

later used on a number of occasions for private hire and special parties, the whole train being used for the opening of the Uxbridge branch in 1904.

At about this time, possibly as a result of the work being undertaken to electrify the line between Harrow and Uxbridge, arrangements were made with the Great Central Railway, who had then only recently opened their new Marylebone station, for the 'Rothschild Specials' to be worked into the latter station rather than Baker Street. Unfortunately by then, the two carriages had been in constant use for some ten years and were beginning to show the fact. Selbie, fearing that their condition might result in their traffic being lost to the Great Central, at a cost to the Met of some £600 per annum, recommended to the Metropolitan Board that, if the situation was to be recovered, the two saloons be not only thoroughly refurbished but also rebuilt into a single carriage on a new bogie underframe, the cost being estimated at £220.

Selbie's recommendations were accepted by the Board and in due course, in early 1907, the reconstructed saloons emerged from Neasden Works as a single carriage, now numbered 1. At 55ft 10in long, it was the longest carriage on the Metropolitan, considerably larger than the Bogie stock with which it was contemporary. The metamorphosis had been achieved by joining the two bodies, each shorn of the luggage compartments, end to end, to form a double saloon divided by a centre bulkhead. The two single compartments remained, now at the outer ends of the carriage. The vehicle was refurnished internally by Messrs Maple & Co. with free-standing settees and an assortment of mahogany armchairs and occasional tables. Specially-made Wilton and Saxony carpets were provided, whilst the furniture was covered in red tapestry in one saloon and blue and yellow in the other. Below, a new steel underframe had been provided, running on 7ft 0in Fox pressed steel bogies set at 38ft 1in centres. Vacuum braking was provided and Stone's electric lighting equipment was fitted in place of the original gas installation. The decision to build a new underframe was evidently not part of the original scheme, for there exists a drawing of an even longer timber underframe which appears to have been derived by splicing together the two original frames and adapting the whole to be mounted on bogies. What the body would then have looked like is unknown since no drawings exist.

Although in its rebuilt form the saloon continued to be used primarily for conveying Lord Rothschild to and from the City, advancing age resulted in his making less use of it, and the train was, to a limited extent, given over to use by private parties and the directors of the Metropolitan Railway. It appeared in the latter capacity sandwiched between the two Pullman cars on the occasion of their inau-

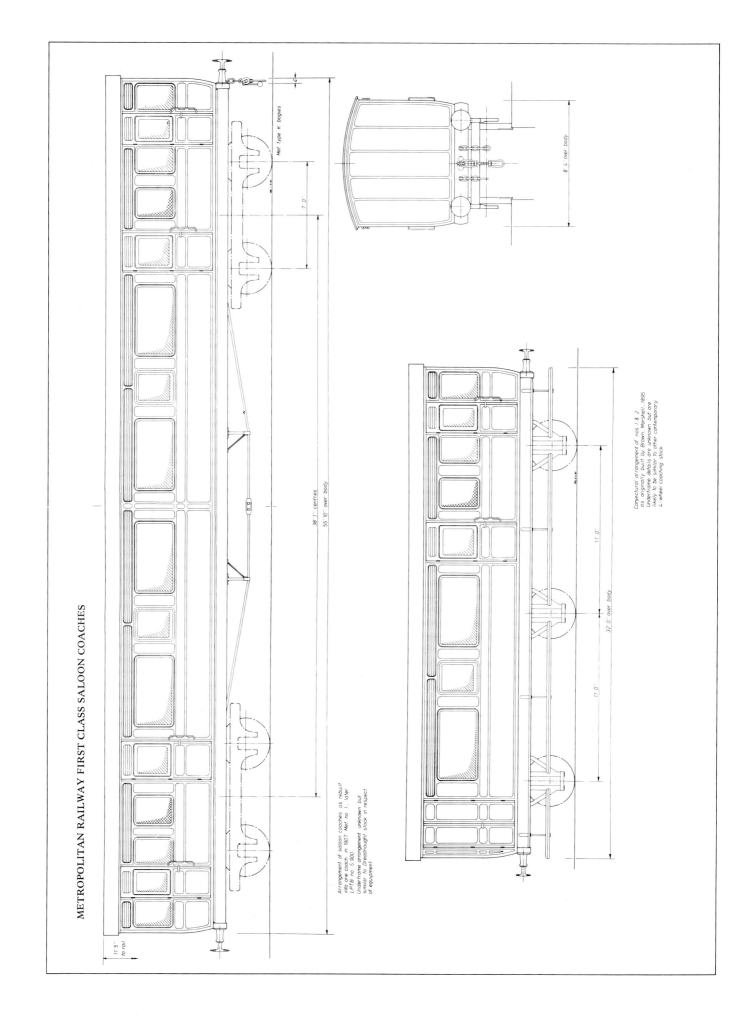

METROPOLITAN RAILWAY FIRST CLASS SALOON COACHES

Met type 'K' bogies

7' 0"

38' 1" centres

55' 10" over body

8' 4" over body

11' 5"
to rail

Arrangement of saloon coaches as rebuilt
into one coach in 1907. Met no 1, later
LPTB no S 900.
Underframe arrangement unknown but
similar to Dreadnought stock in respect
of equipment.

11' 0"

11' 0"

32' 0" over body

Conjectural arrangement of nos 1 & 2
as originally built by Brown, Marshall 1895.
Underframe details are unknown but are
likely to be similar to other contemporary
4-wheel coaching stock.

*By 1907, the two Rothschild saloons were in need of refurbishment, both for their normal duties and to act as a stand-in for the Pullman cars. The decision was taken to combine the two into a single bogie carriage, a new underframe being built for the purpose. Seen here in Neasden car shed, its last act, as LT Saloon S900, was to convey the railway's officers on the closure of the Brill branch in 1935.*

A. CRUIKSHANK COLLECTION

gural run in 1910. When, in 1912, it became necessary to withdraw each of the two Pullman cars for overhaul, the Metropolitan's restricted loading gauge prevented any other cars being used as substitutes, leaving the saloon as the only potentially suitable vehicle. In the absence of any other suitable Pullmans being available which would clear the Met loading gauge, the saloon was selected to act as a temporary replacement. Selbie agreed to hire the vehicle to the Pullman Car Company, at £3 per week, to maintain the service. In the form in which Neasden had rebuilt it, it was not immediately suitable for Pullman duties and various modifications had to be undertaken, the most substantial being the reconstruction of one of the lavatories and the adjoining compartment to a small kitchen, complete with gas and water supplies. Otherwise, the car was refurnished internally, new green carpet being laid and sixteen leather chairs and eight tables being sent from the Pullman Company's Battersea depot for incorporation into the car at Neasden. Externally, the saloon's new, if temporary, status was indicated by the embellishment of the waist panels with 15ft long paper labels bearing the title 'Pullman'. Other, smaller labels on the exterior announced the availability of the car to first-class ticket holders upon the payment of the supplement.

Thus refitted, the Met saloon stood in for *Mayflower* from 11th March 1912 until mid-May, when the Pullman car returned from Brighton, after which its original fittings were restored, save for the retention of the kitchen facilities, and the saloon returned to its normal 'excursion' duties for the summer season. September 1912 saw the other Pullman car, *Galatea*, returned to Brighton for refurbishment, as a consequence of which the saloon was again re-equipped with borrowed furniture and fittings to act as a temporary Pullman car until *Galatea*'s return in November.

The saloons also occupied a prestigious place in the Metropolitan's fleet in that they (or later, it) were used for the conveyance of the directors and other guests of the com-

pany. Their first recorded use in this capacity was in 1906 on the occasion of the opening of the Uxbridge branch, when the two saloons and the three 1897 rebodied eight-wheelers were formed into the inaugural train.

Four years later, in 1910, the by now rebuilt saloon figured in the inaugural Pullman car train, coupled between the two Pullmans on the only occasion that the latter ever ran in the same train. After that, it passed into obscurity, appearing occasionally as substitute Pullman cars until 1925, when it formed part of the inaugural train on the ~~Stanmore~~ Branch. *Watford*

It reappeared again in this capacity in 1932 in the inaugural train on the Stanmore branch, when it and one of the Pullmans were formed into a train with MW type multiple unit stock. Why this stock, rather than the MV stock or one of the electric locomotives, was chosen remains obscure, since neither the Pullman nor the Saloon possessed the centre automatic couplers and Westinghouse brake equipment necessary for proper operation with the MW stock. Quite how these two vehicles were coupled with the rest of the train remains a mystery, although the design of the MW stock underframe and drawgear is such that it could have been modified to take side buffers and screw couplings, a task which Neasden Works could readily have undertaken. Through air brake pipes could have been fairly readily fitted, although there is no evidence to suggest that any Westinghouse brake equipment was actually carried, whilst an extra-long control jumper would have been required to allow both motor coaches to be driven in multiple.

Two and a half years later, the saloon, by now allocated the number S900 by its new owners, the LPTB, was turned out for what was probably its last ceremonial duty, conveying a party of LPTB officers on 23rd July 1935 on a tour of inspection of the Brill Branch prior to its closure on 30th November that year. After that sad occasion, the saloon languished at Neasden, finally succumbing to the scrapman when Neasden Depot was rebuilt in the late 1930s.

A train of 1907 Hammersmith & City stock pictured in the sylvan setting of Addison Road on the Kensington—Edgware Road shuttle service.

# CHAPTER SEVEN

# ELECTRIFICATION & ROLLING STOCK DEVELOPMENT

THE electric rolling stock of the Metropolitan Railway consisted broadly of two distinct families, the saloon stocks and the later slam-door stocks. There were inevitably exceptions, either in the form of the experimental stocks or conversions from surplus locomotive-hauled stock.

The first electric trains operated by the Metropolitan dated from 1904, being used on the tunnel sections of the railway, i.e. the Circle service. Possibly influenced by the new Tube railways, the rolling stock for this service showed a distinct American influence, being of the open saloon type, with access from initially open-end platforms, later enclosed vestibules. Each train was formed of four trailer cars flanked by two motor cars, the latter having four motors of 150, later 200 hp capacity. These trains set a design standard which was to remain largely unchanged over the remaining life of the Metropolitan. Although change did take place between successive batches, most noticeably in regard to window sizing, door layout and roof construction, the essential dimensions as well as many standard parts remained unchanged until the final saloon stock car was built in 1924.

The opening of the Watford branch in 1927 marked a significant change in the design of the Metropolitan's rolling stock. Hitherto, the limit of electric working had been Uxbridge, a journey which was considered tolerable in the saloon stock; the longer journeys to Watford and Rickmansworth were considered to be more suited to compartment type stock. As a consequence, the next generation of electric stock was a development of the Dreadnought stock, the principal change being the provision of a more powerful motor coach at each end of the trains.

## THE INITIAL SYSTEM

In October 1897, the Board of Trade published a report enquiring into methods of relieving the atmospheric conditions prevailing in the then steam-worked Metropolitan tunnels, unreservedly recommending the adoption of electric traction. No action was taken by the Metropolitan other than to secure the necessary statutory powers and, in 1899-1990, to participate in the experimental electrification of the Earls Court–High Street Kensington section. This latter exercise was widely interpreted as a sop to public opinion, but the opening in June 1900 of the Central London Railway, running largely parallel to the Metropolitan's route, resulted in a serious loss of traffic (estimated at £42,000 for the first half of 1901) which could not be ignored.

A consequence was the invitation, in August 1900, of nine leading electrical concerns to provide tenders for the electrification of the tunnel section of the railway. These were assessed by a joint committee set up by the Metropolitan and District Railway companies, the result being a recommen-

dation, adopted by the boards of both companies, for the 3000 volt 3-phase system proposed by the Budapest firm of Ganz and Company. Unfortunately, this decision only marginally preceded the advent of Charles Tyson Yerkes as the controlling influence on the M.D.R. His engineering advisers were not in favour of the proposed 3-phase AC system, which was at that time untried, as well as complicated in terms of its installation, with the result that the District turned instead to the well proven principles of low-voltage DC traction. The Metropolitan pressed successfully for the matter to be taken to arbitration, where the Hon. Alfred Lyttleton, KC, decided in December 1901, after a hearing lasting nearly three weeks, in favour of the DC system.

The Metropolitan loyally accepted this decision and in December 1902 placed an initial order for 50 electric trailer cars with Brown Marshall. This was followed in May 1903 by an order, again to Brown Marshall, by now incorporated into the Metropolitan Amalgamated RC & W Company, for 20 motor cars, the electrical equipment for which was supplied by the British Westinghouse Electrical Company.

The resultant stock was a mixture of British and American practice. Like a number of cars built at around the same time for the Mersey and Lancashire & Yorkshire Railways, the body style was very American, with a dome-ended clerestory roof and access only via end platforms, quite unlike any contemporary British carriage designs. By contrast, teak was used for both the framing and panelling of the body, which was constructed separately from the underframe, itself built from rolled steel sections. Unusually, the solebars were of angle, rather than channel, section, with the flange facing outward, and 7ft 0in wheelbase pressed steel bogies to Fox's patent were used throughout, set at 35ft centres.

The motor cars were provided with a full-width cab at the outer end, the controls being located on the nearside, with the switch panel on the opposite side on the rear partition. Access was by means of inward-opening doors on either side, supplemented by a swing door in the car end. Behind the cab was a luggage compartment, accessed either via large sliding doors in the body side or through sliding doors in the partitions at either end. From here, a single passenger saloon extended unbroken to the single-entry platform at the inner end of the car, entry being gained through double doors which slid into pockets in the bulkhead. The roof, not in fact a true clerestory, since it served not to admit light but to house adjustable ventilators, overhung the open platform and was supported by tubular pillars. Except for the section over the centre buffer, this platform was enclosed by vertically-barred iron panels, those at the side being hinged from the corner pillars to form access gates. By means of suitable levers, the gateman or conductor could, from his position in

# METROPOLITAN RAILWAY 1904 STOCK MOTOR CAR

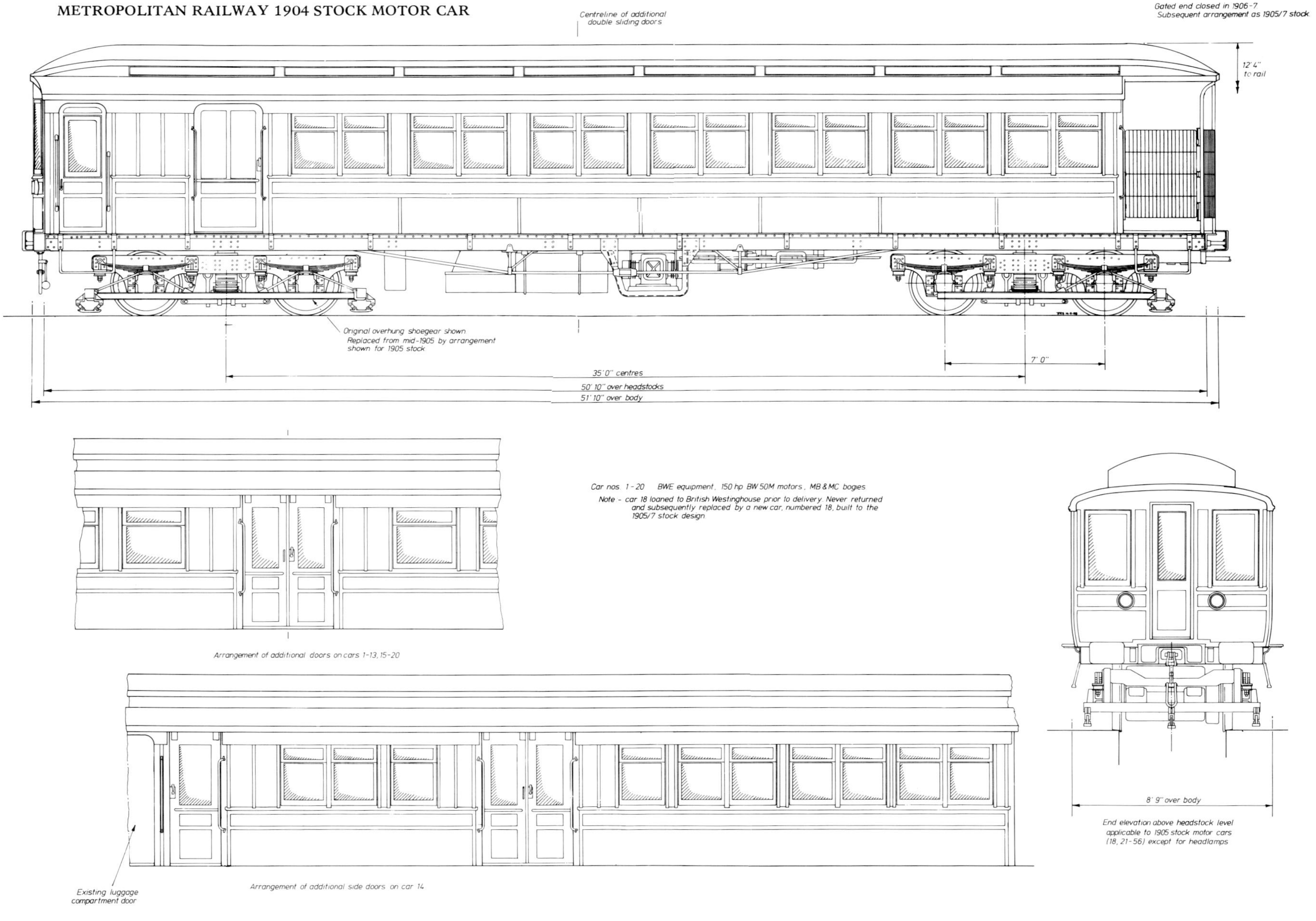

Gated end closed in 1906-7
Subsequent arrangement as 1905/7 stock

12' 4"
to rail

Centreline of additional
double sliding doors

7' 0"

35' 0" centres

50' 10" over headstocks

51' 10" over body

Original overhung shoegear shown
Replaced from mid-1905 by arrangement
shown for 1905 stock

8' 9" over body

End elevation above headstock level
applicable to 1905 stock motor cars
(18, 21-56) except for headlamps

Car nos 1-20     BME equipment. 150 hp BW SDM motors    M8 & MC bogies
Note - car 18 loaned to British Westinghouse prior to delivery. Never returned
and subsequently replaced by a new car numbered 18, built to the
1905/7 stock design.

Arrangement of additional doors on cars 1-13, 15-20

Arrangement of additional side doors on car 14

Existing luggage
compartment door

# METROPOLITAN RAILWAY 1904 STOCK TRAILER CAR

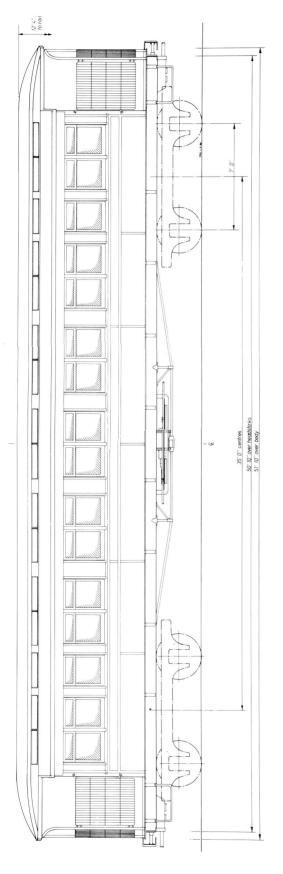

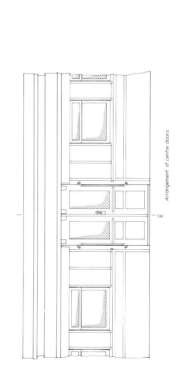

Arrangement of centre doors

Car nos (as built)

1 - 20    First class

1 - 30    Third class

For subsequent renumbering, refer to separate table

Note - detail of body end not shown due to original drawings
        having been lost

Bogies - Met Rly Type I (LT ref MR)

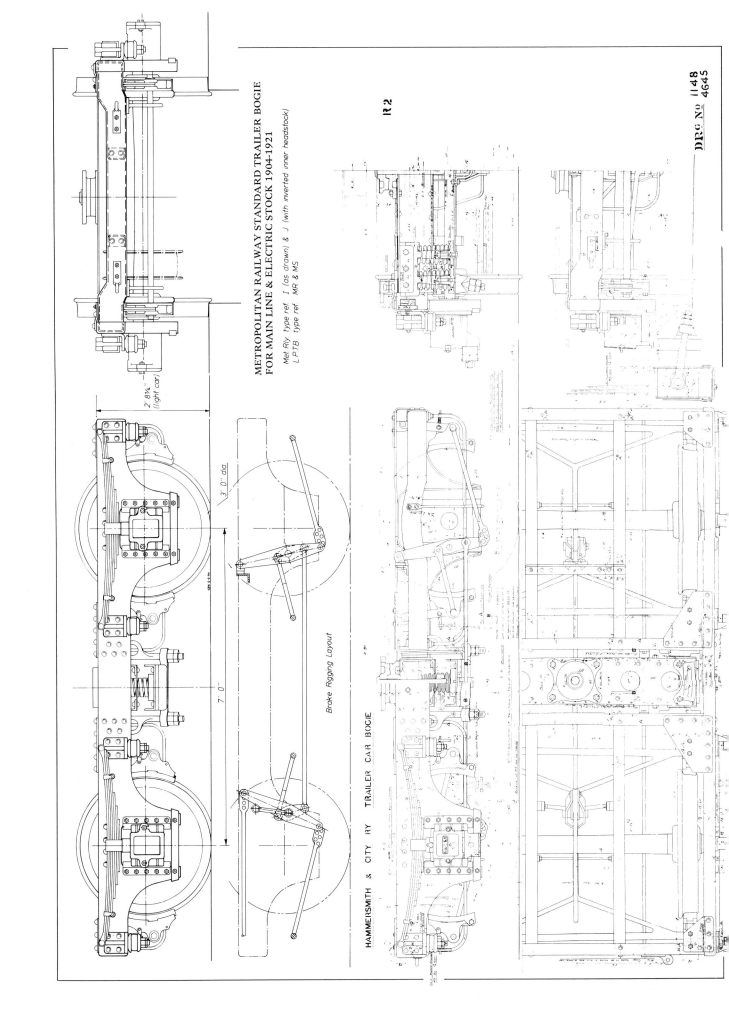

METROPOLITAN RAILWAY STANDARD TRAILER BOGIE
FOR MAIN LINE & ELECTRIC STOCK 1904-1921

Met Rly type ref   I (as drawn) & J (with inverted inner headstock)
L P T B   type ref   MR  &  MS

2' 8¼" (light car)

3' 0" dia

7' 0"

Brake Rigging Layout

HAMMERSMITH  &  CITY  RY  TRAILER  CAR  BOGIE

R 2

DRG No 1148
4645

the centre gangway, control the gates at the adjacent ends of the cars. To prevent passengers falling into the space between the car ends, collapsible lattice gates were fitted, permanently hinged to the diagonally opposite corner pillars and pinned to the adjacent cars after coupling.

A total of 48 seated passengers could be accommodated on a mixture of transverse bays and longitudinal benches, the latter predominating nearer the car ends so as to provide better standing space for passengers as well as facilitating access to the traction motors beneath. Upholstery in these cars, which were rated as first class, was originally of green moquette or green leather in the non-smoking and smoking cars respectively, together with double Wilton carpets laid over the cork linoleum floor. Both first and third class accommodation was finished internally with oak panelling, differing only in the degree of elaboration of the carving, with white painted lincrusta roof panels.

Artificial lighting was provided by a total of twenty 32-candle-power carbon filament lamps wired in series strings of five across the 600 volt traction supply. Various forms of fitting were employed depending on the seating arrangement and location in the car, ranging from two- and three-way electroliers to single lamps in holders attached to the base of the clerestory over the longitudinal seating.

Heaters of Gold's tubular pattern were also provided below the seats; ten 60V 580W in the motor cars and eighteen 33V 360W in the trailer cars.

Motive power was provided by four 4-pole nose-suspended Westinghouse type BW50M motors, each rated at 150 hp driving the 36in diameter wheels via single-stage reduction gearing of 17:54 ratio. Current in the four motors, each pair of which could be connected in series and parallel, was regulated by a controller of Westinghouse patent design, termed a turret controller from its arrangement of the electro-pneumatically operated contactors in a circle around a single arc blowout coil. The reverser was also electro-pneumatic in operation, air for both these switches and the brakes being supplied at 60 psi from a Westinghouse 8 hp compressor — type 8G2 — arranged for automatic operation. Control of the traction equipment was effected by solenoid valves energised from the master controller in the driver's cab. A multi-core cable extending the length of the train, carried between cars by short plug-in jumper cables, enabled the controller to operate each of the traction equipments simultaneously. The power supply for this was initially obtained from a 14 volt lead-acid battery in the cab, later replaced by a small motor-generator set. Automatic control of acceleration was provided. Initially, a second master controller was provided, presumably for shunting purposes, on the rear platform of the motor cars. Other than that, all the 600 volt equipment was slung below the car floor.

Traction current, generated at 11kV $33\frac{1}{3}$ cycles 3-phase, was distributed from the Neasden power station to sub-stations where it was changed by means of rotary converters to 600 volts DC. In accordance with the standard set by Yerkes and the District Railway, there were two rails, the positive being set 16in outside and 3in above the running rails and the negative, or return, being set on the track centreline, raised $1\frac{1}{4}$in above rail level. Current collection was effected by appropriately-positioned spring-loaded cast-iron shoes suspended from transverse oak beams at the ends of the motor bogies, these being carried on longitudinal channel beams suspended from the axle boxes. The beams at the outermost ends carried both negative and positive shoes, a third negative shoe being provided at the inner end of the driving end bogie, presumably to mitigate problems with loss of contact through pointwork when the cars were travelling singly. A through 600 volt bus-line connected the two motor cars in the train, as well as supplying heating and lighting power to the trailer cars.

In common with most electric stock, Westinghouse compressed air braking was provided, with a single cylinder on each car. These cylinders, which were of 10in diameter on the trailer cars, or 12in on the heavier motor cars, operated the brake shoes on both bogies through suitable rigging; two shoes per wheel were provided on the trailer bogies, whilst only one per wheel could be accommodated on the motor bogies. An unusual feature of these was the way in which the pull rod from the brake cylinder operated on a crossbeam at the rear of the bogie, this being curved in order to avoid bogie rotation from applying the brakes. In addition to the driver's controls, there was a release valve for the conductor's use on each end platform to facilitate emergency application of the brakes, whilst each cab had a handwheel allowing manual application of the brakes on that car.

Within the six-car trains the cars were coupled by simple bars, held in tension by a single centre buffer. At the outer ends of the motor cars, a screw coupling and side buffing blocks were provided in addition to the centre buffer, thus allowing emergency coupling with both steam locomotives and other electric trains.

The 1904 stock had been intended for the Inner Circle services, but owing to the practical difficulties which were experienced in the conversion, progress was outstripped by that on the extension lines (the Main Line) and as a result these trains became earmarked for the comparatively very exposed Uxbridge route, for which they were found to be eminently unsuitable.

The first workings of these trains were on the Rayners Lane to South Harrow section of the Metropolitan, using power drawn from the District Railway's temporary generating station at Alperton on their Ealing and South Harrow branch, also electrified at about the same time. This allowed crews to be trained for the full service, which commenced on 1st January 1905 between Baker Street and Uxbridge, although a full 6-car electric train had worked through to Uxbridge on 13th December the previous year.

Initially three trains were operated, the number gradually increasing until steam was eliminated by 20th March on the through services. The shuttle service between Uxbridge and Harrow during the off-peak hours was also converted to

*After the experiments with Motor Car 14, the definitive modification, seen here on 1904 Motor Car 11, was to insert a double doorway slightly ahead of centre. Photographed in 1933 at Neasden after the formation of the LPTB.*
LONDON UNDERGROUND

*As originally built, the 1904 and 1905 Motor Cars had only one vestibule, suffering loading problems as a result. Vehicle 14, seen here in 1934, was used to test solutions to this problem, in the course of which it was fitted with an additional single door at the cab end of the saloon and, later, with centre doors, in which form it remained until scrapped.*
LONDON UNDERGROUND

electric working using a half train. However, the lack of any driving provision on other than the motor cars necessitated the train being propelled in one direction, a situation which the Board of Trade considered unacceptable. As a result, steam was reintroduced on the trains whilst Neasden created a driving trailer car, presumably using similar equipment to that already provided on the non-driving ends of the motor cars. With this modified car, electric working was resumed on 1st June.

Only 19 of the intended 20 motor cars were in fact delivered, the odd one, No. 18, being loaned to the British Westinghouse Electric company in order to allow them to demonstrate their single-phase traction system, for which purpose it was fitted with a pantograph for overhead collection. It was kept far longer than had been anticipated, with the result that following representations by the Metropolitan, British Westinghouse offered to provide a replacement car free of charge. This offer was accepted in December 1905, the car being incorporated in the first order

of what was to be the 1905 stock from the Metropolitan Amalgamated C&W Company.

By the mid-1920s the traction equipments on these cars, particularly the split-frame traction motors, were rapidly wearing out, rendering the cars an operational liability. One proposal, put forward in September 1927, would have resulted in the complete re-equipment of 12 of the 19 motor cars in the same style as the, then, new 1927 stock cars for the Watford extension, ie with the switchgear in a compartment behind the driver and (presumably) new motors and motor bogies. The luggage compartment was to have been retained, and to cope with this, the whole body was to have been rebuilt, using material recovered from the original body. Only 32 seats would have been available, compared with the 50 of the 1927 motor coaches, a factor which, together with the open type accommodation, may have been instrumental in the abandonment of the scheme.

In any event, the acquisition of considerable numbers of new compartment stock trains in 1927 and 1929 allowed

*The interior of a 1904 stock 1st class Driving Trailer car in the 1930s.*

Trailer 3rd 199, converted from 1904 stock Motor Car 10 by removal of worn-out control equipment and motors. The left-hand end was the driver's & luggage compartment as evidenced by non-standard cantrail arrangement and offset centre door. The original motor bogies had been retained, with the motors removed, as can be seen from the arrangement of some of the older motor cars to be withdrawn and converted to trailer vehicles. For this, the cabs and luggage compartments were removed and replaced by an extended saloon and end vestibule. Although the new work copied the style of the original, these cars could always be identified by the vestibule, which lacked the inset at the roof level, and the offset location of the centre doors, which were not moved from their position at the centre of the original saloon. Below floor level, the traction equipment was removed, together with the compressor, although its carrying frame remained, and, on the first two cars converted, the motor bogies were replaced by spare trailer bogies. Later conversions retained the original bogies with the motors removed. Seven cars in all were converted, Nos. 1, 2, 4, 10, 12, 13 & 15 (full details are given in the numerical listings).

Of the seventy 1904 stock cars built, none were actually scrapped by the Metropolitan, although most of the motor cars were either out of service with worn-out motors or had been converted to trailers by the time the LPTB inherited the fleet. Not surprisingly, they were marked down for early replacement and the first withdrawals were made in February 1936. The war inevitably slowed this process, with the result that the last cars were not withdrawn until July 1946.

# THE 1905–7 STOCK:

The ten trains of 1904 stock already ordered by the Met were only the beginning, and would not, in any case, have been sufficient for both the Inner Circle and Harrow/Uxbridge services. Consequently, in January 1904, a second order was placed with the Metropolitan C&W Co. for another 36 motor cars and 62 trailers, with an option, later exercised, to extend this by a further 20 motor cars and 40 trailers within 18 months at the same contract price. These cars, however, differed significantly from the first (1904 stock) order as a result of events on other railways. Disastrous fires involving wooden-bodied stock on both the Mersey Railway and the Paris Metro caused the Board of Trade to ordain that the electrical equipment, at least, on motor coaches should be contained by metal-framed enclosures. In the instance of underfloor equipments, as fitted to the 1904 stock, this resulted in the need to provide a continuous steel sheet between the underframe and the body.

The outcome was a complete redesign of the car body, both in regard to its external appearance and its construction. The 1904 stock cars had followed traditional British practice in that the timber-framed body was a completely self-contained structure, built separately from the underframe, to which it would later be attached using numerous holding-down bolts. To have retained this method of construction for the 1905 stock cars would have led in time to considerable difficulties. The steel sheeting would have prevented adequate ventilation of the timber body rails and floor, so that accumulating dampness would have caused rot in the timber as well as severe corrosion of the steel plating. Instead, the timber body framing was built directly on the underframe, the pillars being bolted via brackets directly to the steel floor, making these cars amongst the earliest examples of integral construction.

As this change necessitated a major redesign of the whole car, the opportunity was taken to incorporate a number of structural modifications. The most obvious and significant changes were the enclosure of the end platforms, thus anticipating the draught problems of the 1904 cars, and the substitution of single large windows for the narrow paired type fitted on the earlier cars, thus greatly improving the passenger's outlook as well as the external appearance of the cars. To minimise the fire risk, the inner and outer lower panels were specified as being of steel, as were the seat frames, and a floor covering of non-flammable kork (*sic*) carpet was to be provided.

It was further decided that the new sets should be more readily divisible, both in traffic into three-car units and into single cars for maintenance purposes. To effect this, the original bar coupling was replaced by a knuckle coupler, similar to, but about half the size of, that adopted by the American railroads. This, together with the sprung centre buffer, which was retained from the 1904 stock, became the standard drawgear arrangement for all of the Metropolitan's multiple unit electric stock, although there were a few exceptions. To facilitate the operation of half, ie 3-car, trains, the first class trailer cars, which were normally marshalled at the centre of the train, were fitted from new with driving controls in one vestibule, this being lockable out of sight to allow public access to the vestibule when it was not in use as a cab. Outwardly, there was little to distinguish between these Driving Trailer cars and the ordinary Third class trailer cars, the car bodies and underframes being virtually identical.

By April 1905, the electrification of the Inner Circle was sufficiently close to completion for arrangements to be made with the District for the commencement of the electric service on 1st July 1905. Trial runs on the Metropolitan's own tracks revealed no difficulties with the rolling stock, but the first incursions into District territory were met with disaster. For reasons which are no longer clear, the collector shoes on the Met trains suffered a propensity to slip off the side of the conductor rails, eventually resulting in their being overturned. It was reported that seven trains got round to South Kensington from Aldgate under their own power, although the last three were very late. The eighth train had to be hauled round by a steam locomotive, arriving after some three hours delay. The District already had enough of its own problems without this, having suffered a derailment earlier that morning at Mill Hill Park (now Acton Town) and severe flooding in the cutting at Hammersmith. Given that no practical service could be run under these conditions, the

# METROPOLITAN RAILWAY 1905 STOCK MOTOR CAR

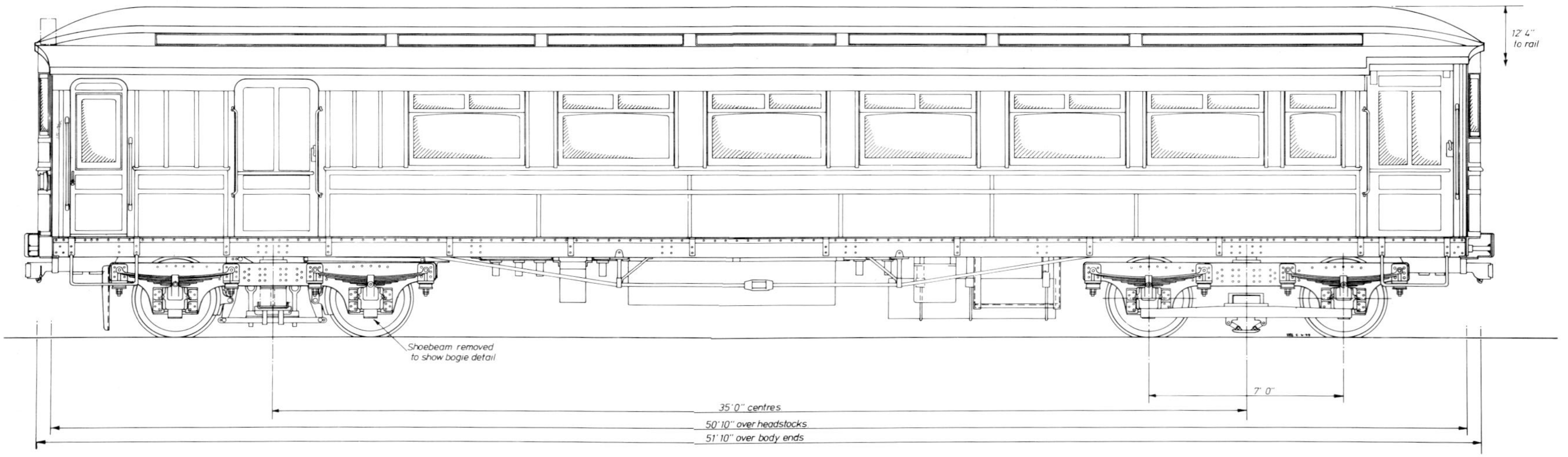

Window 'A'

For non-driving end refer to trailer car

12' 4" to rail

7' 0"

35' 0" centres

50' 10" over headstocks

51' 10" over body ends

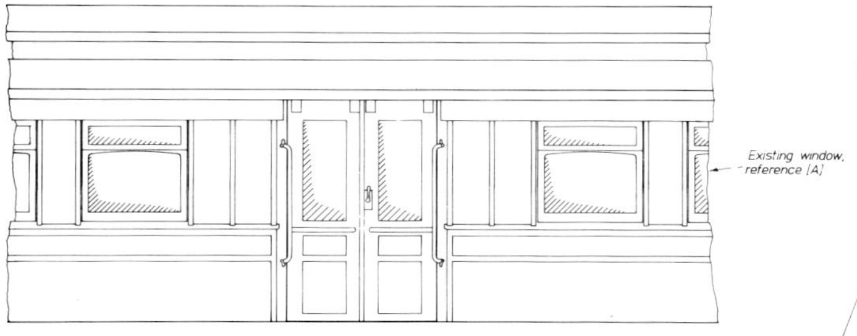

Shoebeam removed to show bogie detail

Outline of destination indicator fitted to cars 57-82 & 126-165

Cars 126-165 only

8' 9" over body

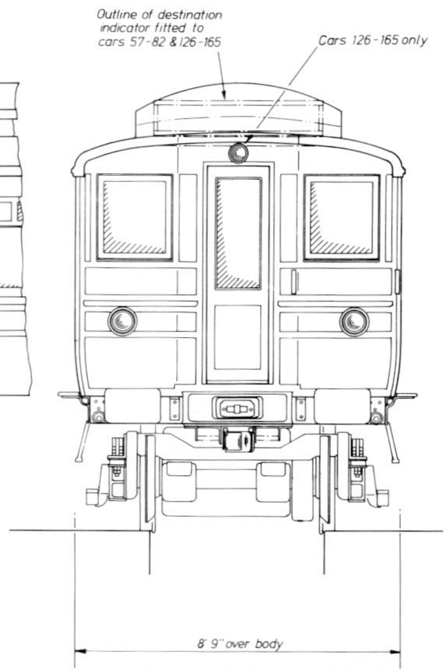

End elevation applicable to cars 57-82 & 126-165
For cars 18, 21-56, refer to 1906 stock

Arrangement of additional side doors on car 32
Opposite side is mirrored from that shown

20°

Existing window, reference 'A'

Existing luggage compartment door

Arrangement of centre doors on all cars except car 18

| Car nos. 18, 21-56 | BWE equipment. | 150 hp BW-50M motors, | MB & MC bogies |
| 57-70 | BTH | 200 hp GE69 motors | ME bogies |
| 71-82 | BTH | 150 hp GE78 | MD |
| 126-165 | BTH | | |

For details of conversions to trailer cars and L.T. renumbering, refer to separate tables.

Note - All cars originally built as shown in main drawing, ie with end doors only. To improve passenger flow all cars were rebuilt from c.1911-12 with additional centre doors as shown in part view (a) except for car 32, for which the arrangement is shown in part view (b).

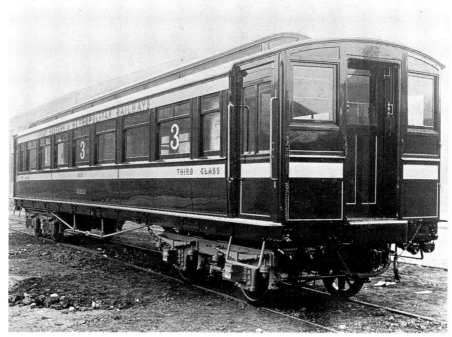

*Hammersmith & City Railway (Met & GW Joint) Composite 1st/3rd class trailer prior to delivery. Although built in 1906/7, these cars were virtually identical to the 1905 stock, the only exception being the composite trailer, which had no equivalent on the Metropolitan.*
R. J. GREENAWAY
COLLECTION

Met withdrew to the safety of its own territory, running an Aldgate–Baker Street–South Kensington shuttle service for the remainder of the day.

Why the Metropolitan trains should have suffered like this is uncertain; whilst mounting the collector shoes outboard of the axleboxes subjected them to greater lateral movement than is the case when they are mounted between the axles, the difference being due to any yawing motion of the bogie, there is no evidence to suggest that they were in any difficulty when working on the Met's own tracks. Instead, this rather infers that the quality of the District Railway track may have been significantly poorer, either in respect of the gauge or the positioning of the conductor rails. Furthermore, many later Metropolitan motor cars had negative shoes which were well outboard from the axles and suffered no problems, even when running on the Circle service.

Whatever the cause, urgent action was required, with the result that whilst a shuttle service of four trains was maintained, supplemented by a reprieved steam Circle service, Neasden was working overtime to modify the shoegear arrangements. In the interim, oak beams replaced the original channel irons, with the shoes being suspended from them at a point midway between the axleboxes. The negative shoes had to remain more or less in their existing position due to the presence of the traction motors in the middle of the bogie. Twelve trains were thus altered, enabling the electrified Circle service to be fully restored on 25th September 1905; the sixteen other trains then working were modified in like manner with the remainder being altered before delivery.

The earliest arrangement of the end vestibules provided for access to the saloon via double sliding doors, and

between cars by means of a single hinged door, the latter being provided for the conductor's use. In March 1906, it was decided that the hinged door should be replaced by one of the sliding type and the internal saloon doors abolished, the aim being to improve passenger movement as well as, allegedly, to reduce draughts. This work, which applied only to the passenger ends of the cars, was carried out as the cars underwent repairs or routine overhaul.

It will be recalled that the 18 trains of 1905 stock were to include the 10 third class trailer cars from the original 1904 stock order which had been rendered surplus by the decision to change the train formation from 7 to 6 cars. Eight of these had been delivered with end platforms, the other two having been built with enclosed vestibules in order to test the design. As the delivery of the 1905 stock predated the decision to modify the 1904 stock cars, the resultant pairing of gates and sliding doors which could occur was not considered acceptable and, accordingly, arrangements were made for 8 motor cars and 8 Driving trailer cars from the 1905 order to be fitted with gated platforms at their non-driving ends, thus keeping like types of car end together. However, as the 1905 cars were all fitted with couplers, it became inevitable that the gated trailer cars would occasionally get loose into trains of vestibuled cars until, by the end of 1907, all the gate ends had been enclosed.

By April 1905 the state of business was such that the company decided to exercise, in part, its option to take up to 10 further trains from the Metropolitan C&W Co. at the previously agreed contract price. Initially, seven complete 6-car trains were ordered, amounting to 14 motor cars and 28 trailers, equally divided between third class and first class. As before, the first class cars were fitted out as Driving trailer

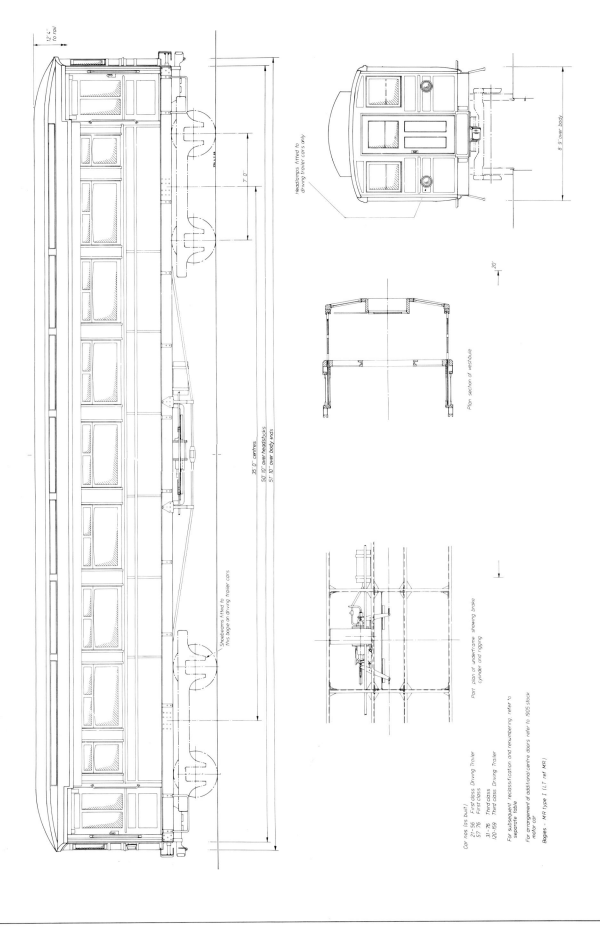

# METROPOLITAN RAILWAY 1905 STOCK TRAILER CAR

12' 4" to rail

35' 0" centres

50' 10" over headstocks

51' 10" over body ends

Shoebeams fitted to this bogie on driving trailer cars

Headlamps fitted to driving trailer cars only

8' 9" over body

Plan section of vestibule

Part plan of underframe showing brake cylinder and rigging

Car nos (as built)

21-56    First class Driving Trailer
57-76    First class
31-76    Third class
120-159   Third class Driving Trailer

For subsequent reclassification and renumbering, refer to separate table

For arrangement of additional centre doors refer to 1905 stock motor car

Bogies - MR type I (LT ref MR)

cars. In all other respects the cars were identical in appearance to the initial batch of 1905 stock, save that the motor cars now had shallower driving end windows and that both the motor and driving trailer cars were fitted with a large roller blind destination indicator at roof level above the cabs. This latter feature did not last long, being replaced by 1911 by the more familiar enamelled plates carried, initially, above the end door and later below the driver's window. The notch which had been cut in the dome of the clerestory roof to accommodate these boxes remained a permanent feature of this batch of stock.

By their nature, motor cars are more susceptible to failure than are trailer cars, and with this in mind, the Met board placed an order for a further six motor cars in September 1905. Considerable difficulties were by then being experienced with the Westinghouse equipment fitted to the fleet, and it is perhaps no surprise to find that of these six cars, two were to be fitted with BTH traction equipments, as a preliminary step to future orders, for which equipment the board were firmly in favour. The continuing troubles with the Westinghouse cars convinced them that to buy any more would be unwise and, as a consequence, instructions were issued to cancel the four equipments on order from Westinghouse, increasing the BTH order to compensate. Westinghouse, however, claimed that by then they had completed the contract, with the result that the Met had to accept delivery of the equipment, which was then placed in store pending a future decision as to their use.

Shortly after this decision was taken, the Met decided in favour of the BTH company's tender for 10 train sets of traction equipment, at the same time increasing the size of the car-body order from 7 to 10 and integrating the 6 spare motor cars into the production order. Delivery was anticipated as being complete by March 1906.

In the meantime, the joint Metropolitan and Great Western committee responsible for the Paddington to Hammersmith branch, had also decided in favour of electrification. Given the Met involvement in this, it was natural that the by now standard design of Saloon stock was chosen, twenty 6-car trains being ordered from the Metropolitan C&W Co, with the BTH company supplying the 150hp motors and their control equipments. Driving trailer cars were not originally provided, and the two centre cars in the formation were first and third class composites, providing the equivalent of a single first class car in contrast to the two on the Met services. The diseconomies of permanently running 6-car trains led in 1908/9 to the fitment of driving equipment to the composite trailers to allow 3-car trains to be formed. Internally, the cars had to have additional partitions erected to provide separate smoking and non-smoking saloons, the cars having been previously wholly of one or other type.

This near simultaneous nature of the two orders was to result in the BTH company's manufacturing abilities to become rather overstretched. In consequence, BTH had to advise the Metropolitan in November 1905, that because of their prior commitment to equipping the Hammersmith &

City trains, they would be unable to supply all of the specified 150hp GE76 motors within the time agreed, offering instead to fit the first 14 motor cars temporarily with GE69 motors, rated at 200hp. These being larger and more powerful machines, the Met was given the option to either rent them until such time as they could be replaced by GE76 motors following completion of the H&C contract, or to purchase them outright. This offer was accepted, and the first BTH equipped train entered service on 1st April 1906, followed by a further six GE69 equipped trains over the next two months. The remaining three trains, together with the six spare motor cars, were not delivered until mid-September, fitted with the intended GE76 motors.

By the end of 1906, BTH were once more in a position to manufacture the outstanding GE76 motors. However, circumstances had by then changed, with the result that these motors were never built. A reduction in the purchase price of the stand-in GE69 motors made it acceptable to purchase them outright, a move which also saved the cost of having to lift the cars concerned. A further factor was the realisation that the additional power of the GE69 fitted motor cars would be sufficient to allow one motor car to work a four-car train on the Inner Circle. The necessity for this had been brought about by an ultimatum from the District Railway to the effect that they intended to work their share of the service with four-car trains only, and that if the Met wanted to operate longer trains they would be required to pay the extra cost of current supplied to them on the South Kensington–Charing Cross–Aldgate section. Furthermore, if they required the District to lengthen its own trains to more than four cars, they would be charged for the additional costs involved in electricity, car-mileage and manning.

In the end, it was agreed that each company would reduce its Circle trains to five cars each, commencing on 18th March 1907, that from 1st April, the service would be operated on the basis of a 50-minute round trip, and that from 1st July, the trains would be further reduced to four cars. It did not take very long to demonstrate that the 50 minutes allowed was quite inadequate, with consequent late-running becoming endemic and intolerable. After much negotiation, the Metropolitan undertook the working of the entire Circle service on the basis of a 55-minute round trip, commencing on 1st January 1908. Although this might have cured the arguments between the two companies, it left the Metropolitan in dire straits for rolling stock, so much so that the Harrow services had to revert to locomotive-hauled trains using either refurbished steam stock or five-car sets of spare trailer cars rendered redundant by the earlier reductions in the Circle trains lengths. It is presumed that in order to provide at least a guard's position as well as a handbrake, these sets must have been made up with at least one driving trailer. In view of their coupling arrangements, the saloon stock sets must have been operated by the BTH type locomotives; with careful selection of the driving trailer cars, these trains could have been worked in the push-pull mode. Whether this was in fact done is not known.

*A group of 1907 Hammersmith & City trailer cars, still in their Met & GW Joint livery but shown here carrying their new LPTB numbers, indicating a date c.1934. The nearest car, 3rd class No. 9239(?) (ex H&C 29) had had the window next to the end doorway blanked off, a not uncommon modification.*
A. CRUIKSHANK COLLECTION

*1905 stock Motor Car 40 in as-built condition, taken in 1934 before becoming LT No. 2526.*

The five-car trains provided for the Circle service were of two formations, occasioned by the availability of suitable rolling stock. Most were formed with a single 200hp BTH motor car paired with a first class driving trailer car and three third class trailers; the remainder were made up from two 150hp motor cars either end of the three trailer cars, one of which was first class. One serious operational difficulty arose from this combination of train formations, in particular with the single motored sets. Traditionally, the first class accommodation had been in the centre of the train; now, because the driving trailer and first class cars were one and the same, the first class section could be in the centre, or at either end of the trains on a random basis. The necessity of transferring themselves from one end of the platform to the other at a moment's notice was something that could not be tolerated for long and complaints poured in until, by February 1909, steps had to be taken. The solution adopted was to exchange the first class internal fittings of 14 driving trailer cars with those on a similar number of third class cars, a move facilitated by the way in which the Met had standardised the design of the various car bodies, the trailer cars being structurally identical. As the saloon stock cars were numbered in three separate series, for motor cars, third and first class trailer cars, the cars involved also had to exchange numbers, resulting in the converted cars being spread randomly through their respective registers until the number series was rationalised *c.*1921. Similar difficulties attended to operation of the H&C 3-car trains, which initially had composite driving trailers; again, the structural similarity of the bodies allowed the interior furnishings of the composite and third class cars to be exchanged, thus putting the first class back close to the middle of the trains.

One other difficulty which had arisen with the purchase of the BTH-equipped trains was their electrical incompatibility with the Westinghouse-equipped cars, making it impossible to mix the two types of motor cars in the same train. Whereas Westinghouse had used a 9-wire control line to operate the solenoid valves on the contactors, which were pneumatically powered, BTH had chosen to use a 10-wire system in which the electromagnetically actuated contactors were driven directly from the control line. Further, because the control wires on the Westinghouse system only operated solenoid valves, little power was needed and a 14 volt supply was sufficient; the electromagnets on the BTH contactors required considerably more power and in consequence were energised directly from the 600 volt traction supply, the use of resistors and series connected coils limiting the voltage at any one contactor to about 100V.

The situation in regard to the trailer cars differed somewhat, in that they possessed no traction equipment. As built, the 1904 cars had been equipped with BW type 9-wire jumper sockets on both sides, making the cars fully reversible. In all probability, the first 1905 stock batch was ordered with the same arrangement, there being no reason to change. The decision to change to BTH equipment for the subsequent batches of 1905 stock resulted in a change to

this, the cars being delivered with BW connections on one side and BTH on the other, the intervening cabling being altered to be suitable for 600V use. All of the subsequent saloon stock, with occasional exceptions, followed this arrangement, as did most of the 1904 stock driving trailers when they were modified. To enable unlike connections to be coupled, special jumper cables were provided, having a BW 9-pin connector at one end and a BTH 10-pin at the other. BW driving trailers could be incorporated in BTH trains and vice versa, under which circumstances the driving controls could not be used.

With the electrification of the District and the H&C in 1905/6, the East London Railway, whose joint committee had decided that they could not afford to follow suit, was effectively severed from the Metropolitan/MDR network, losing its through services to and from the City. Although local services were maintained by the LBSCR, traffic dwindled, and by 1911, it was apparent to the committee that they had to electrify, or fall by the wayside. Of the six companies responsible for the line, only the Met and the MDR had any real experience of the 600V DC system which was considered appropriate. Accordingly, it was agreed that the latter would supply electrical power from its Lots Road station, whilst the Met would provide and operate the rolling stock. The service proposed would have required eight 2-car trains working locally to the ELR, supplemented by four 4-car trains per hour working through from South Kensington. As the only driving trailer cars available were all first class only, the formation of the necessary 2-car trains would have resulted in an unacceptable over-provision of the higher class accommodation. To correct this, it was proposed that a new class of composite driving trailer cars be created by modifying existing cars. Three different internal arrangements were proposed, all necessitating the provision of centre doors to allow direct access to both the first and third class saloons when the driver's vestibule was in use. The eleven cars which were required to cover the ELR needs, as well as providing spares and two for the Uxbridge line, were selected from eight first class driving trailers and three third class trailer cars, all 1905 stock, and were renumbered in a new sequence from 1–10. Apart from their travels on the ELR, little is known of these cars. They were occasionally pressed into service in other Met trains and were often to be found loaned to the H&C, whose trains had incorporated composite driving trailers from new. One car, No 8, was converted by the LPTB in 1934 to a first class driving trailer, having originally been third class. Two others, LT Nos. 6211 and 6582, were loaned to the LMS during the war as emergency reserve stock, and as such, outlasted the remainder by some five years, not being withdrawn until December 1945.

Like the 1904 stock, the motor cars were becoming worn out by the late 1920s, resulting in nine being demoted to trailer cars. Not all of the cars survived the course in the original form in any case. Two, Nos 46 and 69, were to become a unique pair of double-ended composite motor

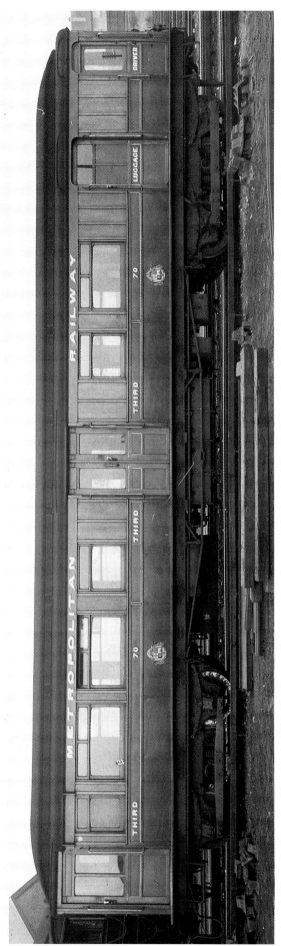

1905 stock Motor Car 70, taken in 1934. The livery still seems to have been varnished teak, although the covering of grime almost totally obscures any detail.

LONDON UNDERGROUND

1905 stock 3rd class Trailer 61 in final condition with centre doors, in 1934 before becoming LT 9527.

LONDON UNDERGROUND

1905 stock Motor Car 64 photographed in 1934 after being renumbered as LPTB 2554 but not yet shorn of its Met livery. Although once fitted with destination blinds, it is distinguishable from the H&C cars by the lack of the centre headlamp, sited above the end door.

G. KERLEY, CTY. A. CRUIKSHANK

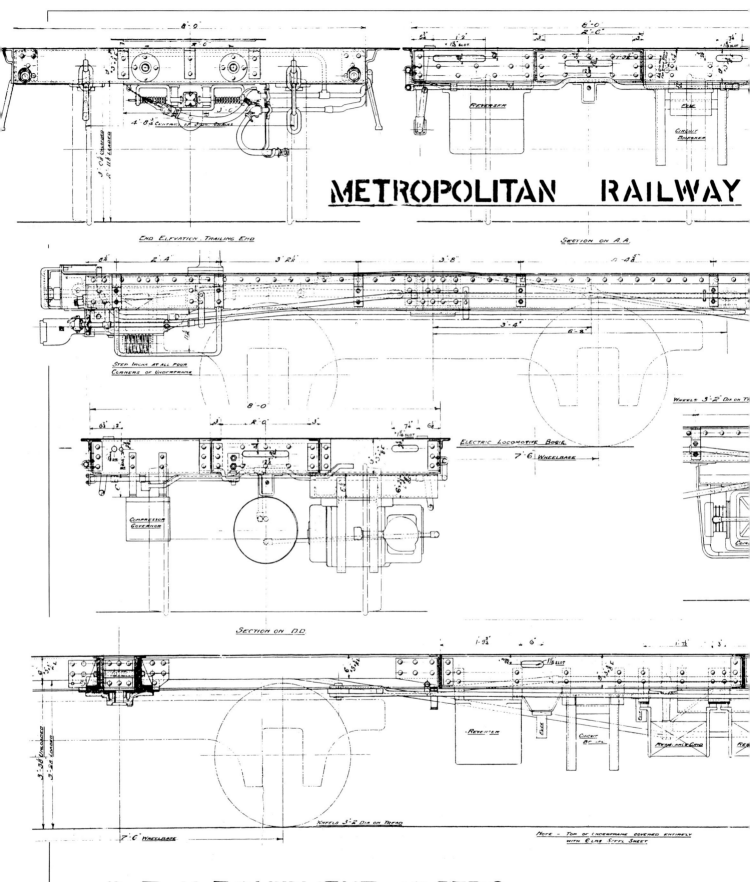

# METROPOLITAN RAILWAY

END ELEVATION. TRAILING END.

SECTION ON A.A.

REVERSER

CIRCUIT BREAKER

4' 8½' CENTRES OF STEP CHAINS

STEP IRONS AT ALL FOUR
CORNERS OF UNDERFRAME

ELECTRIC LOCOMOTIVE BOGIE
7' 6" WHEELBASE

WHEELS 3' 2" DIA ON TREAD

COMPRESSOR
GOVERNOR

SECTION ON D.D.

REVERSER

CIRCUIT
BREAKER

WHEELS 3' 2" DIA ON TREAD

7' 6" WHEELBASE

NOTE – TOP OF UNDERFRAME COVERED ENTIRELY
WITH ELMS STEEL SHEET

# B T H EQUIPMENT 10 SETS

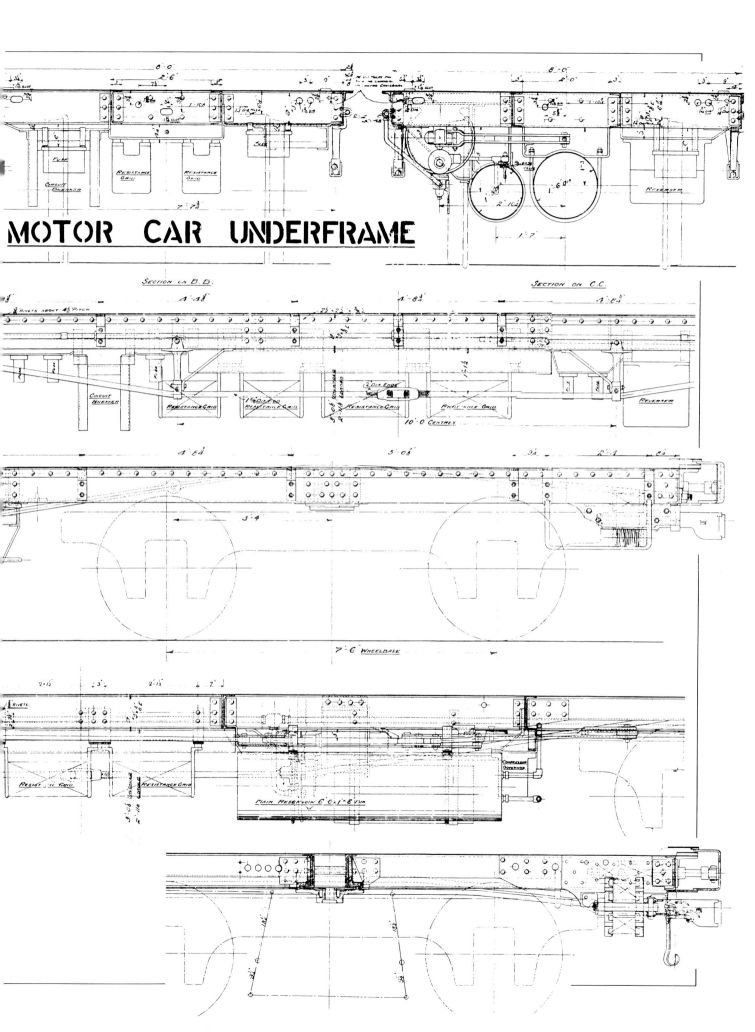

# MOTOR CAR UNDERFRAME

SECTION ON B.B.

SECTION ON C.C.

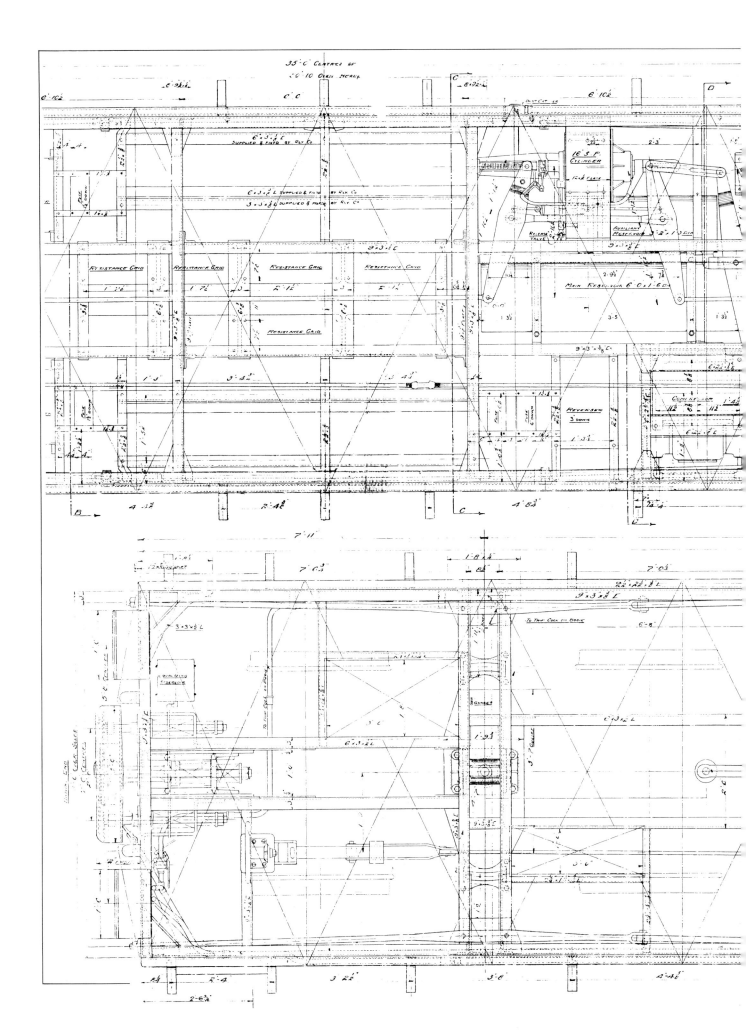

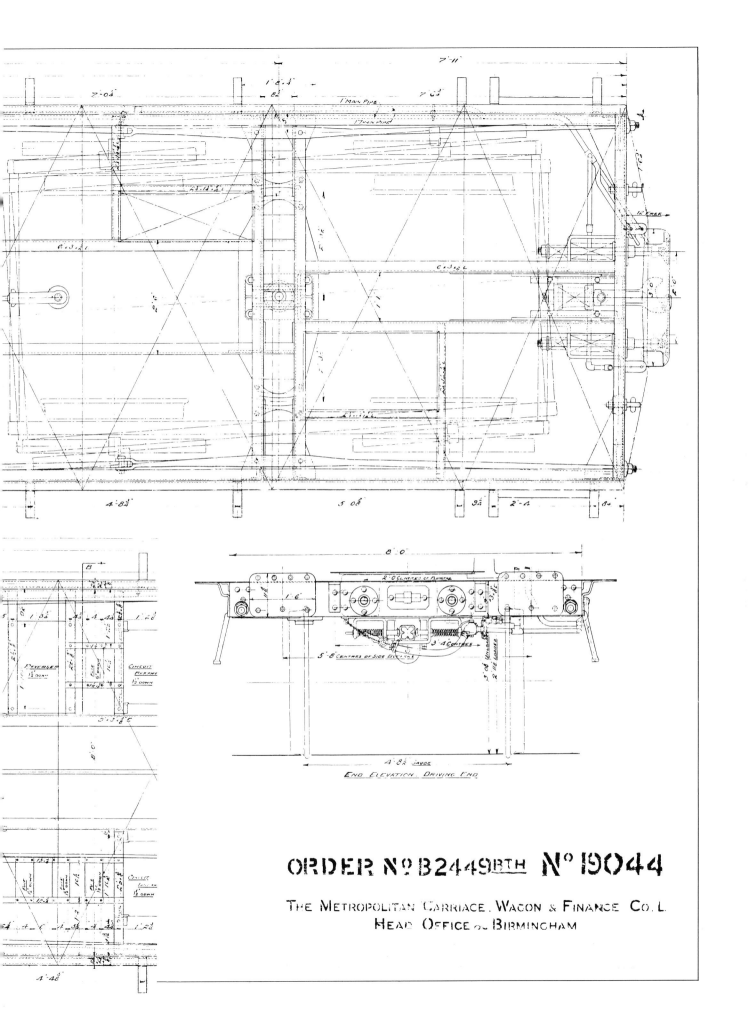

END ELEVATION. DRIVING END

ORDER Nº B2449 BTH Nº 19044

THE METROPOLITAN CARRIAGE, WAGON & FINANCE CO. L.
HEAD OFFICE ᴀᴛ BIRMINGHAM

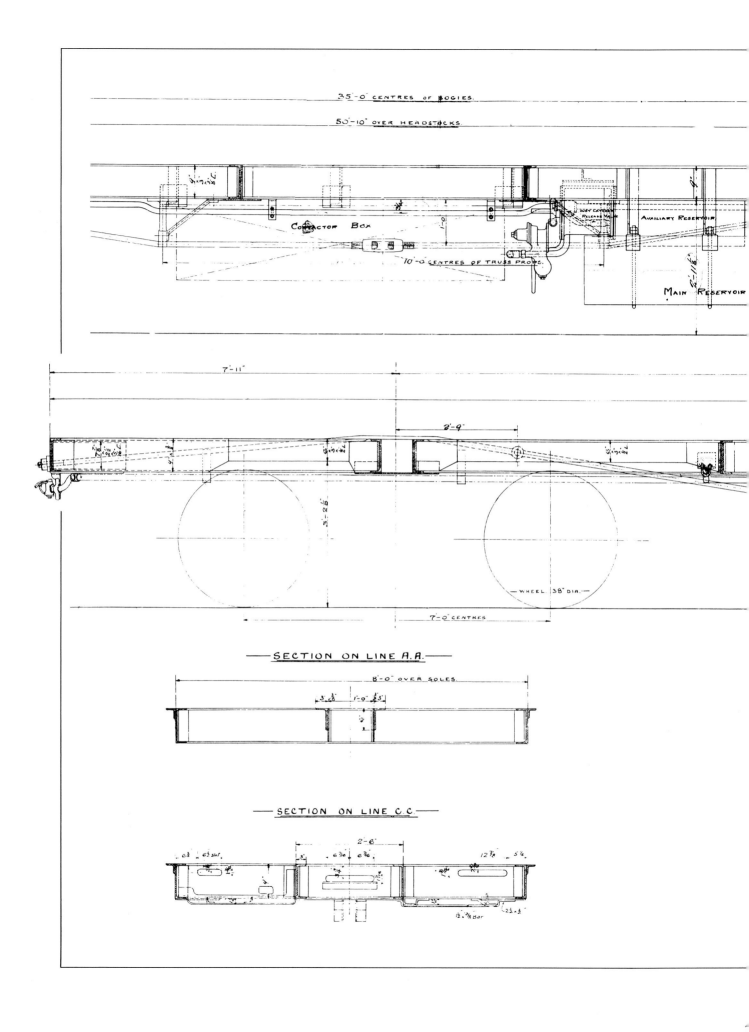

35'-0" CENTRES OF BOGIES.

50'-10" OVER HEADSTOCKS.

Contactor Box

Auxiliary Reservoir

10'-0" CENTRES OF TRUSS RODS.

Main Reservoir

7'-11"

2'-9"

WHEEL 38" DIA.

7'-0" CENTRES

— SECTION ON LINE A.A. —

8'-0" OVER SOLES.

— SECTION ON LINE C.C. —

2'-6"

1½ x ⅜ Bar

# HAMMERSMITH & CITY RAILWAY

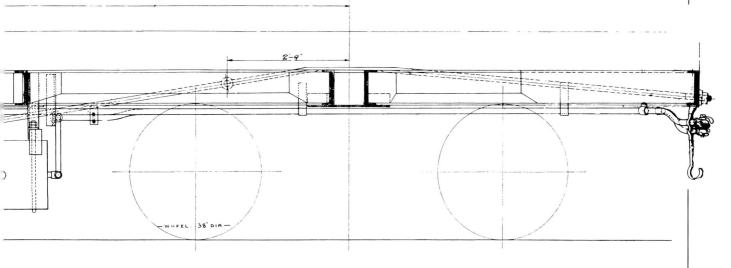

WHEEL. 38" DIA.

2'-9"

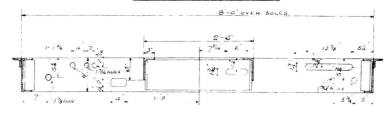

SECTION ON LINE B.B.

8'-0" OVER SOLES.

SECTION ON LINE D.D.

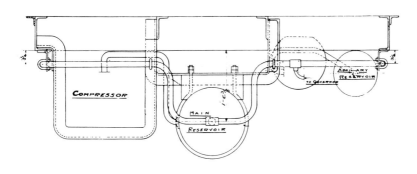

COMPRESSOR

MAIN
RESERVOIR

AUXILARY
RESERVOIR

TO GOVERNOR

SECTION ON LINE E.E.

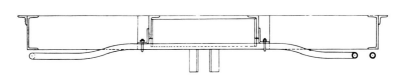

# MOTOR CAR
# UNDERFRAME

R 3

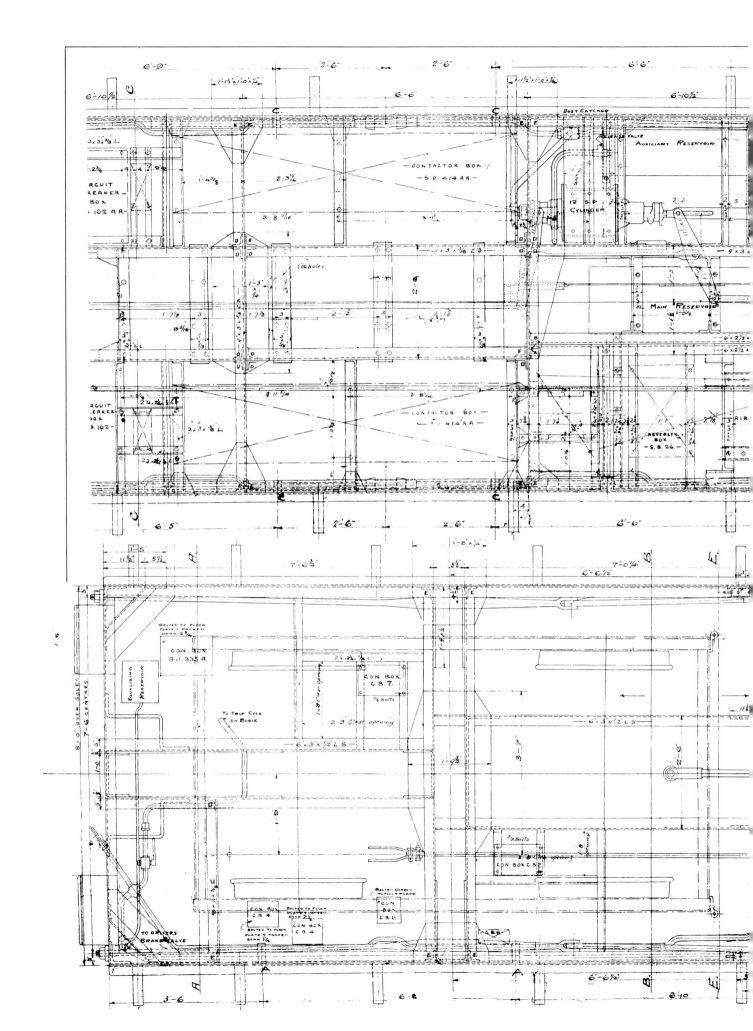

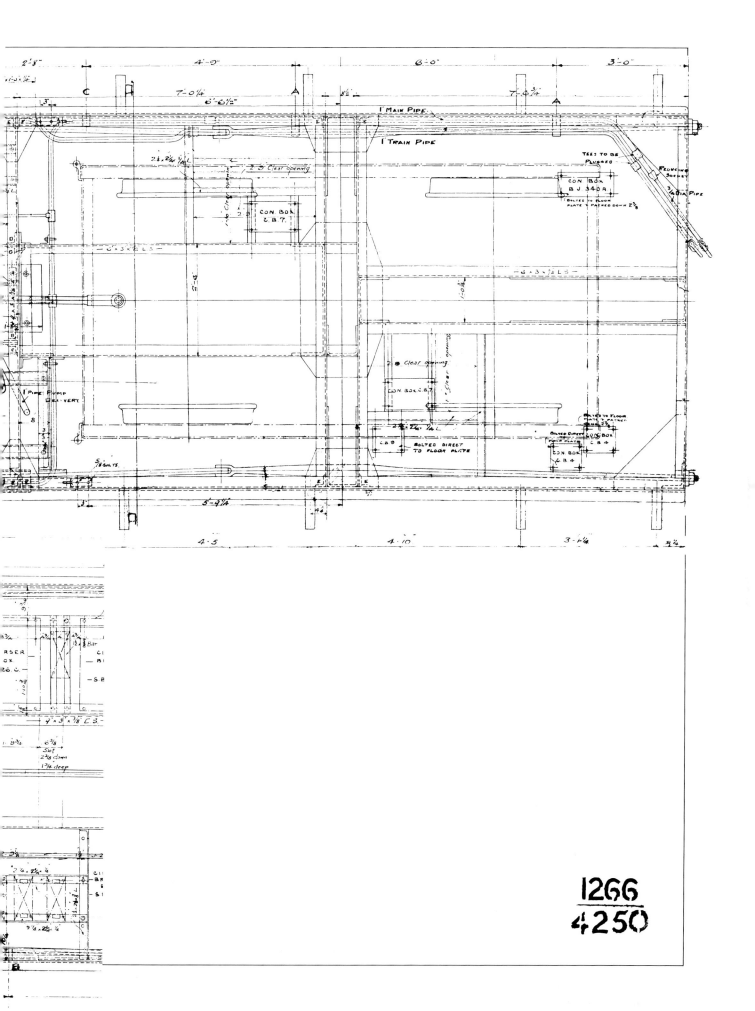

1266
―――
4250

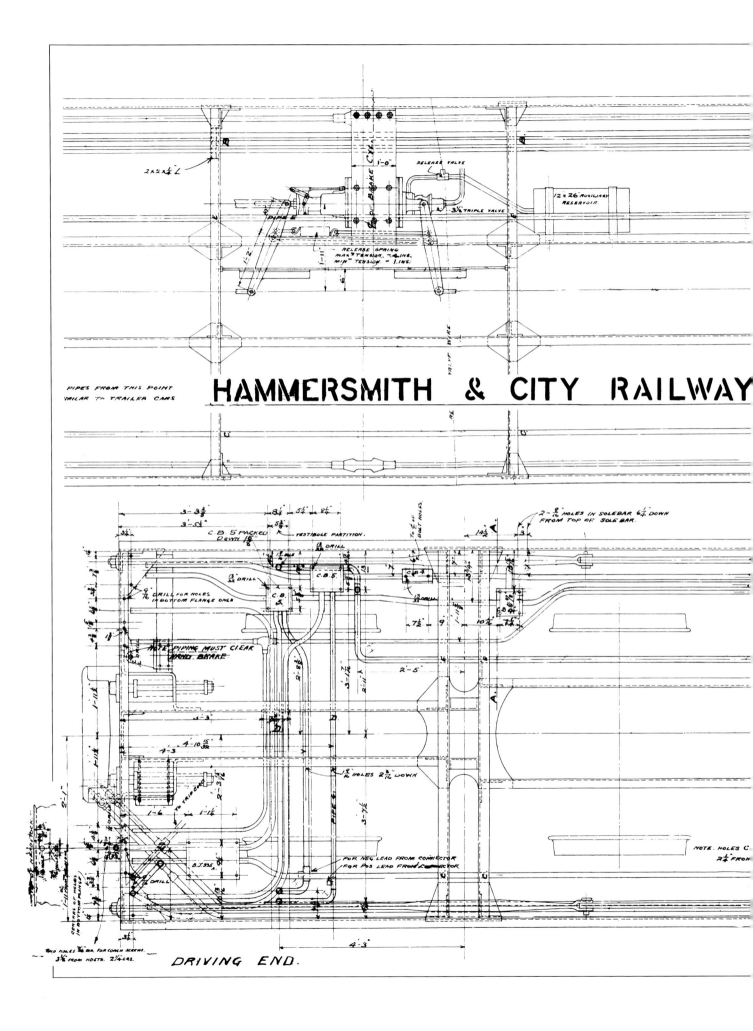

# HAMMERSMITH & CITY RAILWAY

DRIVING END.

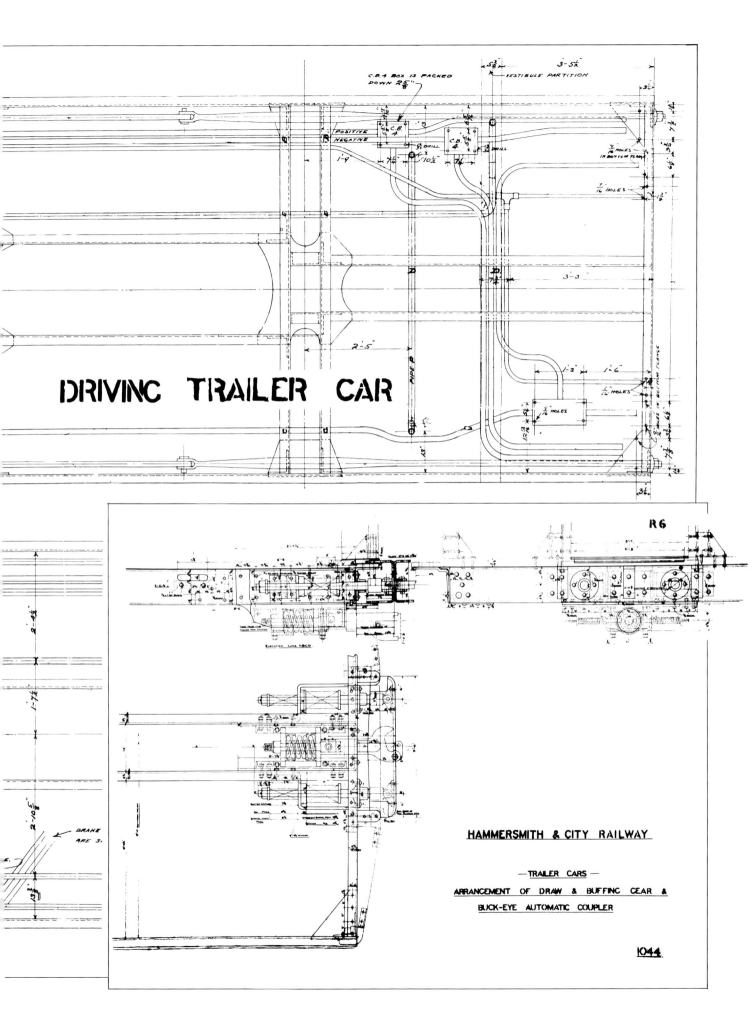

# DRIVING TRAILER CAR

HAMMERSMITH & CITY RAILWAY

— TRAILER CARS —

ARRANGEMENT OF DRAW & BUFFING GEAR &
BUCK-EYE AUTOMATIC COUPLER

1044.

*One of the two double-ended motor coaches built in 1910 on the underframes of accident-damaged 1905 stock Motor Cars 468 and 469, whose numbers and underfloor equipment they retained. The bodies were the prototypes for the Dreadnought stock and, in respect of the ends, for the later MW stock.*

LT COLLECTION

cars with, effectively, the prototype Dreadnought stock bodies. Two more, 36 and 44, were rebuilt in 1919 with an experimental arrangement of swing doors and intermediate seating bays. Of the trailer cars, ten of the first class cars were scrapped in 1910 to provide the underframes and running gear for the first two trains of the Dreadnought stock, whilst another four, two first and two third class, were rebuilt as part of the 1919 experimental stock train. Driving trailer 66 was destroyed by fire, probably in 1925, on the basis of an otherwise unaccounted decrease in the annual rolling stock returns; its underframe is believed to have survived as the LPTB surface line gauging car G662, which is known to have carried a 1906 building plate.

The acquisition of new electric stock in the 1930–32 period created a surplus to the Metropolitan's requirements, as a result of which four complete BTH trains were loaned to the Hammersmith & City Railway. Prior to this transfer, it had not been unusual for Met cars to be loaned, for a suitable charge, to the H&C to cover maintenance needs, as its original fleet of twenty 1905 stock trains was never more than barely sufficient. Another four Westinghouse BW50M motor cars were transferred to the GN&C, which had been taken over by the Met in 1913. There, suitably modified with GN&C couplings and shoegear, they were used to increase the peak time service level.

The remainder survived to pass into the hands of the LPTB, in whose hands all but six of the remaining motor cars remained in service until their withdrawal between May 1936 and February 1938. The six other 1905 motor cars finished their days as an experimental train to test the viability of the Metropolitan–Vickers Metadyne system of control. The train, which was converted in 1934, consisted of three 2-car units, each operable independently. One car retained its original body layout and accommodation, whilst the other was converted into a composite car, losing the luggage compartment in the process and gaining an additional sliding door to facilitate access to the new first class saloon. The traction equipment was, of course, replaced completely, with the new Metadyne set being carried under the composite car, feeding the traction motors of both cars. Test running over the following two years was successful, leading to the adoption of this form of control for the later LPTB O&P stocks which replaced much of the older Met saloon stock on the H&C and Uxbridge services from 1938 onwards. The three experimental units are presumed to have been scrapped following the completion of this work in 1936, since their Metadyne machines, control gear and bogies were incorporated in three of the new battery electric locomotives (L41–43) built for the LPTB in 1937.

The trailer cars lasted somewhat longer, aided by wartime needs, being withdrawn between August 1940 and March 1952. Twenty-four cars were loaned to the LMS as emergency stock, being numbered E1–24 in a special series, and kept at strategic points to cover the possibility of large-scale damage to the regular fleet.

# EXPERIENCE WITH THE EARLY ELECTRIC STOCK

Although it was originally intended that the 1904 stock trains should be used predominantly on the Inner Circle service, the progress of the electrification programme was such that they entered service on the Main Line, the Circle tracks not being ready until well into 1905. Whilst they might have been tolerable on the sheltered reaches of the Circle tunnels, their draughtiness on the comparatively exposed route to Harrow and Uxbridge made them distinctly unpopular, to the extent that action had to be taken.

Two proposals were put forward — one, to alter the gate ends to enclosed vestibules, the other, to completely reconstruct them as compartment stock. The latter would have allowed an increase in accommodation from the existing 320 seats to 480 seats, or 50%, together with the elimination of the gatemen, but at a considerable cost and, after only two years of operation, at considerable potential embarrassment to the company. Perhaps not surprisingly, Sir Charles MacLaren, then newly elected as Chairman, decided in favour of enclosed vestibules, with the costs incurred in modifying the existing cars being debited to the Capital Account as the difference between their original cost and that of cars built with vestibules. Two 1904 stock third class trailer cars were modified by the builders, presumably as the prototypes for the new arrangement, which was adopted from new in the second batch of trains, ordered in December 1904, for delivery in 1905. Four of these trains were, however, intended to run with the eight surplus, and unmodified, 1904 stock trailers and were in consequence provided with gated platforms at the inner ends of their motor and driving trailer cars. The 1904 stock cars themselves were not altered until 1906–1907, the work being done during their first overhaul. This was to have been undertaken by Neasden Works, but the extent of the work, together with the necessity for it to be completed before the next winter dictated that the bulk of the work was done by the Metropolitan Carriage Company.

Another inconvenience of the original 1904 stock was its use of bar couplings, the indivisibility of which rendered the reformation of a train a workshop task, rather than a simple depot shunting task. Further, it positively prevented the 6-car trains being split for off-peak operation. The subsequent 1905 stock was ordered with knuckle-type couplers from the start on all the cars, whilst the 1904 cars were modified as they were given their first overhaul/rebuild.

One feature which had already caused difficulties on the 1904 stock trains was the lack of any driving facilities other

*The interior of a 1905 stock 1st class trailer in the 1930s. Compared with the present day, almost every usable space was occupied by advertising, even the toplights and draught screens. Although well lit in daylight, the lighting was distinctly sparse — travelling at night, or on the Circle, must have been a dim experience.*
AUTHOR'S COLLECTION

*1905 stock 1st class Driving Trailer car 43, the position of the driving end being given away by the outside mirror. The shoe gear had been provided to ease the problems inherent in operating with only one motor car over conductor rail gaps. The oval first class markings on the windows were unusual, although from the number of notices, it would seem as if the Met had problems with unruly third class passengers.*

LONDON UNDERGROUND

than on the motor cars, thus making it doubly impossible to operate half trains off-peak. The concept of a driving trailer had been tried with the special modification of one first class car for the Uxbridge–Harrow shuttle service. Now that automatic couplings were to be provided, this concept could be extended. The existing 1904 stock first class trailer cars, which normally occupied the centre positions in the train, were modified by the provision of driving controls, the equipment being taken from the inner ends of the motor cars. The 1905 stock first class trailers were provided with driving controls from new.

Meanwhile, considerable difficulties were being experienced with the Westinghouse traction equipment; several motor failures were traced to faulty construction of the armature, leading to the rebanding of the entire batch. The turret controllers were also a major source of trouble, the never-ending failures leading to an undertaking in February 1906 by the Westinghouse company to replace, at their expense, all of these controllers by more orthodox equipments using individual contactors. Similar troubles also afflicted the ten 'camel-back' locomotives which had been acquired in 1906; they, too, were modified.

Another aspect of the Westinghouse system was its use of batteries to supply the 14 volt control circuits. In the early years of the century, these devices had not reached their present state of development, being essentially messy, fragile (by railway traction standards) and expensive. After initial experimentation, they were replaced in 1908 by small motor-generator sets, one being located in each luggage compartment, the batteries being dispensed with altogether. These

machines were critical to the operation of the train, with the result that after a later failure, when a generator failed to excite, a second, standby, machine was provided in each motor car.

One of the other fundamental disadvantages of the early saloon stock, as compared with its compartmented predecessors, was that entry and exit was confined to the car ends only. Whilst this essentially American influence could be tolerated on the other British railways where similar stock had been introduced, ie the Mersey and the Lancashire Yorkshire railways, it was not at all suited to the conditions of the Inner Circle, where large numbers of passengers had to be got off and on to the trains at each stop in a limited time. By 1910, the loading difficulties were clearly reaching a level where a solution had to be found, particularly on the motor cars, where one door had to serve the entire saloon. More doors were necessary, and proposals were put forward for double-leaf sliding doors to be fitted in the centre of the cars, both motor and trailer. This was adopted, with the result that a programme was put in hand in 1911 to modify all the 1904 and 1905 stock cars, as well as embodying the change in future builds of saloon stock, ie the 1913, and in a modified form, the 1921 stocks. The extensive nature of the work, which involved completely rebuilding and strengthening the centre section of the car body, together with the effects of the First World War, meant that progress was slow; by 1918, only 113 of the 222 Metropolitan cars involved had been modified. The remainder, along with the H&C cars, were not completed until 1921.

*An Inner Circle train post 1945 with (leading) a 1913 stock Motor Car, with the luggage area converted to passenger use, followed by a 1921 trailer, a 1912 trailer, another 1921 trailer and, at the rear, a 1904 or 1905 stock motor coach.*

# SUBSEQUENT DEVELOPMENTS — THE 1913 STOCK

*1912 stock Motor Car 92, of the batch equipped with the 7ft 6in bogies from the BTH locomotives. Photographed in 1933 in pristine Met livery.*
A. CRUIKSHANK COLLECTION

From 1907 to 1912, the saloon stock trains were sufficient to supply the Metropolitan's needs for the Circle and H&C services, together with the Uxbridge branch, where they were assisted by the converted Bogie stock sets. However, by 1912, an expansion of the fleet was required, not only for the forthcoming electrification of the East London Railway (actually completed on 31st March, 1913), but also to allow for the extension of the Uxbridge Line services to the City following the rebuilding of Baker Street and its junction with the Inner Circle. Consideration was also being given to a revival of the service to Richmond, using the running powers over the LSWR tracks from Hammersmith Junction, which had been retained, despite the cessation of the Met service in 1906 as part of the electrification of the H&C. These plans were not to come to fruition, however, being frustrated by both the District and the LSW railways, the former of which had then recently acquired the Central London Railway and was possibly considering future plans for extending that line by a connection at Shepherds Bush into the LSWR's Addison Road–Hammersmith line.

To cope with this expansion, an order was placed in 1912 with the Metropolitan C&W Co. for a further ten 6-car trains of saloon stock, together with three spare motor cars, to be delivered over the following two years. The cars were a development of the established 1905 stock design, the only major differences being the abandonment of the clerestory

roof for the elliptical form, as had already been designed for the Dreadnought stock, and the fitting of centre sliding doors on all the cars. Nominally intended for this new stock, twenty-three sets of traction equipment, incorporating 200hp motors, were ordered from the British Westinghouse Co. Not all were, however, actually fitted to 1913 stock cars; ten were diverted upon delivery to the 1907 BTH locomotives in exchange for their existing BW equipments, the object being to standardise the locomotive fleet, as well as to maintain a balance between BTH and BW equipped motor cars.

As a result, motor cars 83–92 received the BTH type GE69 motors and 7ft 6in wheelbase pressed-steel bogies from the 1907 locomotives (Nos 11–20), whilst the remainder, together with the locomotives, were fitted with the new BW86M motored 7ft 9in wheelbase plate-framed bogies.

Although the East London Railway had been one of the factors which justified the acquisition of the 1913 stock, it never saw any of the new cars. All it got were the older saloon stock cars, displaced from the Inner Circle by the new cars.

Although ordered as complete trains, their complete interchangeability with the 1904 and 1905 stocks meant that mixed formations were not uncommon. They remained as built until 1935, when the LPTB undertook a complete revision of the Inner Circle, displacing the older cars in favour of

A 1913 stock Motor Car, seen in 1934 still in Met livery but with its new LPTB number. This was one of the other batch of Motor Cars fitted with the 7ft 9in bogies recovered from the Westinghouse locomotives.
A. CRUIKSHANK COLLECTION

The 1913 saloon stock, of which a 3rd class trailer is seen here, was effectively only the 1905 stock updated by the substitution of a full elliptical roof in place of the clerestory.
LONDON TRANSPORT

trains formed from the more modern, ie 1913 and 1921, saloon stock cars. The luggage compartment, which had become virtually redundant on the Inner Circle services, was stripped out on the sixteen motor cars thus allocated and replaced by new seating; this was intended to have been transverse, accommodating eight passengers, but was altered in the conversion to longitudinal seating for four passengers. Considerable rebuilding of the car frame in this area was required, including the provision of a complete new window in the same style as the remainder of the car. Only part of the luggage compartment was converted to passenger use, a small section immediately behind the cab being retained for the use of the guard, as well as the stowage of the emergency equipment and, on the Westinghouse cars, the 14V motor-generator sets. Only those cars allocated to the Inner Circle trains were thus altered; the remaining seven,

working the Uxbridge and Harrow services, were not altered in this manner, as there was still a need for the luggage accommodation.

By then, the BW86M motors fitted to cars 93–98 were some 28 years old, and beginning to become a liability through their deteriorating condition. Numbers of BTH GE212 type motors, rated at 240hp, were becoming surplus at the same time as a result of the scrapping of the District B-class cars and the LER/LNWR Watford Joint stock and the decision was taken that these should, in turn, replace the ageing BW86M motors. At a rated 240hp, the GE212 motors were roughly 20% more powerful than the BW86M motors they were replacing, and to avoid an excess of power, only six were to be used to each train. This was achieved by converting cars 96–98 to single equipments, ie two motors only, the inner end bogie being demotored to become a trail-

*The interior of a 1913 stock 3rd class Driving Trailer car in the 1930s.*

METROPOLITAN RAILWAY 1913 STOCK TRAILER CAR

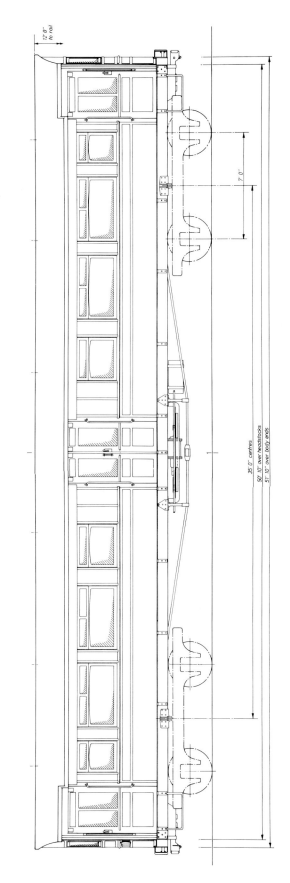

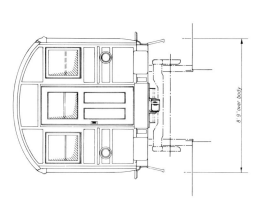

12' 8" to rail

7' 0"

35' 0" centres

50' 10" over headstocks

51' 10" over body ends

8' 9" over body

Car numbers :-
77-86    Third class
77,79-86  First class    Driving Trailer
78        First class    Not fitted with driving controls

For subsequent renumbering by L.T. refer to separate table

Bogies - Met Rly type I ( L.T type MR )

# METROPOLITAN RAILWAY 1913 STOCK THIRD CLASS MOTOR CAR

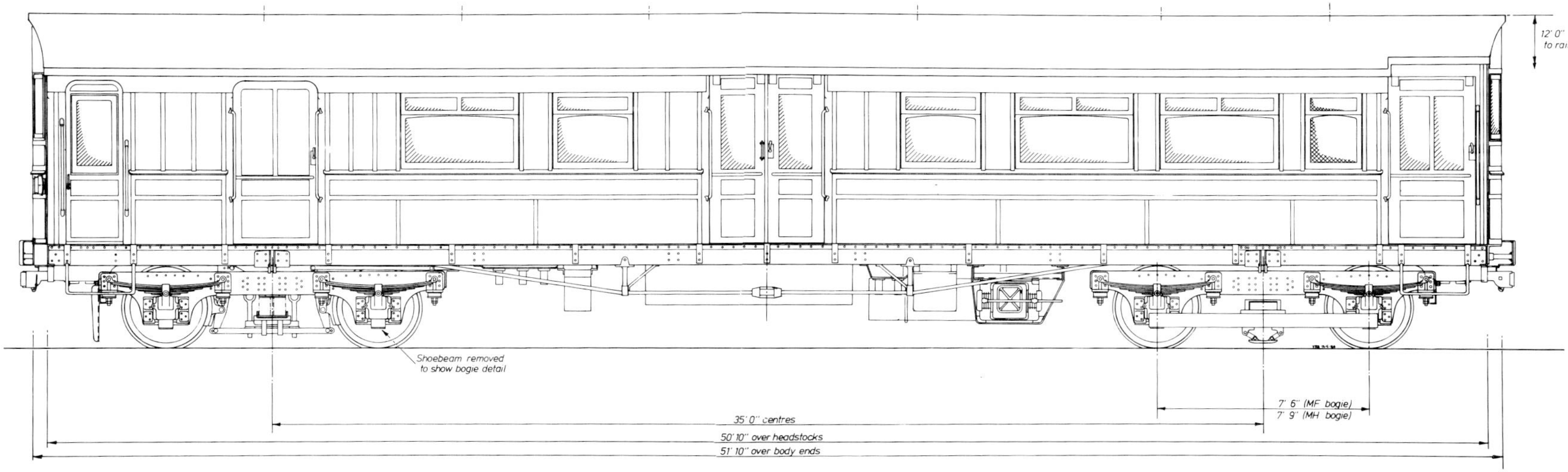

For non-driving end
refer to trailer car

12' 0"
to rail

7' 6" (MF bogie)
7' 9" (MH bogie)

35' 0" centres

50' 10" over headstocks

51' 10" over body ends

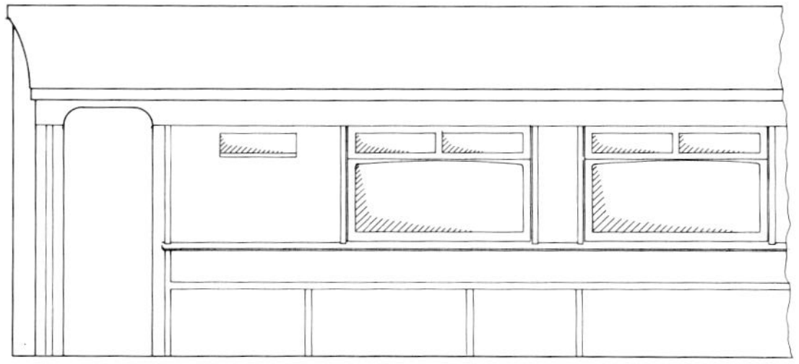

Shoebeam removed
to show bogie detail

8' 9" over body

Car nos 83 - 92 (LT 2587 - 2596)   BTH equipment.  GE 69 motors
        93 - 98 (    2581 - 2586)   BWE equipment.  BW86M motors
        99 - 105 (   2545 - 2552)

Main drawing shows BTH equipped car running on MF bogies recovered
from electric locomotives 11 - 20. BWE cars 93 - 105 fitted with MH
bogies. for details refer to 1920 stock motor car

Subsidiary drawing shows arrangement following conversion in 1935
of luggage compartment for passenger use on cars 2581 - 2596.
Cars 2545 - 2552 not allocated to Circle services remained as built

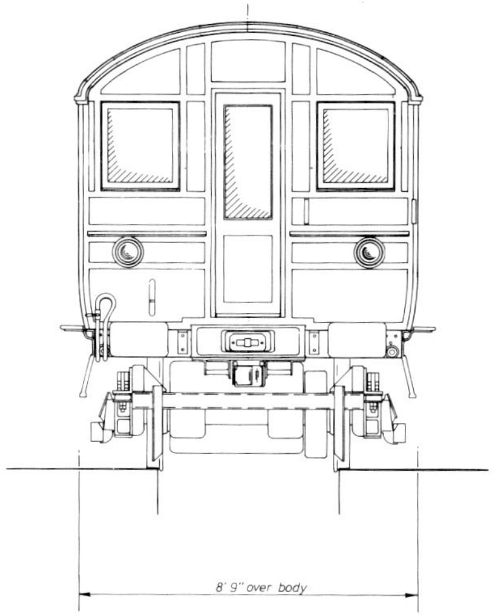

# METROPOLITAN RAILWAY

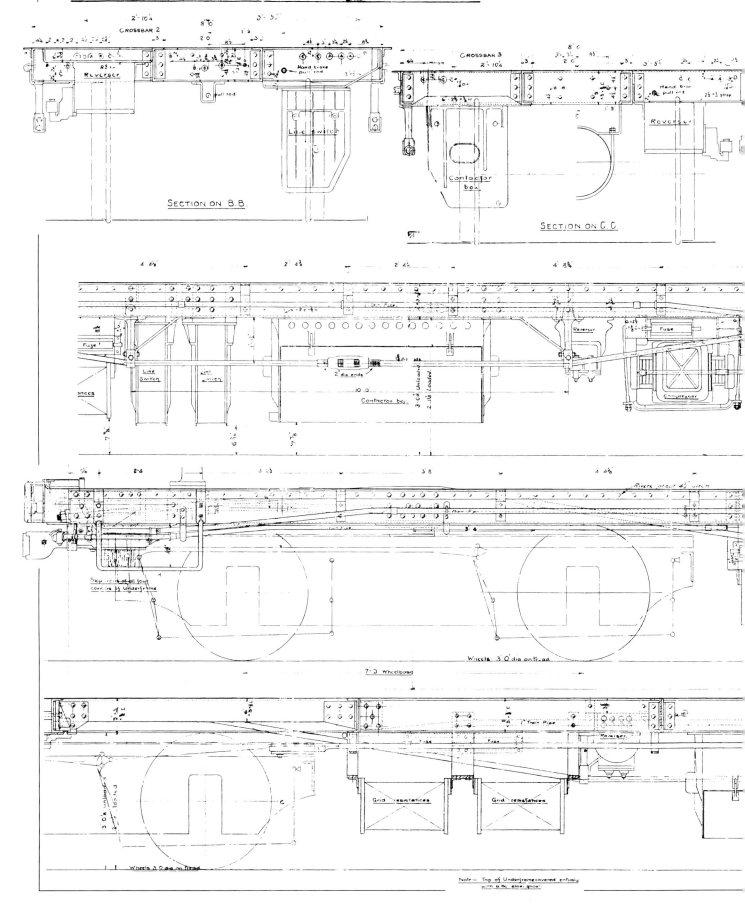

SECTION ON B.B.

SECTION ON C.C.

# MOTOR CAR UNDERFRAME

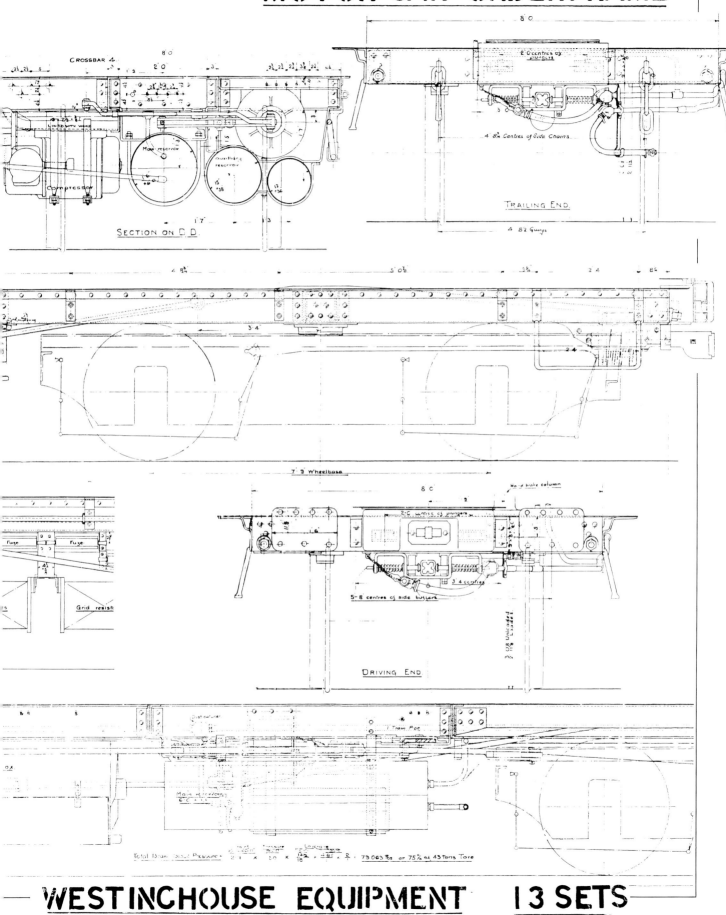

WESTINGHOUSE EQUIPMENT 13 SETS

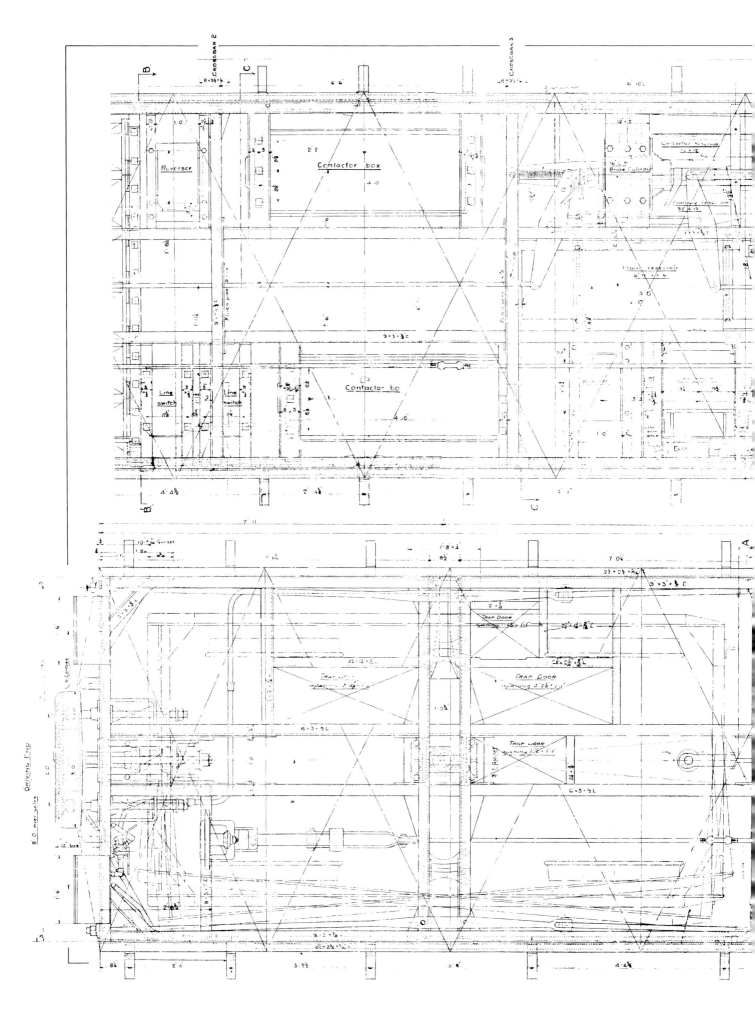

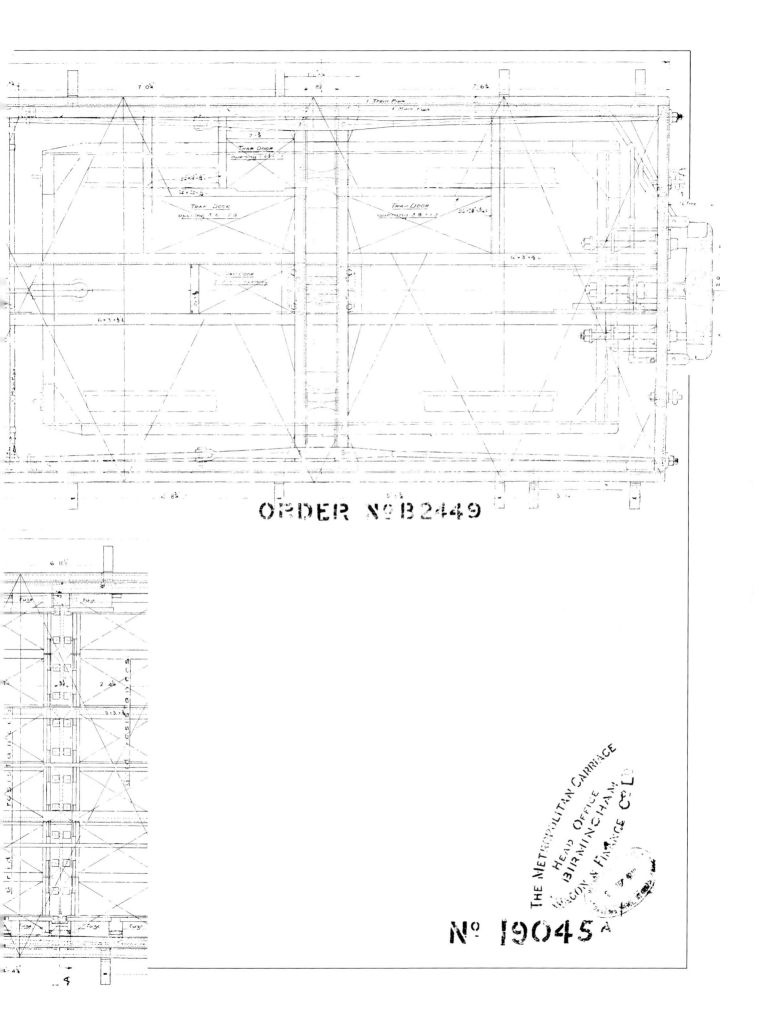

ORDER Nº B 2449

Nº 19045 ᴬ

First class Driving Trailer No. 55 was one of the four trailers and two motor cars rebuilt to form the 1919 experimental stock.

A. CRUIKSHANK COLLECTION

er bogie. The other three cars involved, 93–95, remained equipped with four motors.

Three trailer cars, 80[1], 86[1] & 79[3], were modified in 1942–3 by the fitment of District K2 type bogies, surplus from withdrawn H-class cars, their own Fox type bogies having become structurally unsound.

At least two motor cars were involved in accidents; No 95 collided with motor car 46 in Neasden Yard in 1917, whilst No 88 was hit by five runaway wagons of a GER goods train which it was following towards Shadwell. Both cars survived and were repaired. Car 105 inherited the motors and bogies from 1921 stock car 117 after it had been written off in June 1939 following a collision with a District train due to a wrong-side signal failure at Embankment in May the previous year. It survived in this form until March 1951, becoming the last 1913 stock motor car to remain in service, the rest having been scrapped over the previous ten years.

# SLAM vs. SLIDING DOORS
# THE 1919 EXPERIMENTAL STOCK

Within five years of the inauguration of electric services on the Metropolitan, the saloon stock arrangement of access/egress at the car ends only was proving to be a bottleneck. The greater number of passengers being carried was extending station stop times and frequently causing the following train to be stopped at the home signal in rear. This not only caused delays which, by the nature of the Inner Circle, could spread rapidly through the whole service, as well as outwards into any of the various lines connecting with it, but also increased the electricity demand, leading to higher coal consumption and, therefore, costs. As train lengths could not be increased, the solution had to be based on providing a better flow of passengers on and off the train. To achieve this, it was decided, after some experimentation, that the saloon stock cars should have additional doors at the centre of the car. Existing cars were to be modified, the programme taking some ten years to complete, whilst future cars were to incorporate this feature from new, as shown by the 1913 saloon stock.

Whilst this may have effected some improvement, there is reason to believe that, possibly exacerbated by the increased loadings, this arrangement was not wholly satisfactory. Mr Holt, the Line Superintendent, raised the issue in May 1916, and again in January 1918, as a result of which Mr Jones, the CME, was instructed to investigate alternative arrangements, particularly on the motor cars. Drawings were submitted and authority granted in April of that year for one motor car to be modified. A 1905 stock car, No 32, which had not yet been fitted with centre doors, was selected and became the subject of extensive rebuilding by Neasden Works. To accommodate an additional 3ft 0in single sliding door in each side, the saloon was lengthened by relocating the luggage compartment partition some 2ft nearer the driving cab, the two seating bays between it and the new door being moved correspondingly, together with their associated windows. One seating bay was lost completely, but partly made up for by the provision of longitudinal seating adjacent to the new door pocket. Thus rebuilt, the car went into traffic in September 1918, only to be condemned by Holt, who considered that the existing double-door conversion was better value, the additional cost being more than justified by the wider door opening.

At this stage, the matter was referred to the Carriage and Traffic Departments, who were instructed to form a Committee to consider the question more fully. By December they were able to put forward four schemes for the reconstruction of the 1904/5 saloon stock cars. These offered either four sliding doors or five swing doors per car side, each with either all longitudinal or mixed seating. The vestibules and inter-car communicating doors were to be removed altogether, whilst the luggage compartment was to be shortened to enable its doors to be used by passengers.

As the cars would have to cope not only with the heavy short-distance traffic of the H&C and Circle services, but also with the Uxbridge and Harrow traffic, this swing door arrangement was considered the most suitable compromise. This was accepted, and in March 1919, a six-car train was despatched to the Metropolitan C&W Co. for reconstruction to the new designs prepared by Neasden. The car bodies were completely rebuilt, using much of the original framing and components such as window frames to create an arrangement with alternating doors and seating bays; the trailer cars, of which there were the customary two types, each had five doors per side, whilst the motor cars had four swing doors in addition to the sliding door, which had been made available for passenger use by an internal rearrangement of the luggage compartment. The only parts to remain largely unaltered were the luggage compartments and both driving cabs, the latter retaining their bow-fronted construction. As the train could only operate as a block set because of its unique arrangement, there was no need to retain the end door in the driving cabs of the motor cars, which were rebuilt in a full-fronted style which set the pattern for the 1921 and subsequent stocks. Curiously, the cabs of driving trailer cars retained their original fronts, including the centre door. It had been the original intention to retain the clerestory roof, but in the event, this, too, was replaced by a roof of semi-elliptic form, as had been fitted to the 1913 stock.

Internally, the design was completely novel, single and double bays of seats being placed between the swing doors, protected against draughts by glazed screens. Handrails were provided on the seat backs in place of the original overhead straps for the benefit of standing passengers and the

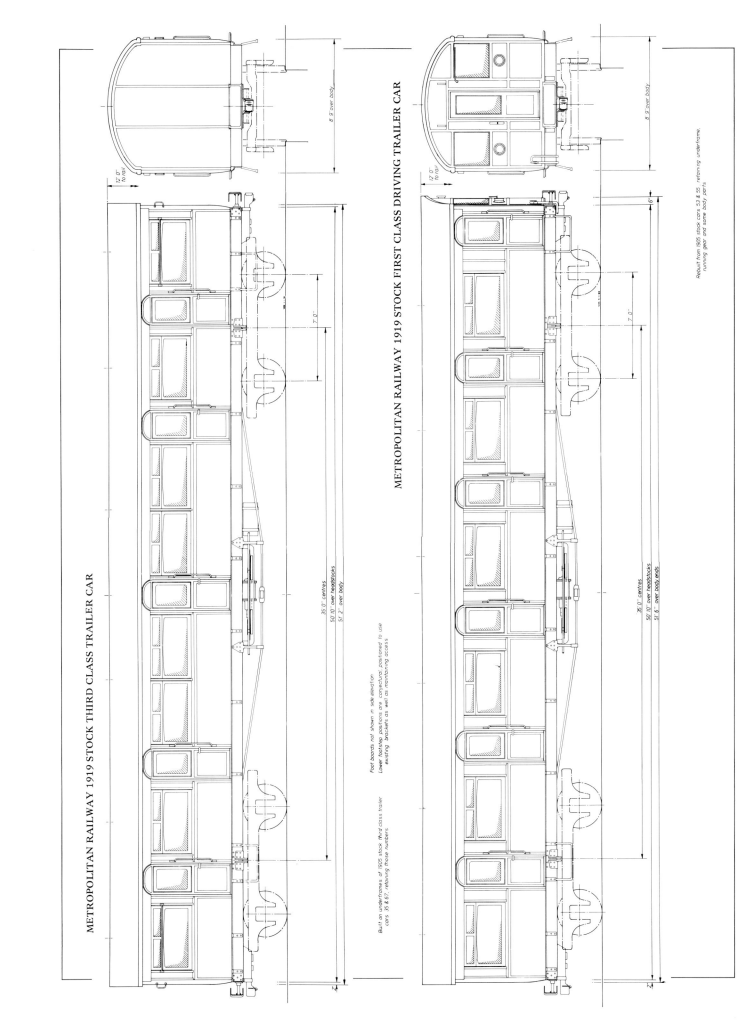

METROPOLITAN RAILWAY 1919 STOCK THIRD CLASS TRAILER CAR

METROPOLITAN RAILWAY 1919 STOCK FIRST CLASS DRIVING TRAILER CAR

12' 0" to rail

8' 9" over body

35' 0" centres

50' 10" over headstocks

51' 2" over body

Foot boards not shown in side elevation

Lower footstep positions are conjectural, positioned to use
existing brackets as well as maintaining access

Built on underframes of 1905 stock third class trailer
cars 35 & 67, retaining those numbers

12' 0" to rail

8' 9" over body

6'

7' 0"

35' 0" centres

50' 10" over headstocks

51' 6" over body ends

Rebuilt from 1905 stock cars 53 & 55, retaining underframe,
running gear and some body parts

# METROPOLITAN RAILWAY 1919 STOCK MOTOR CAR

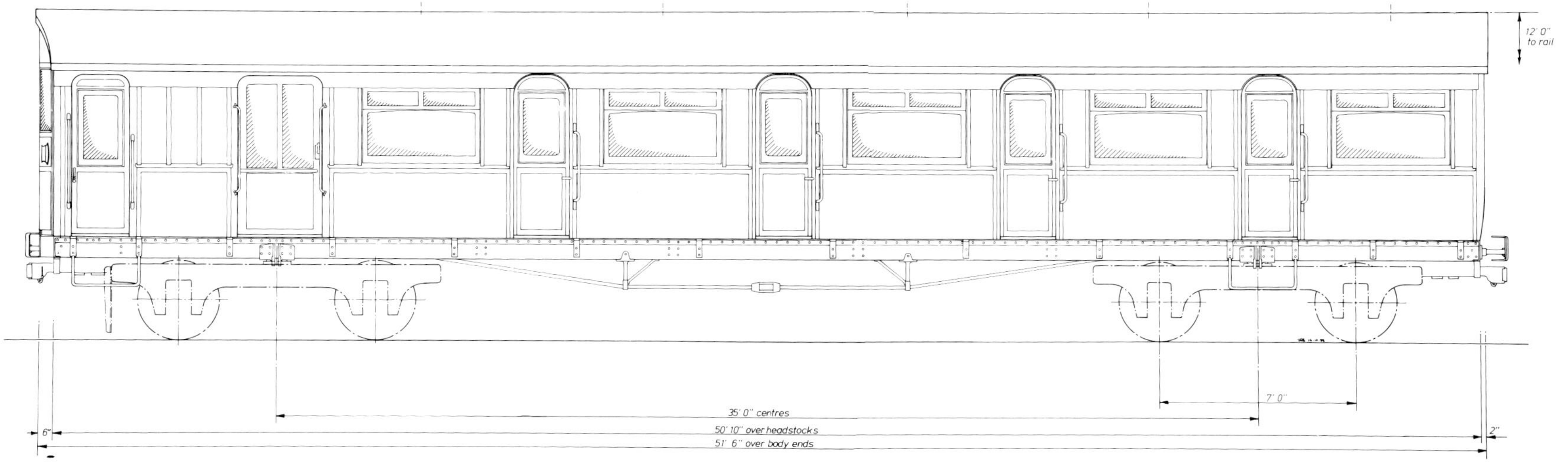

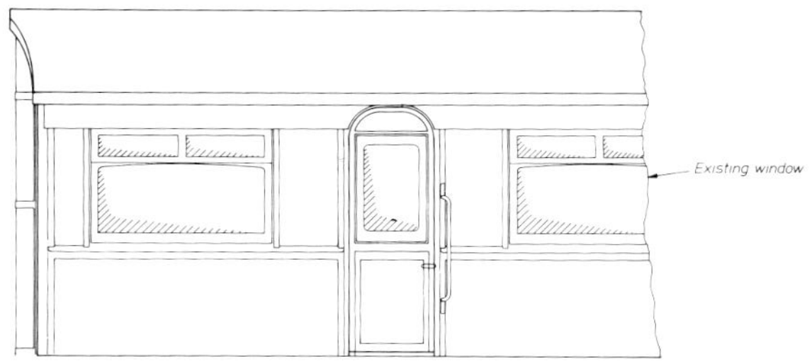

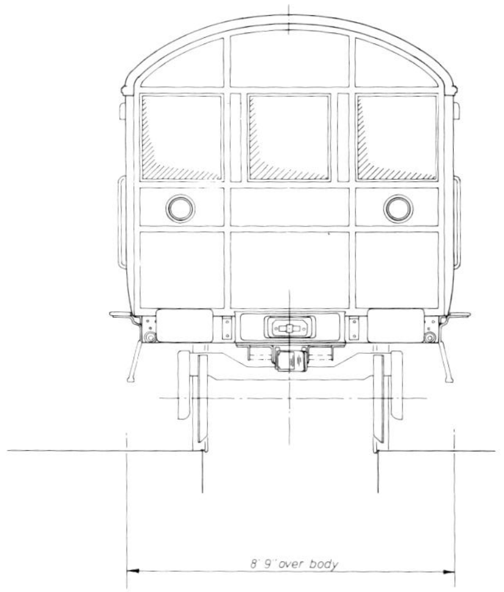

12' 0" to rail

7' 0"

35' 0" centres

50' 10" over headstocks

51' 6" over body ends

8' 9" over body

Existing window

Rebuilt from 1905 stock motor cars 36 & 44, retaining the
original underframe, bogies and power equipment.
Further rebuilt in 1931 as 3rd class trailer cars 197 & 198
by the removal of the luggage and driving compartments.
Subsidiary drawing shows arrangement of rebuilt driving
end of car body.

The interst in this photograph lies not in the motor car, which was a standard 1912 stock car, but in the trailer set behind it. This, the S stock set, was formed from the 1919 experimental stock, of which there had been but a single train. This had been an unsuccessful attempt to reduce station times by increasing the number of doors. Unfortunately, the constricted vestibules provided too much of an obstruction – the 1921 stock reverted to large sliding doors, three per side.

LURS COLLECTION

general appearance improved by the substitution of frosted bulbs and opal reflectors for the original bare lamps. To facilitate passenger movement through the sliding doors, the luggage compartment was divided, Bostwick type collapsible gates being provided to prevent unauthorised tampering with any luggage or parcels contained therein.

Whilst this work was in progress, a further proposal was put forward by the General Manager, R.H. Selbie, which involved the provision of an additional sliding door immediately behind the luggage compartment, in addition to the double centre doors. One motor car, No 14, was thus modified, but although the passenger flow was improved as a result, the considerable expenditure involved more than offset the benefits. No further cars were modified in this way, although the arrangement was to reappear later in the 1921 stock.

The 'Hustle Train', as it was to become known, was revealed to the Press at Baker Street on 18th December 1919, receiving favourable reports. In traffic, it achieved its intended purpose of providing a comparable number of seats to the existing stock (286 as compared to the 268 of centre-doored saloon stock) whilst at the same time reducing station times by 50% to roundly 25 seconds. This achievement was not without its disadvantages, however. The narrow door openings, 2ft as against 3ft 6in, together with the restricted space between the seat backs, created congestion within the doorways, whilst the number of entries caused a degree of hesitation whilst passengers decided which one to make for. In consequence, whilst the train was a technical success, the cost of such a major rebuilding was not in practice considered to be worthwhile, and opinion swung in favour of sliding doors. The rebuilt train remained in service in its full form until 1931, when, because of the deteriorating condition of the traction equipment, the two motor cars were rebuilt as trailers, giving a 6-car trailer set, designated as S-stock. This ran until February 1941, sandwiched between the two 1924 experimental motor coaches, 198 and 199, although the lower-powered 200hp 1913 or 1921 stock motor cars were used on occasion.

## THE 1921 STOCK

By the end of the First World War, the Metropolitan's passenger traffic had risen to the point where the existing rolling stock fleet was only barely sufficient. Seven-car trains had been introduced on Main Line workings in 1915, with some 8-car workings following in 1916, and when, at the end of 1917, the Metropolitan had agreed to the District's proposal to lengthen the Circle trains to five cars, it found itself in the embarrassing position of having insufficient stock to follow. At the same time, the poor passenger-handling capabilities of the unmodified 1904/5 saloon stock cars, of which there were still some 109 in operation, raised doubts over the suitability of the existing saloon stock designs. After a tentative modification of one car, a joint committee of the Carriage and Traffic Departments proposed two new forms of body arrangement, each having more doors than the current saloon stock. As has been described in the previous chapter, the swing-door proposal was favoured, and a complete 6-car train of 1905 stock rebuilt to the new design, becoming the 1919 experimental stock. For various reasons, this train was not as successful in service as had been hoped, resulting in a revival of interest in sliding doors.

Consequently, when the decision was taken to expand the fleet, the additional stock ordered for the Circle was of the saloon type with sliding doors. It was not, however, merely a repeat order to the established 1913 stock design, which had been found wanting in two important aspects in regard to the door layout. On all the cars, the existence of the partition between the end vestibule and the saloon had been found to restrict the free flow of passengers, whilst on the motor cars, difficulties arose with the driving end of the saloon, which was served only by the centre doors. The extra door fitted to car 32 previously had shown the way toward solving the latter problem, whilst the 1919 stock layout, with its doors more evenly distributed along the car, had improved the directness of access to each seat.

The new cars, designated 1921 stock, drew upon the experience gained with these experimental cars, seeking to avoid the problems which were acknowledged to be inherent in the existing standard saloon stock design. The end vestibule/centre door layout gave way to three sliding doors spaced along the body side, each opening directly into the saloon and serving no more than 1½ seating bays either side. With the disappearance of the vestibule, the car ends became flat and without inter-communicating doors, although these were later provided when the LPTB modernised the Circle fleet in 1935. The trailer cars also broke with tradition in that, for the first time on saloon stock, different bodies were designed for the third class trailers and the first class driving trailer cars, the latter reverting to the earlier practice of providing more space per passenger than in third class, as well as having a dedicated compartment for the driver, rather than sharing what was otherwise a public space.

In all, 59 1921 stock cars were ordered, this being made up from 20 motor cars, 33 third class trailers and 6 first class driving trailer cars. As much of this stock went to increasing the train length, mixed formations of 1913 and 1921 stock cars became the rule; only with the later replacement of the Westinghouse traction motors was there any restriction on the operation of the motor cars.

History repeated itself with the traction equipment for these cars; although twenty cars were ordered, only the second ten were fitted with new equipment and plate frame bogies, identical to those supplied for the 1913 cars. The first

*1921 stock 3rd class Motor Car 115. The body panelling was a masterpiece of the painter's art, for although appearing to be of teak, it is actually only steel, very skilfully painted to reproduce the wood grain, including the knots!*
R. J. GREENAWAY
COLLECTION

*1921 stock 3rd class Trailer 103. Although still in full Metropolitan livery, it presents a much more drab appearance than the motor coach did when it was new.*
LT COLLECTION

ten inherited the equipment and pressed-steel bogies from the Westinghouse locomotives, Nos 1–10, which were then being replaced by the new 1200hp Metropolitan–Vickers locomotives. As with the 1913 cars, the BW86M motors were becoming life-expired by the time the LPTB undertook its review of the Circle fleet in 1935, and since numbers of the more robust BTH GE212 motors were by then available from scrapped District and LER stock, the opportunity was taken to refit all the 1921 motor cars. As these motors were more highly rated than the Westinghouse machines, 240hp as against 200hp, half the cars were converted to have two motors only, the inner end bogie being unpowered. The remaining ten cars retained four motors, so that, when operated as pairs, each five-car train had six motors, totalling 1440hp, slightly less than the 1600hp of the original arrangement.

A further modification carried out at this time was the removal of the luggage accommodation and its replacement by a small saloon with seating for four passengers, similar to the arrangement provided on the 1913 motor cars in the Circle fleet.

One additional first class driving trailer car was constructed in 1923 for display in the Palace of Engineering at the 1924 Empire Exhibition at Wembley, following which it was absorbed into the Metropolitan fleet, becoming car 106. For a while, it formed part of the Circle fleet, but, presumably following the withdrawal of the 1919 stock cars in 1941, it was transferred to the East London Line, where with the two 1925 motor cars 198 and 199, it formed a three-car train until scrapped in the 1950s, in the process evading the 1935 modernisation, so that it never received end doors.

*The interior of a 1921 stock 3rd class trailer car, in LT days, after the insertion of the end door, not an original feature. Compared with the 1905 stock, the lighting had been improved, but the interior decoration was much more basic. Matchboarding apart, the style was halfway to the LT C69 stock, fifty years later, and destined for the Circle service.* AUTHOR'S COLLECTION

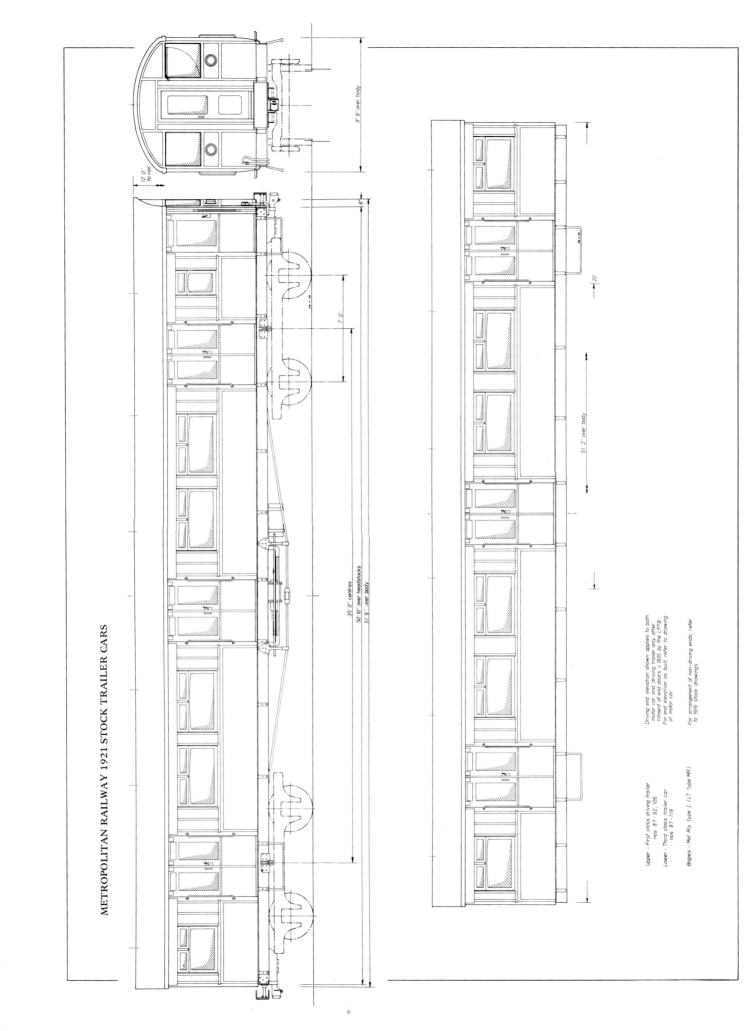

# METROPOLITAN RAILWAY 1921 STOCK TRAILER CARS

8' 9" over body

12' 0" to rail

35' 0" centres

50' 10" over headstocks

51' 6" over body

51' 2" over body

7' 0"

20"

6"

Upper - First class driving trailer
nos 87-92, 106
Lower - Third class trailer car
nos 87-119

Bogies - Met Rly type I (LT type MR)

Driving end elevation shown applies to both
motor car and driving trailer only after
fitment of end doors c.1925 by the LPTB
For end elevation as built, refer to drawing
of motor car

For arrangement of non-driving ends, refer
to 1919 stock drawings

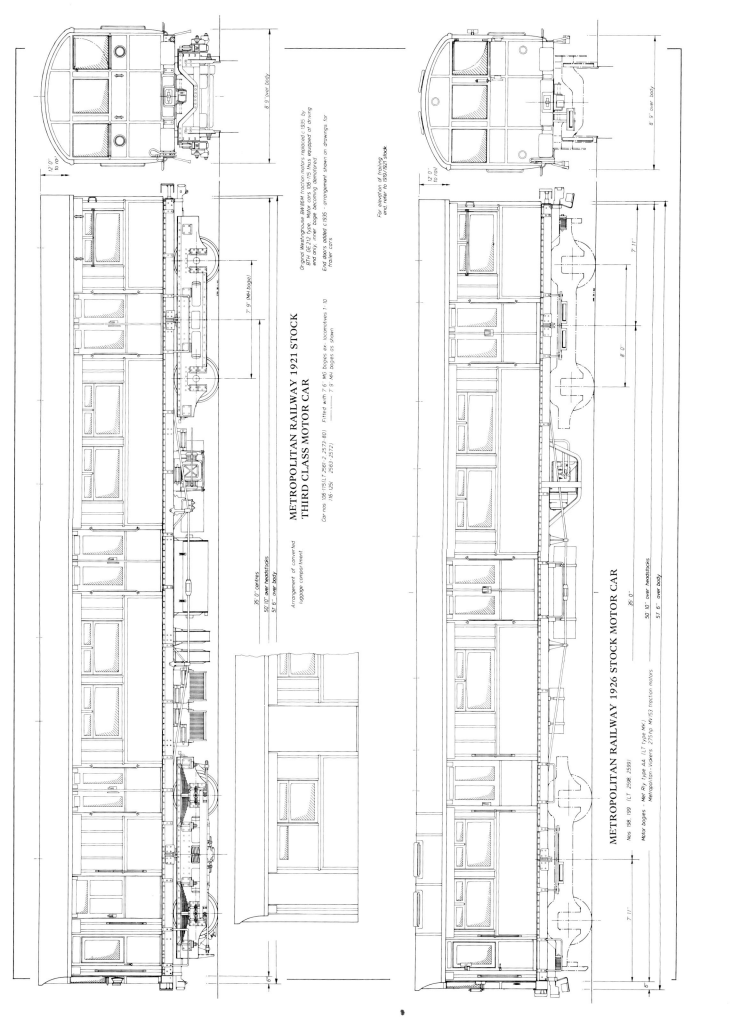

## METROPOLITAN RAILWAY 1921 STOCK
## THIRD CLASS MOTOR CAR

Car nos. 106-115 (LT 256/1-2, 2573-80)
116-125 (2563-2572)

Fitted with 7' 6" MG bogies ex-locomotives 1-10
7' 9" MH bogies as shown

Original Westinghouse BW85M traction motors replaced c.1935 by
BTH GE212 type. Motor cars 106-115 thus equipped at driving
end only, inner bogie becoming demotored.

End doors added c.1935 - arrangement shown on drawings for
trailer cars

For elevation of trailing
end, refer to 1919/1927 stock

Arrangement of converted
luggage compartment

8' 9" over body

12' 0" to rail

7' 9" (MH bogie)

35' 0" centres
50' 10" over headstocks
51' 6" over body

6"

## METROPOLITAN RAILWAY 1926 STOCK MOTOR CAR

Nos. 198, 199   (LT 2598, 2599)

Motor bogies - Met Rly type 44   (LT type MK)
Metropolitan - Vickers 275hp MV153 traction motors

8' 9" over body

12' 0" to rail

7' 11"

8' 0"

7' 11"

35' 0"
50' 10" over headstocks
51' 6" over body

6"

*The ultimate development of the saloon stock was to be found in the two 1924 experimental motor cars, Nos. 198 & 199. These cars, intended as try-outs for the Main Line electric units, developed the 1921 stock by the inclusion of body-mounted control equipment, married to four high (275hp) traction motors. Although technically successful, the use of saloon stock was not to the liking of the Met's longer distance commuters and the design was never repeated.*    A. CRUIKSHANK COLLECTION

*The interior of one of the 1925 experimental motor cars, 198 or 199, looking towards the driving end.*    AUTHOR'S COLLECTION

# THE LAST SALOON CARS
# THE 1925 STOCK

*A train of 1921 stock (apart from one 1913 Driving Trailer) topped and tailed by the two 1924 stock motor cars out in a then very rural Metroland scene somewhere north of Harrow in (probably) the later 1920s.*
A. CRUIKSHANK COLLECTION

With the impending electrification of the Main Line to Rickmansworth and the opening of the joint LNER/Met branch to Watford, more rolling stock was going to be required. The long-distance nature of this new service dictated that a new design of rolling stock was needed, having at least a higher power rating to cope with heavier 7-car trains as well as higher speeds. What was not certain, however, was whether the passenger accommodation should continue to be of the compartment type, as on the steam stock then used on the services north of Harrow, or the saloon type, already established on the Circle and Uxbridge services.

To provide experience before placing the main order, two experimental motor cars were ordered from the Metropolitan C&W Co. in 1925, both to be provided with Metropolitan–Vickers traction equipments based on those previously supplied for the 1200hp electric locomotives and having four 275hp motors. In this latter respect, they were, at the time, the most powerful multiple-unit vehicles in Europe. (In Britain, although equalled by the 1927 MV/MW stock motor coaches, they were not to be exceeded in power until 1967 with the entry into service of the new multiple unit stock for the Bournemouth electrification.)

Although the two cars bore a close family likeness to the preceding 1921 stock cars, they were significantly different in many ways. Most obvious was the transfer of the traction equipment from below the floor to a new compartment situated immediately behind the driving cab. To compensate for the space thus occupied, the passenger saloon was correspondingly shortened, the overall body length remaining unchanged at 51ft 6in. Structurally, the body reverted to conventional practice, being built separately from the underframe, rather than directly on it, as had been standard from the 1905 stock onwards. This had the effect of raising the whole body by 3in, to compensate for which the profile of the elliptical roof had to be altered in order to maintain the overall height for the car within the 12ft 4in limit. New plate-framed motor bogies were provided, together with a new and heavier design of underframe incorporating channel section solebars in place of the angle sections hitherto employed.

The reasons for placing the traction equipment, switchgear as well as resistors, in a compartment rather than below the floor, as had been the practice, are unclear, as there was little, if any, increase in the size and number of components despite the higher rating of the motors, and similarly-sized equipments for contemporary Southern Railway units were of the underfloor type. It is, nonetheless, acknowledged that maintenance access was significantly improved, pit facilities no longer being a necessity, and that greater cleanliness could be assured, leading to improved reliability.

These two cars were considered successful, but the time taken to load and unload, particularly at Baker Street, together with passenger preference, persuaded the Metropolitan to provide compartment accommodation for the new Main Line fleet, the subsequent development of which is covered in other chapters. The two cars themselves had long, if undistinguished, lives, running for a time with saloon stock trailers before, in 1931, becoming paired with the 1919 stock set, by then all trailer cars, until their demise in 1941. Following this, they and the additional 1921 stock driving trailer 106, were coupled as a three-car set and despatched to the East London Line, where they remained until withdrawn by the LPTB some time in the 1950s. Whether or not they retained their full traction equipment on this last duty is uncertain; certainly, the provision of 2200hp for a total train weight of 121 tons would have been excessive, and it is more than likely that they would have been reduced to two motors, ie one equipment group, on each car.

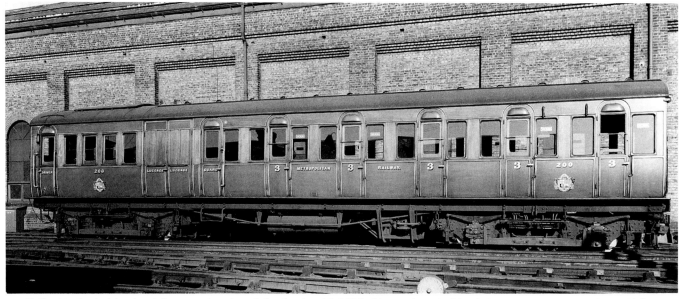

*Following the decision to retain compartment stock for the electrified Main Line services, the Met designed a new motor coach, combining the features of the Dreadnought design with the control equipment and mechanical parts of the 1924 experimental motor cars. The result was the 1927 MW/MV stock. The six MW class coaches, of which 200 is seen here, were equipped with centre buffers and couplers and Westinghouse brake and used to power trains of converted bogie stock.*    A. CRUIKSHANK COLLECTION

*The six MV class motor coaches, of which 207 was the prototype, were equipped with standard screw couplings, side buffers and vacuum brakes so that their trailer coaches, which were modified Dreadnought stock, could be locomotive-hauled if necessary.*    A. CRUIKSHANK COLLECTION

# CHAPTER EIGHT

# THE MAIN-LINE COMPARTMENT ELECTRIC STOCK

FOR the Metropolitan, the years following the First War were marked by the growth of Metroland, both westward along the Uxbridge branch and northward between Harrow and Rickmansworth. To better cope with the increase in traffic which would, with time, result from these developments, as well as the opening, in 1925, of the branch to Watford, it was recognised that electrification would be necessary and that additional rolling stock would be required.

Up until then, the Metropolitan's electrified lines had been essentially suburban in nature, with comparatively short journeys, stopping at most stations, and undemanding performance requirements for which pairs of 800hp motor cars had sufficed for each 5- or 6-car train. For the 6-coach trains contemplated for the Rickmansworth and Watford services, where speeds and distances were higher, this stock would not be adequate; a completely new design of motor-coach would be required.

Working in conjunction with Metropolitan–Vickers, it was decided that 1100hp motor coaches would be required, each having four 275hp traction motors. Not only would new bogies be required to accommodate these larger motors, but the power requirements would be beyond the capabilities of the underfloor equipment used thus far on the various Saloon stocks. Using the 1921 Saloon stock motor car as a basis, designs were produced in 1924 for a new saloon type motor car, the most noticeable feature of which was the mounting of the traction equipment in a separate compartment behind the driver instead of below the floor. After further work, two experimental motor cars, numbers 198 and 199, were ordered from Metropolitan C&W in 1925, both with equipment from Metropolitan–Vickers.

Whilst the new traction equipment on these two cars performed extremely well and set the pattern for the future main-line stock for which they were effectively prototypes, the Metropolitan's choice of a saloon layout for the passenger accommodation was not such a success, proving a source of delay in unloading peak time trains (as the 1919 experimental stock had also borne out in its trials). There was also considerable opposition from the passengers themselves, who were not willing to give up the individual compartments to which they had been long accustomed.

Following the experience gained with these two motor cars, the Met placed an order for a further twelve motor coaches with Metropolitan C&W. These shared the same underframes, bogies and traction equipment as 198 and 199, but instead had compartment-type bodies, the saloon layout of the 1925 cars having been found wanting for main-line duties. Since the prime purpose of these coaches was to gain experience, both with the traction equipment and the operation of multiple unit stock on main-line duties, no trailer coaches were ordered.

Six of the new motor coaches, numbered 200–205, were equipped with buckeye couplers and centre buffers at both ends to allow them to be used at either end of three of the rakes of converted Bogie stock which were at that time being operated with pairs of 200hp Saloon stock motor cars. As these were already equipped with Westinghouse air brakes, the new motor coaches had to be similarly fitted, thus earning them the designation 'MW'.

To work with the other six new motor coaches, numbered 206–211, three five-coach sets of Dreadnought stock were provided, unaltered save for the addition of the through 10-way control cables required to allow them to be operated between pairs of new motor coaches. So that they could still be used as locomotive-hauled stock if needed, they retained their side buffers, screw couplings and vacuum braking, as a result of which the new motor coaches had to be similarly fitted, thus causing them to be designated as MV stock to distinguish them from their Westinghouse-equipped sisters. The use of vacuum braking, unusual in electric multiple unit rolling stock, necessitated their being fitted with an exhauster as well as an air compressor, the latter being still required in order to operate the traction control equipment.

The bodies, each of which had five compartments seating a total of 50 passengers, as well as guard's and luggage compartments, were derived directly from the design of the Dreadnought stock, sharing common dimensions but differing in their construction methods. Whilst both retained the traditional use of teak for the body framing, teak panelling was applied only to the six MV stock coaches (206–211). The other six coaches, 200–205, were flush-clad in sheet steel, the dimensions of the timber body frame being enlarged to compensate for the thinner sheeting. Why the two different forms of body panelling should have been tried is unclear, since steel had been used since 1904 on all the saloon stock, although compartment stock had continued to use teak panelling. It is notable, however, that at the time these motor coaches were designed, steel-panelled coaches were appearing in growing numbers in the fleets of the other main-line railway companies; the Met had a long tradition of design innovation and it may be nothing more than the desire to evaluate this method of construction that led to the use of both this and timber construction for these motor coaches.

The experience gained over the following two years with these twelve 1927 MW/MV stock motor coaches was considered to be very favourable, as a result of which, in 1929, a further order was placed with the Metropolitan Railway Carriage & Wagon Co. for 30 motor and 25 trailer coaches, all to be fitted with Westinghouse brakes and automatic couplings with centre buffers, following the pattern set by the 1927 MW coaches, with which they were interchangeable. Although built as complete trains from new, they retained the traditional methods for control of the heating

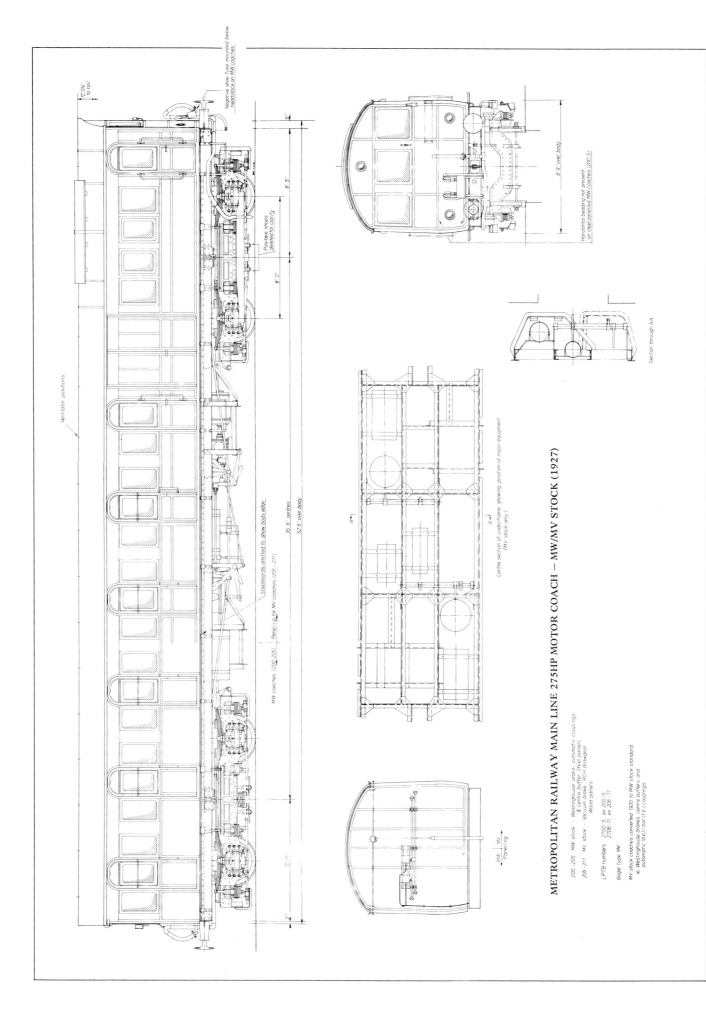

METROPOLITAN RAILWAY MAIN LINE 275HP MOTOR COACH — MW/MV STOCK (1927)

200 -205   MW stock - Westinghouse brake  automatic couplings
                          & centre buffer  Steel panels
206 -211   MV stock - vacuum brake - RCH drawgear
                          Wood panels

LPTB numbers   2700-5  ex 200-5
                        2706-11, ex 206-11

Bogie type MK

MV stock coaches converted 1935 to MW stock standard
ie Westinghouse brakes, centre buffers and
automatic (late)/barrier) couplings

Section through AA

Ventilator positions

MW coaches (200-205)  Panelling for MV coaches (206-211)

Stepboards omitted to show body edge

Positive shoes
deleted for clarity

Negative shoe fuse mounted below
headstock on MW coaches

Horizontal beading not present
on steel panelled MW coaches (200-5)

8' 9" over body

Centre section of underframe showing position of major equipment
(MV stock only)

MW  MV
Panelling

35' 6" centres
52' 6" over body

8' 5"
8' 0"
5"
7' 11"
2'-0½"
to rail

# METROPOLITAN RAILWAY 1929 & 1931 MW STOCK DRIVING TRAILER COACHES

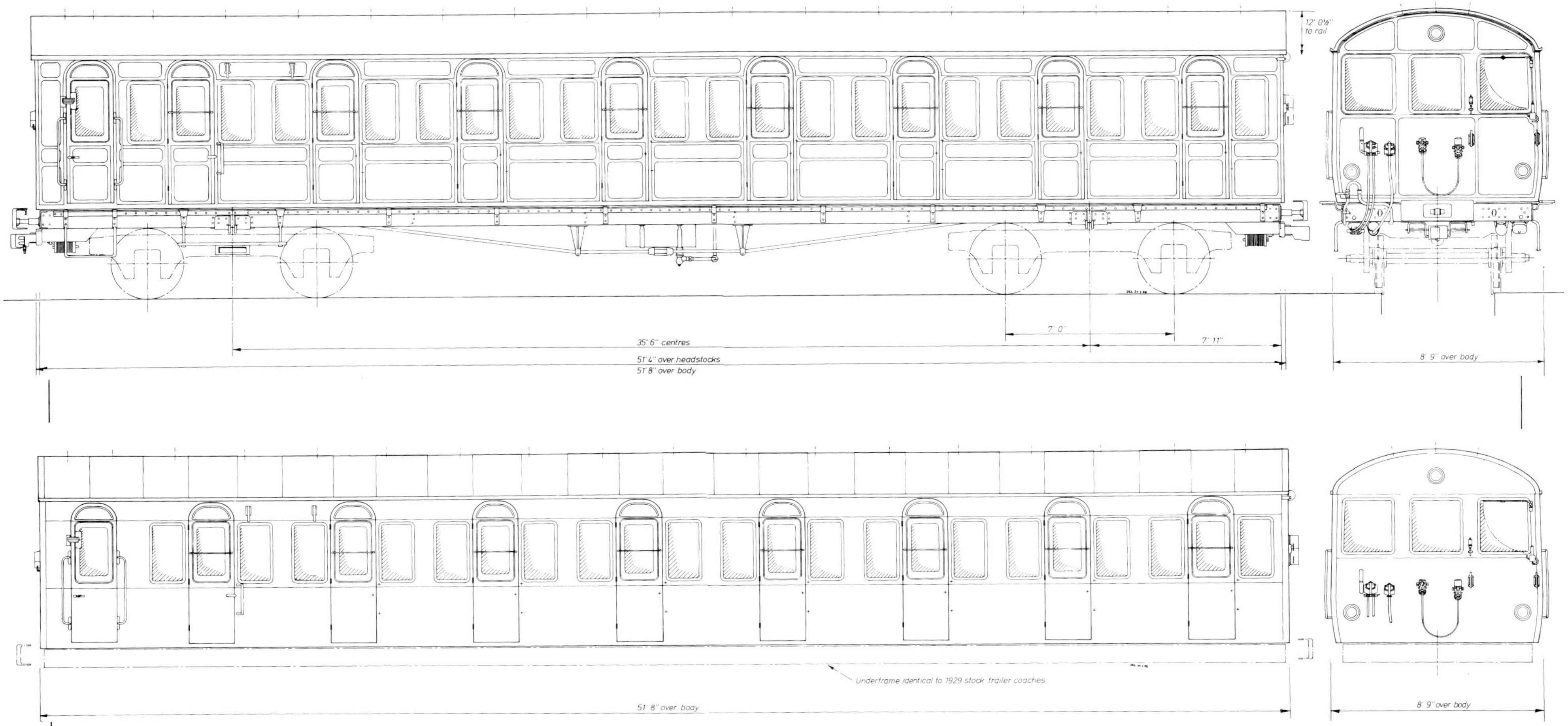

12' 0½" to rail

8' 9" over body

8' 9" over body

7' 11"

7' 0"

35' 6" centres

51' 4" over headstocks

51' 8" over body

51' 8" over body

Underframe identical to 1929 stock trailer coaches

Built by Birmingham Rly Carr & Wagon Co

Numbered – 526 - 535 (LT 6712 -6721) 1929 stock (Upper drawing)
536 -549 (LT 6722 -6735) 1931 stock (Lower drawing)

Bogies:– Type MT (1929 stock), MU (1931 stock). Refer to separate
drawing for details

# METROPOLITAN RAILWAY MW STOCK 3rd CLASS MOTOR COACH, 1929 TYPE

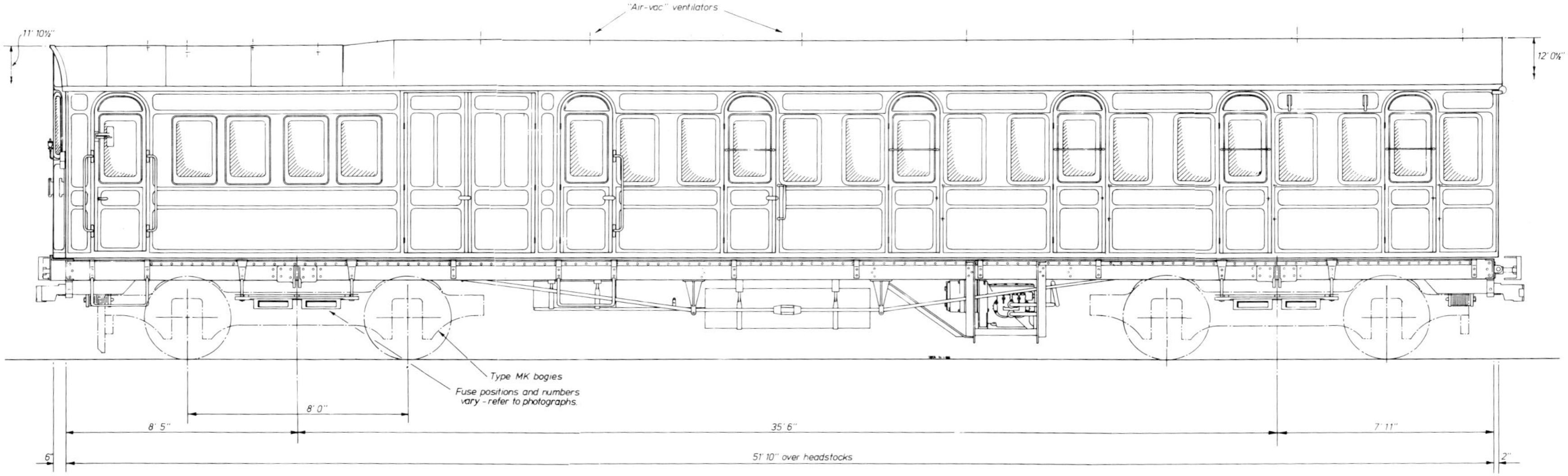

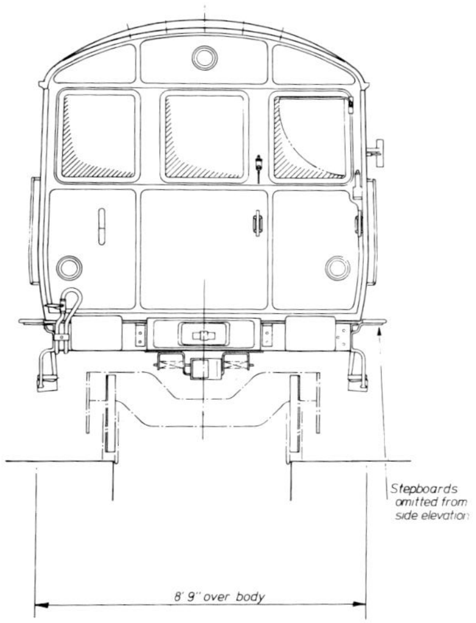

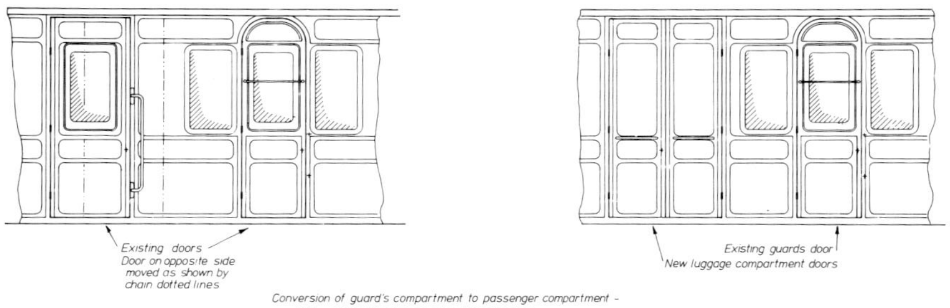

'Air-vac' ventilators

12' 0¼"

7' 11"

2"

11' 10½"

Type Mk bogies

Fuse positions and numbers
vary - refer to photographs.

51' 10" over headstocks

35' 6"

8' 0"

8' 5"

6"

11' 10½"

Existing guards door

New luggage compartment doors

Existing doors
Door on opposite side
moved as shown by
chain dotted lines

Conversion of guard's compartment to passenger compartment -
left - proposed arrangement November 1934
right - arrangement adopted from 1935 (guard's position
moved to driver's cab)

Stepboards
omitted from
side elevation

8' 9" over body

Numbered 212 - 241, renumbered 2712 - 2741 by L.T.
Built by Birmingham R.C. & W. Co. equipped by
Metropolitan-Vickers

Motors - 4 x MV 153, rated at 275 hp/1 hr

Coaches 232 -241 are equipped with roller bearing axleboxes

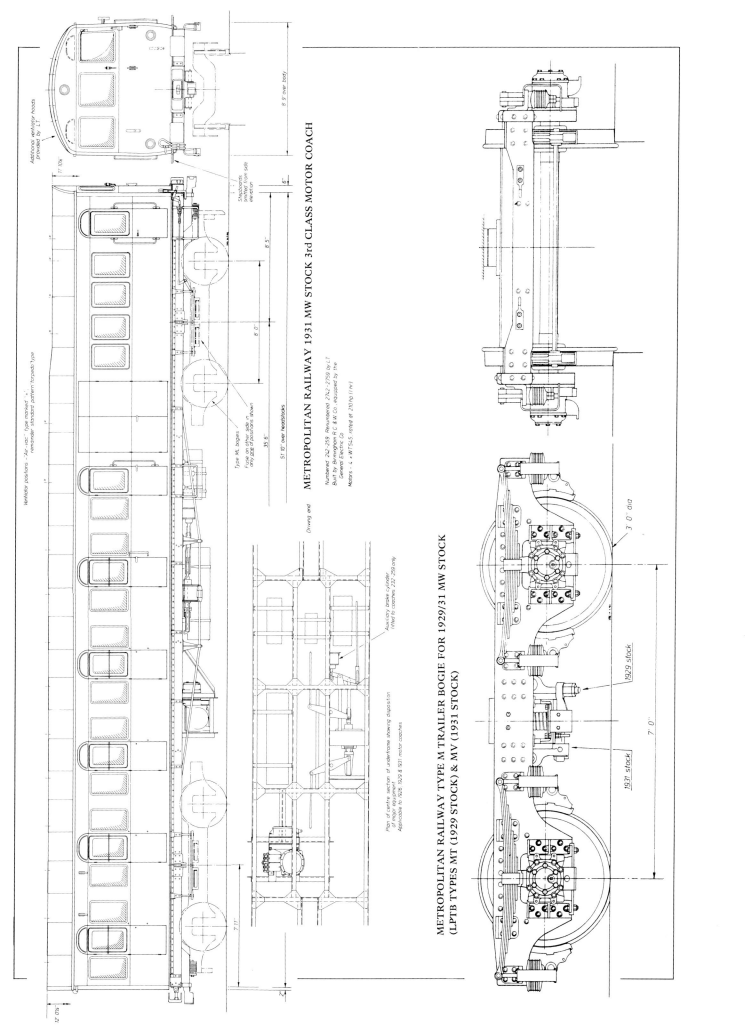

**METROPOLITAN RAILWAY 1931 MW STOCK 3rd CLASS MOTOR COACH**

Numbered 242-259. Renumbered 2742-2759 by LT.
Built by Birmingham R.C.& W.Co., equipped by the
General Electric Co.

Motors – 4 x WT545 rated at 210 hp.(1 hr.)

Ventilator positions – "Air-vac" type marked '*':
remainder standard pattern 'torpedo' type

Additional ventilator hoods
provided by LT

Driving end

Stepboards omitted from side
elevation

Type Mt. bogies
Fuse on other side in
only one of positions shown

Auxiliary brake cylinder
(fitted to coaches 232-259 only)

Plan of centre section of underframe showing disposition
of major equipment
Applicable to 1926, 1929 & 1931 motor coaches

**METROPOLITAN RAILWAY TYPE M TRAILER BOGIE FOR 1929/31 MW STOCK**
**(LPTB TYPES MT (1929 STOCK) & MV (1931 STOCK)**

3' 0" dia

1929 stock

1931 stock

7' 0"

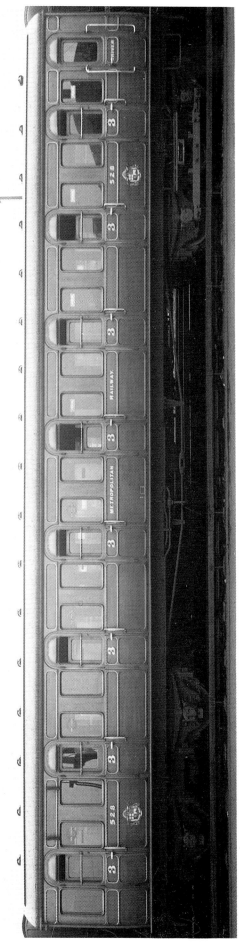

*1929 MW stock Driving Trailer 528. Again this was a direct development of the Dreadnought all-Third, differing only in that one compartment had become a cab, the remaining eight being slightly larger to compensate, and the substitution of a new bogie, replacing the older 7ft Fox design, which was to prove to be at its limits with the Dreadnought vehicles.*
A. CRUIKSHANK COLLECTION

*The production version of the 1927 stock emerged as the 1929 MW stock, air braked, and clearly showing its descendancy from the earlier Dreadnought stock. Although almost 20 years younger, the general appearance of these coaches was very little different from that of the two prototype Dreadnoughts, motor cars 46 and 69.*
A. CRUIKSHANK COLLECTION

A complete 1929 MW stock train in pristine fully lined crimson livery in Neasden car shed. This was a full 7-coach set, formed (M3–1–DT3) + (DT3–3–1–M3), divisible for off-peak workings.

*One of the 1927 MV stock motor coaches after conversion in 1935 from vacuum to air brake and replacement of the side buffers and screw coupling by the standard miniature buckeye and centre buffer arrangement.*
LURS COLLECTION

and lighting, each coach being fitted with external rodding at one end, a feature that was later to prove a significant disadvantage in their operation.

Although a new design of bogie was used, finally replacing the 7ft Fox type which had become standard on the Met, the design of the rest of the coach was virtually identical to that of the Dreadnought stock, which had itself originated in the two double-ended composite motor coaches of 1910.

The twenty-five trailer coaches and ten of the thirty motor coaches were used to form five 7-coach trains, each made up as 3M-3-1-3DT-3DT-1-3M, the intermediate driving trailer coaches allowing each train to be split for off-peak working into a 3- and a 4-coach portion. Of the remaining twenty motor coaches, four were used to displace the saloon stock motor cars from the remaining two W stock sets (6-coach sets of converted Bogie stock), thus making a total of five MW/W stock trains. The other sixteen were used to displace worn-out saloon stock motor cars, being formed up either end of 5- or 6-car sets of saloon stock trailer cars, the complete trains being designated as VT stock.

The main-line electric fleet was further augmented in 1931 with the ordering, this time from the Birmingham RC&W Co., of a further 18 motor and 47 trailer coaches to the same general design as the 1929 stock. These were used to form seven 8-coach trains, the extra five third class trailers being used to bring the existing 1929 stock trains up to the same 8-coach length.

These 1931 stock coaches, although identical in layout to the earlier 1927 and 1929 MW stock vehicles, differed in two major respects. As well as the change of car-builder, two other significant changes had been made to the detail design of these vehicles; the traction equipment was supplied by the General Electric Co., whilst, more obviously, the bodies were clad with sheet steel panels, originally painted in an imitation grained-teak finish. Although from a different source, the traction control equipment was also electro-pneumatically operated and was designed to work in multiple with the Met–Vick equipment fitted to the 1926/27/29 MW stock motor cars, thus making all the MW stock coaches fully interchangeable with each other. In practice, this was not the case, the characteristics and gearing of the MV153 (Met–Vick) and WT545 (GEC) motors being sufficiently different as to make multiple operation of the two different types of motor coach impracticable. The two types of MW stock motor coaches had therefore to be kept segregated. Later, under the auspices of the LPTB, this situation was resolved by the fitment of new 18:65 gearsets on the 1926/27/29 motor coaches in place of the 21:62 ratio originally fitted on the Met–Vick equipped coaches. The gearing on the 1931 coaches was unchanged at 20:62.

*1929 MW stock motor coach 2722 (ex-Met 222) after conversion of the guard's compartment for passenger use, apparently for ladies only to judge by the inscription on the quarterlight. The livery of varnished teak is probably seen here in the later 1930s, there being as yet no LT overhaul date on the body end.* LURS COLLECTION

*The final stock designed by the Met was the 1931 MW stock, represented here by Driving Trailer No. 543 and all-Third No. 556. These were derived from the 1929 stock design by the substitution of steel for teak sheeting. Despite the full lining out, these carriages were fully flush-sided, as well as being painted in maroon livery.*　　A. CRUIKSHANK COLLECTION

*1931 MW stock 3rd class motor coach 248, the last Met stock, still fully lined out although totally flush-panelled. At this stage, the guard still enjoyed his own compartment — before long, LT would convert this into a normal passenger compartment, consigning the guard to the back cab and reducing the luggage space by almost one fifth.* LONDON UNDERGROUND

The arrival of this stock also signalled a step forward in railway bearing technology, in that all of the 1931 motor coaches, as well as the last ten of the 1929 order, were fitted with roller bearings in the axleboxes as well as in the traction motors. This was one of, if not the first significant application of rolling element bearings to railway axleboxes, involving Timken, Ransomes & Marles and SKF, at least, all of whom provided designs. Not only did the use of these bearings greatly reduce maintenance requirements but they also reduced the frictional losses to the point where the traction motors fitted to the later 1931 stock were only rated at 210hp as against the 275hp of the original 1927 coaches.

When the Met had embarked on its development of main-line electric multi-unit trains, the twelve 1927 motor coaches were essentially pre-production prototypes for which complementary trailer stock was not a justifiable expense. The only air-braked compartment stock available at the time consisted of the five sets of converted Bogie stock, so that either one train would have to have used saloon stock, or coaches would have to be withdrawn from the Dreadnought stock fleet. Saloon stock had already been shown to present loading difficulties, as well as incurring the displeasure of passengers and was not therefore a preferable solution. As a consequence, fifteen Dreadnought stock coaches were allocated to form three of the six trains.

Because there were no spare motor coaches at that time, a failure would have resulted in a complete train being taken out of service; the decision to retain the vacuum brake on six of the motor coaches not only allowed the trailer coaches to be converted at the minimum of effort but also allowed them to be returned immediately to locomotive-hauled operation if the need arose. Conversion to air braking would have required the coaches to have been fitted with automatic

couplers and centre buffers in order to allow operation with saloon stock motor cars, assuming that spare cars were available. Not only would this have been more expensive, but, apart from the two 1925 motor cars, the saloon stock motor cars were rated at 300hp less than the 1927 motor coaches, which would have caused time-keeping difficulties.

The subsequent acquisition by the Met of the twelve 1929 and 1931 MW stock trains, together with the thirteen other MW stock powered trains of Bogie and Saloon stock, meant that, by the time the Met passed into the LPTB, the three vacuum-braked MV stock trains were becoming an inconvenient minority. The ability to run their trailer coaches in the locomotive-hauled fleet, once a point of flexibility, was now outweighed by their not being interchangeable with the rest of the MW stock fleet, as a consequence of which the LPTB took the decision to convert all three trains to MW stock standard, commencing in 1935 as individual vehicles were overhauled. The method of conversion was unusual in that the necessary air brake equipment and drawgear were fitted alongside the existing equipment, but not finally commissioned until the whole fleet was changed over, after which the original vacuum brake and screw couplings were removed when convenient. The opportunity was also taken to bring these three sets into line with the rest of the MW stock fleet by the conversion of three Dreadnought stock coaches from the loco-hauled fleet, each set being lengthened to eight coaches.

The main-line electric fleet that the LPTB inherited was composed of two distinct groups, each distinguished by their average age. Not quite half the fleet was composed of the various 1927/29/31 MW stock trains, all relatively new, although some of the trailer coaches, being ex-Dreadnought stock, dated back to 1920. The remainder was composed of

The final batch of MW stock, in 1931, presented a decidedly plain appearance, being steel panelled with no mouldings. The second coach, a 1929 stock Third, illustrates the difference.
LURS COLLECTION

1931 MW stock motor coach 259 in its final form in 1955 as LT 2759. The guard had been relegated to the cab in order to free his compartment for passengers, whilst, in an attempt to remedy the rough riding of these coaches, the original single axlebox springs had been replaced by the distinctive triplex type seen here.

*Rickmansworth in 1960, with an unidentifiable MW stock motor coach from the 1933 batch heading a Baker Street train.*

various trains formed either from converted Bogie stock, dating from the turn of the century and powered by MW stock motor coaches, or from Saloon stock dating from the 1905–13 period. By the late 1930s, many of these vehicles were nearing, if not at, the end of their useful lives and in need of replacement. Relief came in 1938 with the arrival of the LPTB P stock, allowing the five MV/VT stock trains, which used Bogie stock trailers, and the eight MV/Saloon stock trains to be disbanded, the ageing trailer vehicles being scrapped. Of the twenty-six MW stock motor coaches released by this process, four were absorbed by the re-organisation of the MW stock fleet from seventeen 8-coach trains to nine 8-coach and ten 6-coach trains, by then designated by the LPTB as T stock.

As part of the LPTB's intended expansion in the 1930s, it had been anticipated that electrification would be extended from Rickmansworth to Amersham and Chesham, requiring in turn an expansion in the Metropolitan Line electric rolling stock fleet. At the same time, the replacement of much of the 1904–7 generation saloon stock by the (LPTB) O&P allowed the thirteen MW/Saloon and MW/VT stock trains to be disbanded in favour of unified saloon stock trains, thus rendering twenty-six motor coaches spare. It was intended that the new trains required would be formed by converting Dreadnought stock coaches to run with these surplus motor coaches, as had been done with the three original MV stock trains. At the same time the existing MW stock fleet, now numbering nineteen trains, was to be the

subject of a renovation programme which included the fitment of electro-pneumatic brakes and through heating and lighting control circuits.

In the event, this programme was hardly under way, one train having been converted to through lighting control, before Germany's invasion of Poland and the consequent declaration of war put a virtual stop to the whole 1935 expansion programme, of which this was a part. Nonetheless, it was presumed at that time that work would restart after hostilities had ceased, and in anticipation of this, all twenty-two spare MW motor coaches were kept in full running order during the war years, so as to avoid the problems which would be incurred in their subsequent recommissioning. When peace finally returned, conditions had changed such that the Amersham electrification was postponed indefinitely, not in fact being undertaken until the very late 1950s, when the arrival of the A60 stock and the abandonment of the Aylesbury service finally rendered both the loco-hauled 'steam' and the MW stock trains redundant.

Although the motor coaches had been extensively tested in their development from the two 1925 experimental cars to the production batch in 1929, prolonged and changing service conditions revealed several problems which resulted in modifications being made. The first of these concerned the riding qualities of the motor coaches themselves, which although initially thought tolerable, were becoming unacceptable by the time the 1931 batch was ordered. The difficulties were attributed to the primary suspensions, which,

*The end? A 6-coach train of 1929 MW stock heading towards Baker Street in the last days before the LT A60 stock took over the Met, consigning all the remaining Met stock to oblivion.*
                                                                                          LURS COLLECTION

given the 49 ton weight of the motor coaches, were leaf springs of relatively massive proportions, with a stiffness to match. As the car weight could not be altered, the solution lay in redesigning the springs, as a result of which they were replaced by a new design of triplex leaf spring, thought to be unique in railway applications, which, whilst retaining the strength needed to support the coach, was more flexible than the single-leaf spring which it replaced.

Although modified by the need to accommodate a driver's and an electrical switchgear compartment, these motor coaches were direct derivatives of the Dreadnought stock. As such, and in recognition of their main-line role, they retained the separate luggage and guard's compartments, although the latter was reduced in width. By the early 1930s, however, it was apparent that the space could be better used for passenger accommodation, resulting in proposals being made to enlarge the guard's compartment to full size by the resiting of the partition separating it from the luggage compartment, thus creating space for ten seats. The remaining part of the luggage compartment, now about two-thirds of its original size and distinctly cramped, would have been given over to the guard. This scheme did not find favour, and was replaced by a second proposal which, although it retained the concept of enlarging the original guard's compartment for passenger use, differed in that the guard was moved into the driving cab, the luggage compartment being retained for its original purpose, albeit in a reduced form. This scheme was evidently considered satisfactory, all sixty MW stock motor coaches being altered.

Towards the end of the war, whilst electrification through to Amersham remained a probability, the suitability of the MW stock for operation on the Circle Line stations east of Baker Street was becoming questionable. There were two fundamental reasons for this, firstly, that, as compartment type coaches, there was no facility for the emergency evacuation of the train along its length, and secondly, the difficulties of ensuring the safe departure of a train having, typically, 50–60 separate doors, were becoming intolerable by comparison even to trains formed of stock with hand-worked sliding doors.

In consequence of this, the original pre-war plan to expand the MW stock fleet had to be abandoned in favour of the construction of new sliding door stock. Various designs for new stock, including some which virtually amounted to sliding-door compartment stock, were considered in the early stages of the design of what would have been the 1952 Surface stock. This never, in fact, reached the construction stage, so that it was not to be until the arrival of the LPTB A60 stock that slam-door operation finally ceased. However, during the design process, the opportunity was taken to construct two full-size experimental coaches in order to test reaction to various types of saloon layout. This had arisen as a result of there being available two MW stock motor coaches which had been withdrawn from service during the war and stored in an unserviceable condition. Their underframes, stripped of all their traction equipment and modified to run on ex District K2 trailer bogies, were fitted with new bodies built by the LPTB's Acton Works. Car 17000, as it was now numbered, was the first to appear, entering service in late-January 1946, being followed eighteen months later, in June 1947, by the second car, numbered 20000. Both incorporated saloon-type internal layouts, but differed radically in that whilst 20000 was arranged as a centre-gangwayed saloon, 17000 was the reverse. Its seating was arranged in self-standing islands with gangways running along both sides of the body. Air-operated sliding doors were fitted to both cars, as well as remotely controlled fluorescent lighting, as a result of which both had to be operated coupled to a MW stock driving trailer coach which had been fitted with the necessary equipment. They remained in operation, with minor modifications, until 1953, largely because of the difficulties in providing the additional guard required to work the door controls, and were eventually scrapped in 1955, having provided valuable experience toward the design of the A60 stock which was finally to replace both the MW and Dreadnought stocks, by then the only Metropolitan Railway stock remaining in service.

# CHAPTER NINE

# NON-PASSENGER STOCK

FOR the first fifteen years of its life, the Met used town gas as its standard means of carriage illumination, carried at low pressure in large inflatable reservoirs mounted on top of the carriage roof. Despite the bulk of these roof gas-bags, the low pressure available meant that the volume of gas available, and hence the endurance of the lighting, was relatively limited. The inconvenience of regular gas replenishment stops, together with the rise in the price of town gas in the 1870s led the Metropolitan to experiment with alternative systems, the Pintsch high-pressure oil-gas system finally being adopted in 1878. To provide the necessary supplies, small oil-gas plants were set up at Baker Street, Liverpool Street and Hammersmith. Unfortunately, the obnoxious smells emitted by these plants were not to the liking of the local residents, who successfully obtained injunctions against the company, effectively preventing the further production of gas at these locations. However, the Met was at this time well advanced in the development of Neasden as a works and main depot; it was relatively easy for a new gas works to be accommodated on the site in order to replace the original three plants.

The drawback to siting the gas supply at Neasden was that, at the time, only a small proportion of the total carriage stock was stabled overnight there. To supply the remainder of the fleet, outstabled at various locations, it was therefore essential to provide some means for the bulk transport of gas to the outlying stabling points. The result was the supply, in September 1881 by Ashbury, of two wagons, described as 'carriage trucks'; three more followed in July 1882 and a further eight in August 1884. The final total of 14 wagons was reached with the construction of a single wagon by Neasden Works, probably the first vehicle to be constructed by the new works. Only in December 1891 were these wagons acknowledged as being 'gas-holder trucks'.

Their construction was simple, two large cylindrical tanks capable of holding the gas under high pressure being mounted on top of a standard design wooden underframe. The tanks, which were about 18ft long and 4ft in diameter, were carried on a 22ft long, 12ft 6in wheelbase, underframe; hand brakes only were provided, although for operation in passenger trains, through vacuum brake pipes were fitted.

The adoption of electric lighting for the Bogie stock, together with the electrification of the Circle, Hammersmith and Uxbridge services, rendered many of these wagons redundant. One was sold to the Cambrian Railway, who also acquired a number of the B class 4–4–0T locomotives, in early 1907; four more, after being on hire for a year to the LB&SCR, were sold to that company on July 1907. Another was scrapped in 1911. The remaining eight survived for much longer, being required to service the original

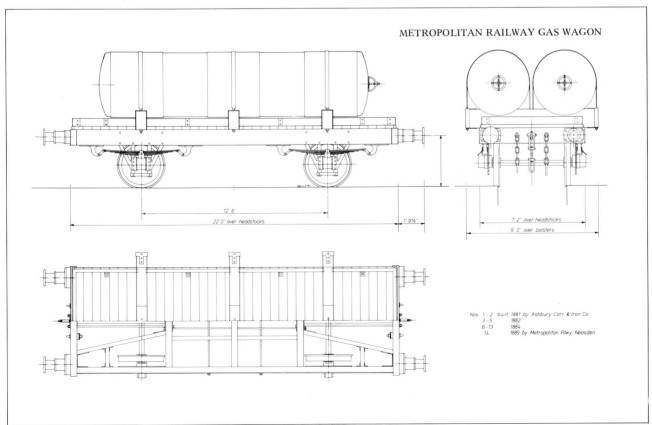

METROPOLITAN RAILWAY GAS WAGON

12' 6"
22' 0" over headstocks
1' 9½"
7' 2" over headstocks
9' 0" over bolsters

Nos 1 - 2  built 1881 by Ashbury Carr & Iron Co
3 - 5        1882
6 - 13       1884
14           1889 by Metropolitan Rlwy, Neasden

Dreadnought stock, the 1910 and 1912 batches of which reverted to gas lighting. The use of gas for passenger stock lighting was effectively discontinued with the arrival of the 1919 Dreadnought stock coaches, which were electrically lit from new, and the earlier coaches being converted shortly afterwards. As a result, three were withdrawn in 1919, two being converted to workshop vans for weighing machine maintenance, with the remainder being withdrawn in 1921 and sold two years later.

As the Metropolitan gradually advanced northwards from Harrow to Aylesbury, ever deeper into the Hertfordshire and Buckinghamshire countryside, so it was able to develop new traffic which reflected the more agricultural nature of these areas.

One of the earliest passenger train traffics to be developed was the carriage of milk, in churns, to the dairies of inner London. Initially, this had had to travel in the brake compartments of the ordinary carriages, where space was at a premium. By the early 1890s, this was evidently becoming a problem, and the opportunity was taken to convert six 4-wheeled first class carriages, which had been rendered redundant some ten years earlier, by the conversion of the twin-carriages to run as single vehicles. The conversion work, which was undertaken in 1892–3, consisted of stripping out the interior and providing a pair of outward opening double doors on each side where the centre compartment had been. The remaining doors at one end were sealed up; those at the other end were retained to allow access to

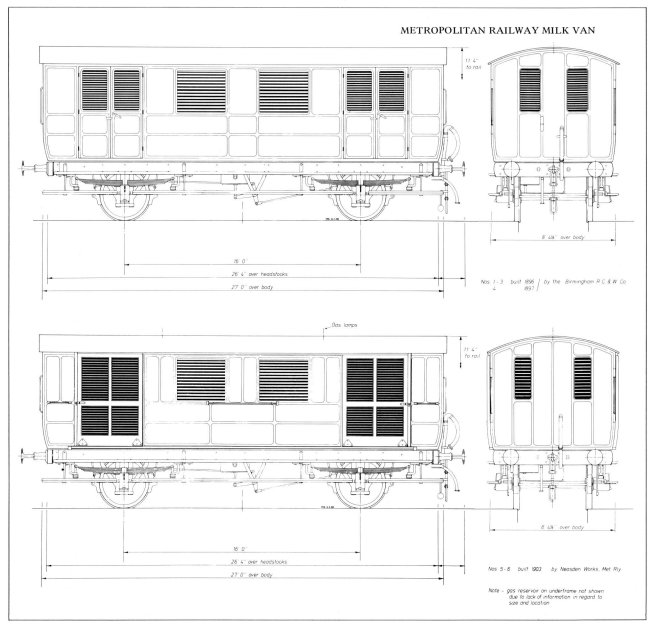

METROPOLITAN RAILWAY MILK VAN

C class No. 68 on the way to Verney Junction with a train of 8-wheeled stock, headed by one of the sliding door milk vans, either No. 5 or 6. The original photograph is undated, but the adoption of the teak and white livery throughout would suggest the later 1890s. Curiously, though, the upper parts of the luggage doors on the Brake 3rd appear dark to their full height.
A. CRUIKSHANK COLLECTION

the handbrake, which had been added as part of the conversion.

These carriages had used the same suspension and axleboxes as the 8-wheeled rigid stock, where a high degree of lateral movement was essential. On these 4-wheeled carriages, this lack of lateral restraint, together with a relatively short wheelbase, resulted in their being very lively riders indeed, so much so that it was not long before they were banned from running at the rear end of trains. The consequences of this, together with their severely restricted load capacity (3 tons), did not endear them to the operating staff, as a result of which they were replaced by a new purpose-built design, four examples of which were constructed by the Birmingham Carriage & Wagon Co. and delivered in 1896–7. These vans, whose design followed on from that of the Jubilee stock, were altogether more substantial, being 27ft long by 8ft 4½in wide. Two pairs of hinged doors were provided on each side, whilst these and both the side and end panels were liberally provided with louvred ventilation openings. They were vacuum braked and equipped with interior illumination in the form of two Pintsch gas lamps.

Two more vans, to the same general design but with sliding doors in place of the hinged type previously fitted, were built by Neasden in 1903. Other minor changes were made to the ventilation arrangement and to the panelling layout. Curiously, however, whilst these two vans post-dated both the Bogie stock and, more significantly, the Passenger Brake Vans, their design remained that of the Jubilee stock, including the equally divided waist panelling of that and earlier stocks.

By 1914, the milk traffic had declined to such an extent that four of the six vans were standing out of use at Neasden. Consideration was given to taking them into the general goods stock fleet, but their relatively light body construction (compared to contemporary Met goods stock)

made this impractical. They were to remain unused until 1920, when two of them were apparently taken into departmental service, although one was later restored to the revenue fleet in 1923. Ultimately, all six survived to be inherited by the LPTB, although Nos. 1, 2 and 4 were scrapped in 1936. The remaining three, Nos. 3, 5 & 6, were more fortunate. Nos. 3 and 5 were converted to serve as tool vans for the Neasden breakdown train, becoming LPTB Nos. BDV700 and BDV701 respectively. No. 6, now renumbered SC632, worked in the quarterly stores train between Ealing Common and Little Ilford (East Ham) depots. All three were repainted into grey, the two Breakdown vans having a red stripe, edged with black, at waist level. No. 5 (BDV701) was scrapped in June 1944, whilst No. 6 (SC632) lasted until July 1958. No. 3, as BDV700, was more fortunate, surviving long enough to be restored to its original teak livery to take part in the 1963 Centenary celebrations and, in consequence of this, was subsequently preserved. This last vehicle is interesting in that it now has sliding doors instead of the hinged type with which it was originally built. Whether this is a consequence of its having been in the breakdown train, or the result of a deliberate modification by Neasden, is not known.

Coincident with the introduction of the Bogie stock, the opportunity was taken to replace the three remaining converted milk vans, this time with six new Passenger Brake Vans. Although to the same general dimensions as the 1896 milk vans, these vans were provided with a central compartment for the guard, equipped with a screw handbrake and the usual vacuum brake controls. On either side were two compartments, access to which was afforded by pairs of outward opening doors. No windows were provided, save for the droplight in the guard's doors, so that the sole means of illumination was through two roof-lights, one to each stowage compartment, supplemented by electric lamps pow-

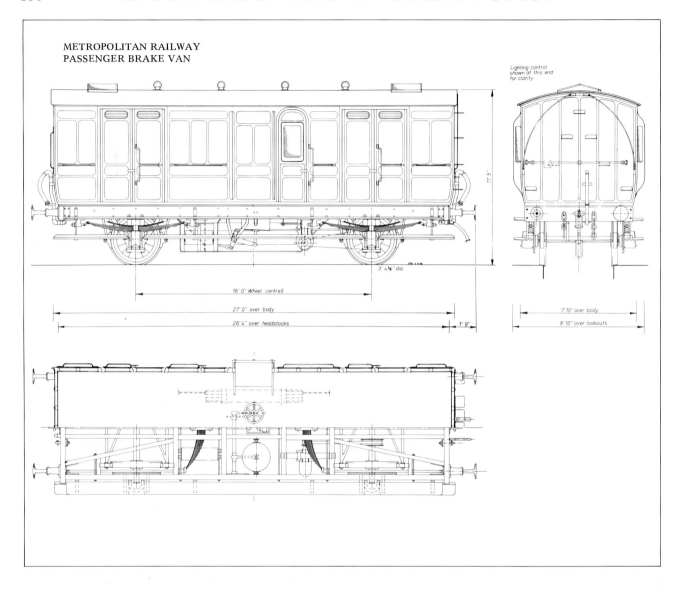

METROPOLITAN RAILWAY
PASSENGER BRAKE VAN

Lighting control
shown at this end
for clarity

11' 5"

3' 4¾" dia

16' 0" Wheel centres

27' 0" over body

26' 4" over headstocks

1' 9"

7' 10" over body

8' 10" over lookouts

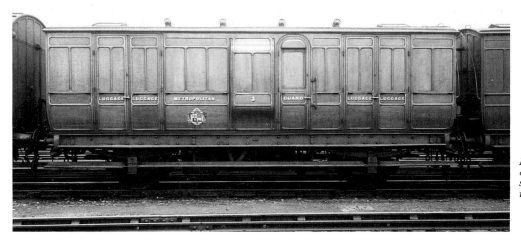

*Passenger Brake Van No. 3, one of six built in 1898 seen in 1934 after acquisition by the LPTB.*
LURS COLLECTION

*Metropolitan Horse-boxes Nos. 1 and 6. The first batch, for which no drawings remain, were more in the style of the 8-wheel stock, being straight-sided with turned-under ends. The later, standard design was in the style of the Jubilee stock, with turned-under sides and straight ends.*
A. CRUIKSHANK COLLECTION

ered from batteries, a dynamo being provided to charge these and generate current while on the move. Like the Bogie stock, gas lamps were originally to have been provided, but this was dropped in favour of electric lighting before the vans were built.

These vans, which were normally used on their own, attached to main-line trains of either Bogie or Dreadnought stock, all survived long enough to be inherited by LT, although their subsequent lives were very short. Nos. 1–4 were scrapped in February 1936, whilst 5 and 6 were absorbed into the service vehicle fleet, becoming B576 and B577 respectively in January 1938. Of these two, B576 survived until November 1939. The last survivor, now painted grey, found its way into the Stores train, where it remained until withdrawn in July 1958.

As it progressed northwards, the Metropolitan was able to establish a small but significant traffic flow conveying both the horses and the carriages of the gentry, the former particularly during the hunting season. Initially, the company borrowed suitable stock from the Midland Railway. Before long, however, the ever-increasing empty mileage worked by these vehicles between the Finchley Road exchange yard and the northern parts of the Met rendered these arrangements uneconomic, in consequence of which the Met took the decision to acquire its own fleet of horse-boxes and carriage trucks.

Three horse-boxes were constructed in August 1892, followed by a further four, built at Neasden, in June 1898 and a

final batch of three, built by G R Turner, in May 1904. All ten were to the same, conventional, design, with separate compartments at each end for the groom(s) and for the stowage of fodder and spare partitions. The centre section, to which access was gained by the usual combination of a drop flap and hinged top doors, could accommodate up to three horses in longitudinal stalls. The groom's compartment was provided with gas lighting and sliding hatchways in the internal partition to allow attention to be given to the animal's needs. Also accommodated therein was a screw-type handbrake. The underframe, which was derived from the Jubilee stock design, was fitted with vacuum brakes, whilst some, at least, were also later fitted with a through Westinghouse brake pipe and, after 1918, with through 600V power cables to facilitate working with electric locomotives.

Nos. 8 & 9 were withdrawn in 1914 as surplus to requirements, being sold to the Brecon & Merthyr Railway, in whose ownership they remained until condemned by the GWR in the mid-1920s. The remainder survived, albeit rarely used, well into LPTB ownership, not being written off until January 1938. Throughout their lives, the horse-boxes were allocated on an individual basis to specific stations over the length of the main line.

Allied to the horse traffic was a small fleet, numbering four in all, of carriage trucks, also designed for operation in passenger trains. The first two, built by the Birmingham Carriage & Wagon Co. in 1896, were of the open type, with low height fixed sides. Only one drawing of these trucks sur-

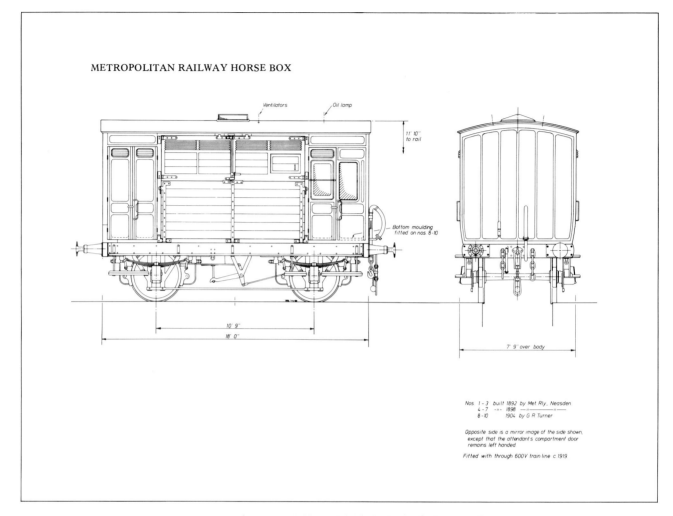

METROPOLITAN RAILWAY HORSE BOX

Ventilators

Oil lamp

11' 10"
to rail

Bottom moulding
fitted on nos. 8-10

10' 9"

18' 0"

7' 9" over body

Nos. 1 - 3   built 1892 by Met. Rly., Neasden.
      4 - 7   -"-  1898   —"—————"—
      8 -10         1904  by G R Turner

Opposite side is a mirror image of the side shown,
except that the attendant's compartment door
remains left handed.

Fitted with through 600V train line c.1919

*The Met owned ten horse-boxes, stationed in ones and twos all over the system. No. 6, to the later design, built in 1898 by Neasden Works, is seen here at its home station, Willesden Green, in 1937.*

A. CRUIKSHANK
COLLECTION

vives, showing the lettering arrangement on an outline of the side elevation only; no detail drawings are known to have survived to the present. Nonetheless, it is almost certain that the underframe would have been a derivative of the Jubilee stock frame and, given the commonality of dimensions, might well have been identical to that fitted under the horse-boxes.

These were followed in 1902 by two more carriage trucks, this time of the covered variety, built by Ashbury. These two vehicles, which were significantly larger at 27ft over the headstocks and 8ft 1³⁄₄in wide, were vertically boarded on a timber frame and provided with double doors in each side.

Nos. 1, 2 and 4 were withdrawn in 1929, whilst No. 3 survived to be converted to a 7 ton capacity flat wagon (LPTB No. F301) in June 1935 before being finally scrapped in June 1940.

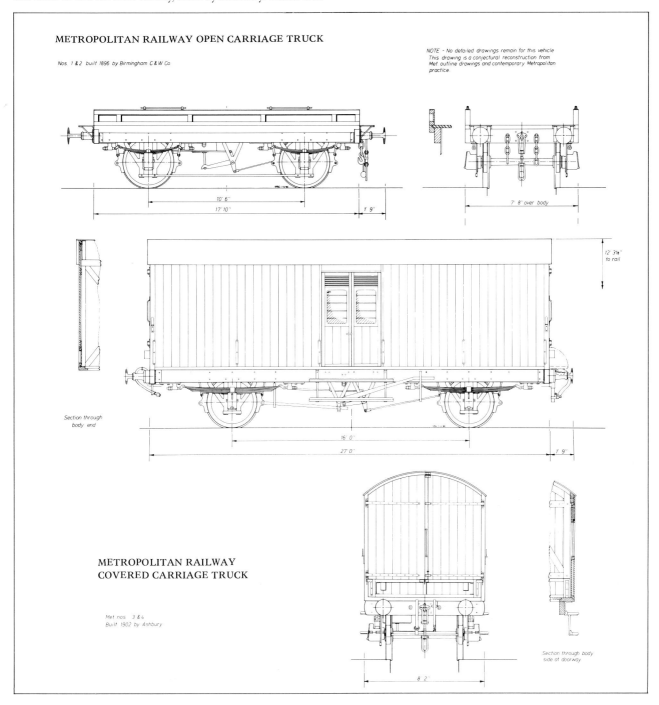

**METROPOLITAN RAILWAY OPEN CARRIAGE TRUCK**

Nos. 1 & 2 built 1896 by Birmingham C & W Co

NOTE - No detailed drawings remain for this vehicle
This drawing is a conjectural reconstruction from
Met outline drawings and contemporary Metropolitan
practice.

10' 6"
17' 10"
1' 9"
7' 8" over body

12' 3½"
to rail

Section through
body end

16' 0"
27' 0"
1' 9"

**METROPOLITAN RAILWAY
COVERED CARRIAGE TRUCK**

Met nos. 3 & 4
Built 1902 by Ashbury

Section through body
side at doorway

8' 2"

STORES.

One of a series of overlapping views, probably taken in 1933, of the Neasden Works, showing a large part of the Metropolitan's more specialised goods stock, a great part of which would be transferred to the LNER in 1937. Prominent in this view are two of the cattle wagons, some of which were vacuum-piped, and, in the middle distance, two of the short rail and timber wagons. The van beyond them, although clearly a Met vehicle, remains an enigma, there being no remaining drawings. From the outside stepboards, it would appear likely to have been a workshop van.

A. CRUIKSHANK COLLECTION

# CHAPTER TEN

# GOODS STOCK

*Part of Neasden Works in 1933, containing a wide variety of Metropolitan goods stock.*

ALTHOUGH generally thought of as a passenger railway, the Metropolitan, from its earliest days, also supported a variety of freight services. Although it was initially only connected to the Great Western at Paddington, it was not long before connections were developed at King's Cross, with the GN and Midland Railways, and at Farringdon, to the LC&DR. Goods stations also appeared at Whitecross Street (MR), at Farringdon (GNR) and below Smithfield Meat Market. Thus, the Met, particularly at its eastern end, was able to support a growing traffic in cross-London goods trains, to the extent that the King's Cross–Farringdon section had to be quadrupled by the building of the City Widened Lines before the Metropolitan's original line was opened.

To begin with, the Met itself did not operate goods services, confining itself to the carriage of parcels on passenger trains. Nonetheless, by 1890, it had built up a fleet of some 50 open wagons, rated at 6T each, together with 6 brake vans, for use in the maintenance of the railway. The origins of these Ballast wagons, as they were known, are obscure, since they bear none of the hallmarks of later Metropolitan design. It is possible that the earliest examples, which date back to 1866, were either acquired from, or copied from, wagons used by the contractors building the railway. They

were evidently to the Metropolitan's liking, since the design was perpetuated, unchanged for some 16 years, spread over up to seven different batches.

In addition to these wagons, the Met also owned a small number of single bolster wagons whose original purpose was to carry lengths of rail for the maintenance of the permanent way, although they were later redesignated as Rail & Timber wagons, a change reflecting Metropolitan's later involvement in the transport of timber felled from the Chiltern hills. Like many of their contemporaries, these bolster wagons were originally built with dumb buffers, although, as with the ballast wagons, these were later replaced with self-contained spring buffers. From the Metropolitan's six-monthly rolling stock returns, it would appear that there were only six of these wagons, a view substantiated by the later rebuilding of six timber (*sic*) wagons into covered goods vans. (Given the small size of the bolster wagons, the rebuilding may have been more a case of re-use of the running gear and parts of the underframe.)

The possible use of small single bolster wagons appears to have been re-considered during the 1920s, since a Met drawing has survived showing a 1926 dated proposal for such a wagon using RCH standard components. That this is not simply a potential modernisation of the earlier wagons is

## METROPOLITAN RAILWAY 6 TON BALLAST WAGON

Nos. 1 - 5   Built 1866
   6 - 10       1869
  11 - 15     1878 by Ashbury C & I Co
  16 - 20     1880 ——————
  21 - 30     1881 ——————
  31 - 50     1882

Note :-
a  Wagon is shown in post-1927 condition, double brakes
   shown, replaced original brake of unknown type
b  Sprung buffers shown are a self-contained type,
   unconfirmed replacements for original dumb buffers

Lower drawing shows the Metropolitan Rly Stores Van,
built on the underframe of a 6T Ballast Wagon
Original MR number unknown, became LPTB no SC630
Very little is known of the detailed design of this wagon,
although major dimensions are accurate, ironwork details
are conjectural, based on typical Met practice and
limited photographic evidence

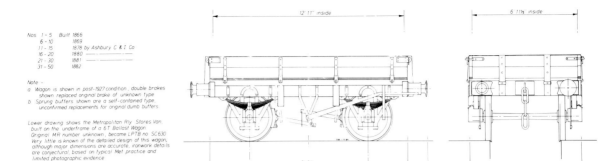

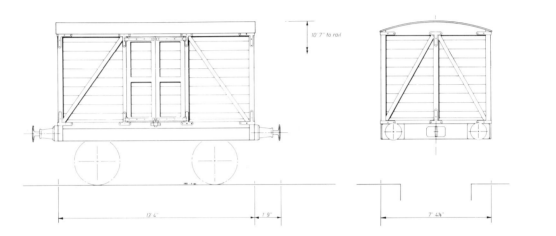

*Not the best, but the only known picture of the Met Stores Van, rebuilt from a Ballast wagon. This wagon, found lurking in the background of a photograph of a C class locomotive, survived into LPTB ownership, becoming Stores Van SC630.*

**A. CRUIKSHANK COLLECTION**

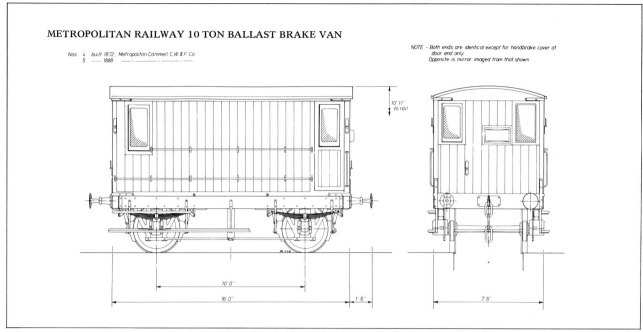

**METROPOLITAN RAILWAY 10 TON BALLAST BRAKE VAN**

Nos  4   built 1872, Metropolitan Cammell C,W & F Co
     5   —-- 1888   ——————————————

NOTE - Both ends are identical except for handbrake cover at
door end only
Opposite is mirror imaged from that shown

10' 11"
to rail

10' 0"

16' 0"

1' 6"

7' 6"

*Ballast Brake Van No. 5, in LT days as B552, paired with Met F class 0–6–2 No. 93, in LT livery as L52, at, judging by the cleanliness, sometime in the late 1930s or early 1940s.*

evidenced by the way in which the 1926 wagon differs significantly in its major dimensions. The idea evidently did not meet with approval, for none were ever built.

To run with these trains, the Metropolitan acquired six goods brake vans, each rated at 10 tons, over the period between 1866 and 1890. There were two different types, a double-ended general purpose van, distinctive by its outside body framing, and a fully enclosed type for ballast train working, when it would have served not only as a brake van but also as a travelling and mess van. They were allocated the numbers 1–6, and, from remaining records, it is believed that Nos. 1–3 were Goods Brakes, whilst 4 and 5, at least, were Ballast Brakes. No. 6, which was not built until 1890, cannot be identified with any certainty.

Unlike their contemporary wagons, these vans were almost certainly designed by the Met, given their similarity

in terms of dimensions and standard fittings to the later Met vans and to other Met-designed goods stock.

The northward expansion of the Metropolitan, from its St John's Wood terminus through Harrow to Aylesbury and beyond, marked a significant change in the nature of the railway. Whereas before it had been a predominantly commuter railway, it now began to take on some of the characteristics, if not the stature, of a main-line railway. Most of the new stations were then in generally rural areas and as a consequence were provided with goods facilities to service the need for freight cartage to and from their surrounding areas. To begin with, the Metropolitan acted essentially as a distribution/collection agency, making use of its connections with the Midland Railway, with whom it shared an exchange yard at Finchley Road. Although there was no difficulty in distributing loaded wagons coming onto the Met, problems arose whenever anything required to be loaded and dispatched from a Met station, due to the restrictions imposed on wagon back-loading by the various Common User arrangements coordinated by the Railway Clearing House.

During the 1880s it is believed that the Met, through its links with the Midland, particularly at Finchley Road, made use of the latter company's rolling stock in order to effect outward traffic. This had its complications, particularly as the increasing empty mileages worked made the economics of freight working unattractive. Consequently, by 1891, the Met accepted the need for a wagon fleet of its own, from which it could gain the maximum revenue of its own.

From a modest start in 1891, the Met gradually built up a fleet which, by the turn of the century, included some 255 10T open wagons, together with 6 covered goods vans and supported by a fleet of 23 Goods Brake vans. As was normal at the time, the greater proportion of these open wagons were of the low-sided type, 16ft long and 1ft 8½in deep inter-

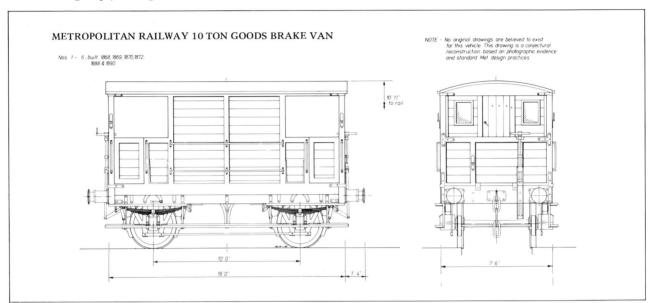

METROPOLITAN RAILWAY 10 TON GOODS BRAKE VAN

Nos 1 – 6 , built 1868, 1869, 1870, 1872, 1888 & 1890

NOTE – No original drawings are believed to exist for this vehicle. This drawing is a conjectural reconstruction based on photographic evidence and standard Met design practices

10' 11" to rail

10' 0"

16' 0"

1' 4"

7' 6"

*Goods Brake Van No. 1, probably in the 1920s. Although unique in having outside framing, it set the basic standard from which the later Met vans differed little until the time the ex-WD vans were purchased.*

nally, with full length drop sides; wheelbase was 9ft 6in. The remainder were classified as high-sided, having an internal depth of 3ft 0in. Two sizes were built, the earliest being 14ft 11in long (conforming to the RCH standards set down in the 1870s) whilst the later wagons were 16ft long. The wheelbase, curiously, did not follow that of the low-sided wagons, being only 9ft 0in. Although both types are shown as being goods wagons, there are references to some being designated as coal wagons, although for what purpose is not clear, since the Met used outside contractors for its supply of locomotive

and power station coal. Over time, however, the larger wagons became more useful for general traffic, leading to a substantial number of low-sided wagons being rebuilt into the high-sided form, in which guise they retained their original dimensions.

At first sight, there was a degree of similarity between these wagons and their Midland Railway counterparts, but this was only superficial. Neasden's wagons differed not only dimensionally, but also in their detail design, many aspects of which were distinctly Metropolitan.

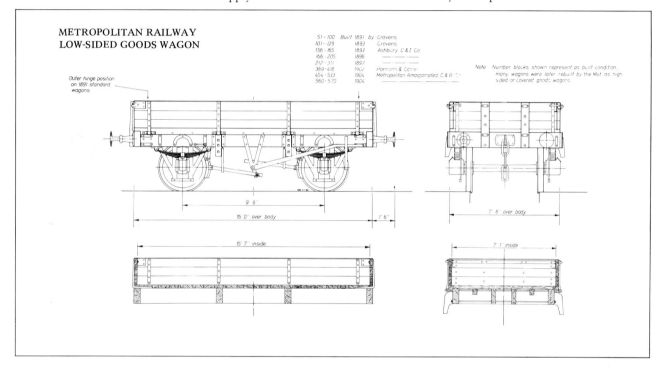

10T Low open goods wagon 121, built in 1893 by Cravens, in later life as LT ballast wagon BW147. No paint date is visible, but it would appear to have been freshly outshopped, complete with through air pipes and 600 volt cables, but still only with single-sided hand brakes.

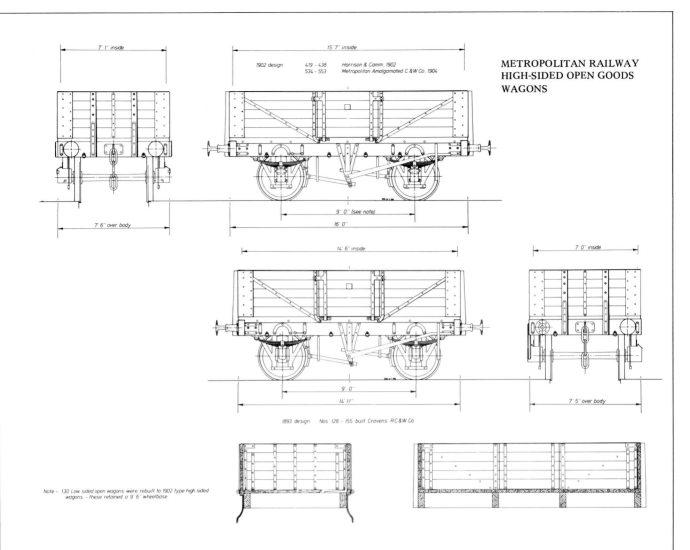

METROPOLITAN RAILWAY
HIGH-SIDED OPEN GOODS
WAGONS

7' 1" inside

15' 7" inside

1902 design     419 - 438     Harrison & Camm, 1902
534 - 553     Metropolitan Amalgamated C & W Co. 1904

9' 0" (see note)

7' 6" over body

16' 0"

14' 6" inside

7' 0" inside

9' 0"

14' 11"

7' 5" over body

1893 design    Nos 126 - 155 built Cravens RC & W Co

Note - 130 Low sided open wagons were rebuilt to 1902 type high sided
wagons - these retained a 9' 6" wheelbase

Met open goods wagon
542 at Neasden in 1951
as LT ash wagon A945.
Built in 1911 by Metro-
politan    C&W    and
finally     condemned
c.1970.

Further substantial additions were made to this fleet during the following decade, so that by 1910 the goods stock fleet, including the service wagons had almost reached its final total of some 600 wagons, most of which were open wagons.

In keeping with the rural nature of its northern extremities, the Metropolitan was also called upon to transport livestock from time to time, for which purpose a fleet of six cattle wagons was acquired from Cravens in 1894, again to Neasden designs. A further six wagons to the same design were added in 1912, followed by six more in 1914, the latter

being converted from redundant twin bolster wagons, a consequence of which was that they were 22ft long, significantly longer than any of the 'large' cattle wagons in service on any other railway.

The impending electrification of the Met required the provision of new, longer, rail wagons to cope with the laying of the new conductor rails. Because of the relatively greater length of the rails, as well as the workload involved, the existing single bolster wagons were neither large nor plentiful enough to be useful. Consequently, a new design appeared from Neasden, consisting of two permanently coupled sin-

*Open Goods wagon 547, photographed soon after the LPTB takeover, as shown by the freshness of its new LPTB livery. Built in 1912 by the Metropolitan C&W Co. in Birmingham, this wagon survived the 1937 handover, eventually being withdrawn in February 1964 as Slurry wagon SL967. A peculiar Met feature, seen here, is the way in which the diagonal strap was joggled to fit behind the verticals, necessitating rebates being cut in the side planks.*
A. CRUIKSHANK
COLLECTION

*Originally built as an Open Goods wagon in 1904 by Metropolitan C&W, as Met No. 539, and later modified by LT by the addition of a sixth plank to become Slurry wagon SL936, then Power House wagon PH936, for use in Neasden Power Station.*

METROPOLITAN RAILWAY CATTLE TRUCKS

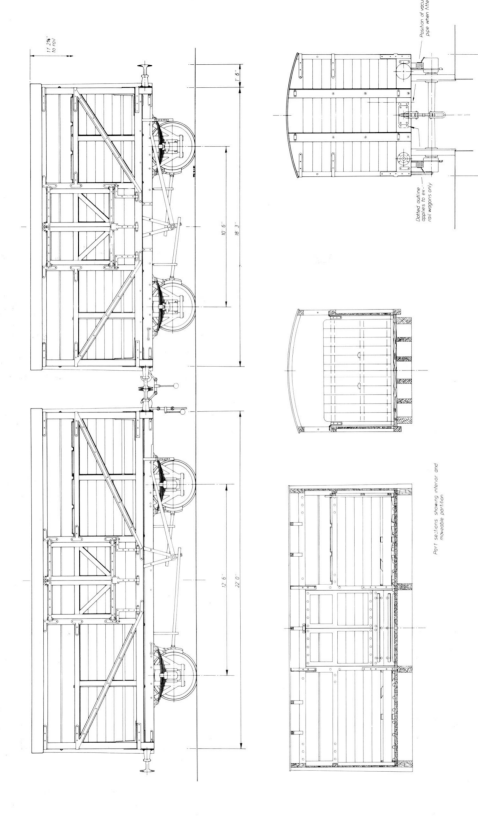

Position of vacuum
pipe when fitted

8' 0"

Dotted outline
applies to ex-
rail wagons only

Part sections showing interior and
moveable partition

Nos 1 - 6    Built 1894  I- 18' 3" long
7 -12         1902
13-18  Converted from rail wagons 1912 - 22' 0" long

Note - wagon nos. 5, 8 -12 are fitted with through
vacuum brake pipes

11' 2⅞"
to rail

1' 6"

10' 6"

18' 3"

12' 6"

22' 0"

*Another of the 1933 views of Neasden works showing a range of Metropolitan goods stock, with a standard cattle wagon, showing much evidence of lime wash, in the centre and, at the right, one of the long goods vans converted from redundant rail wagons.*

*Cravens 1894 built cattle wagon No. 5, apparently in ex-works condition, coupled to 10T Goods brake van No. 16, also built by Cravens in 1895. Interestingly, the cattle wagon appears to have been painted white over the lower part of the sides, a feature not seen on other railways in the days when lime wash was used to disinfect these wagons.*

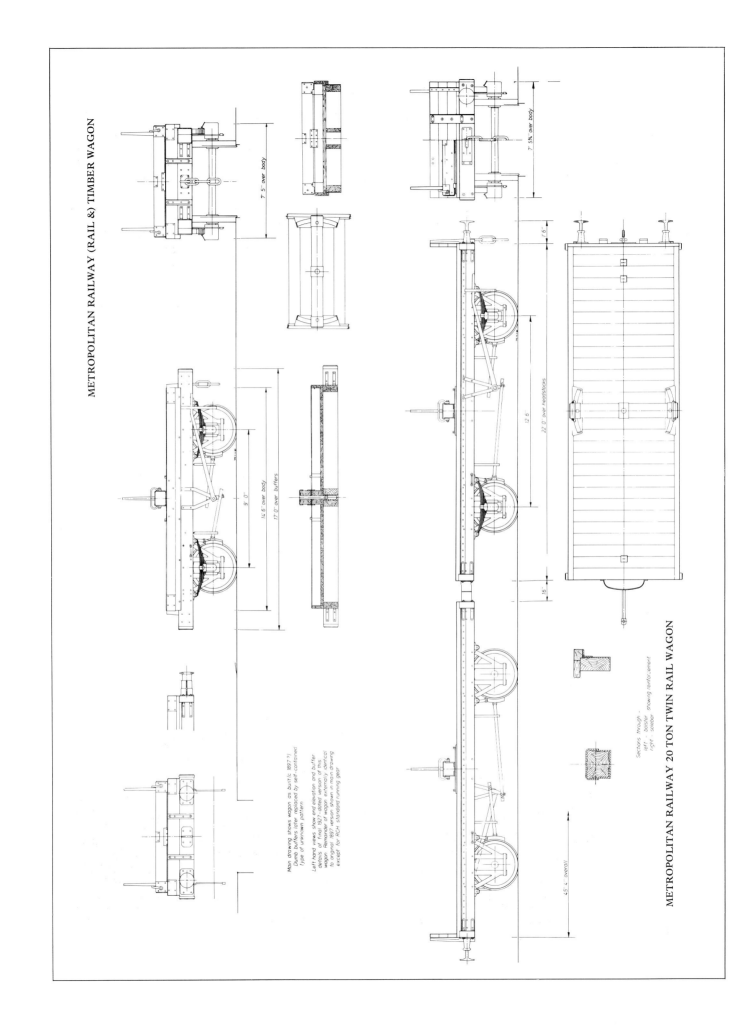

METROPOLITAN RAILWAY (RAIL &) TIMBER WAGON

7' 5" over body

7' 5¾" over body

1' 6"

12' 6"

22' 0" over headstocks

1' 6"

9' 0"

14' 6" over body

17' 0" over buffers

45' 4" overall

Main drawing shows wagon as built (c 1897?).
Dumb buffers later replaced by self-contained
type of unknown pattern

Left hand views show end elevation and buffer
details of final 1927-dated version of this
wagon. Remainder of wagon externally identical
to original 1897 version shown in main drawing
except for RCH standard running gear

Sections through -
left - bolster showing reinforcement
right - solebar

METROPOLITAN RAILWAY 20 TON TWIN RAIL WAGON

gle bolster wagons, each 22ft long and rated to carry 10 tons. Unusually for a bolster wagon, fixed ends were provided to help contain the load. Twenty-two of these wagons were built c.1903, formed into eleven dedicated pairs to give the length required for carrying 45ft rails. Design followed standard Met practice, except that, to cope with the greater wheelbase and higher load capacity, the timber solebars were not only flitched but fitted with substantial reinforcing angles throughout their length.

The need for these wagons reduced considerably once the electrification of the Circle, Hammersmith & City and Uxbridge lines was completed, as a result of which all but a few were rebuilt for other uses. Six were converted to cattle wagons in 1914, using parts from the existing design modified to fit the greater length of the bolster wagons, resulting in a wagon some 25% larger than normal 'large' wagons. Eight more went in 1913–14 to be converted to covered goods vans, again of generous proportions. In both cases, the original underframe, together with its distinctive offset brake gear, remained unaltered save for the provision of new, deeper, headstocks and drawgear at the previously bar-coupled end. Another pair were converted in 1914 as Ballast Train Brake Vans, for which purpose a completely new body was built on the existing frame, with full clasp brakes replacing the original lever type.

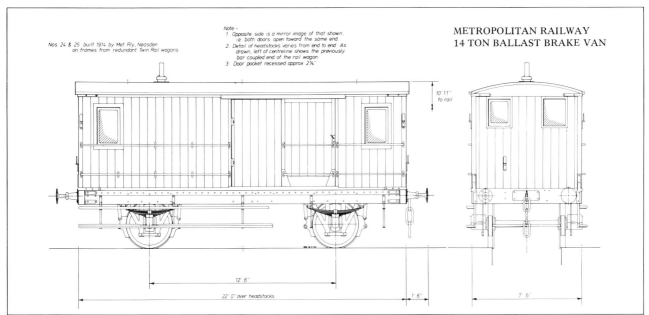

Note -
1. Opposite side is a mirror image of that shown. i.e. both doors open toward the same end
2. Detail of headstocks varies from end to end. As drawn, left of centreline shows the previously bar coupled end of the rail wagon
3. Door pocket recessed approx 2¼"

Nos. 24 & 25 built 1914 by Met Rly, Neasden on frames from redundant Twin Rail wagons

METROPOLITAN RAILWAY
14 TON BALLAST BRAKE VAN

10'11" to rail

12' 6"

22' 0" over headstocks

1' 6"

7' 6"

*10T Ballast brake van B553, ex Met 24, rebuilt in 1914 from a 22ft rail wagon, next to B567, ex Met 15, built in 1895 by Cravens as a 10T Goods brake van.*

Only three wagons remained to be inherited by the LPTB in their original form, two later being transferred to LNER ownership in 1937, with the third remaining with the LPTB, ending their days as crane runner wagons.

The six older short rail and timber wagons also succumbed at this time, being quoted as being rebuilt as covered goods wagons. However, since these bolster wagons were several feet shorter than the standard Met goods van, as well as having a number of other fundamental dimensional differences, it is probable that these wagons were not rebodied, as with the 22ft wagons, but dismantled to provide parts for the construction of new goods vans.

A further 268 wagons were added to the Metropolitan's fleet over the next five years, ie to 1905. The great majority were open wagons as before, although a higher proportion were of the high-sided variety. The remainder fell into three types, covered goods vans, of which there were a further 18, the 22ft twin rail wagons, described earlier, and three Machinery wagons. These latter were typical of their period, with a slightly depressed floor into which wheeled vehicles could be loaded over the wagon ends, or bulky items lowered by crane. Their precise purpose is no longer known, but it is reasonable to suspect that their probable use was the transport of agricultural machinery, for which an ordinary open wagon would be inadequate.

After this period, the size of the wagon fleet remained virtually static, only a few open wagons being added in 1910–12. Excepting the rebuilt rail wagons, no additions

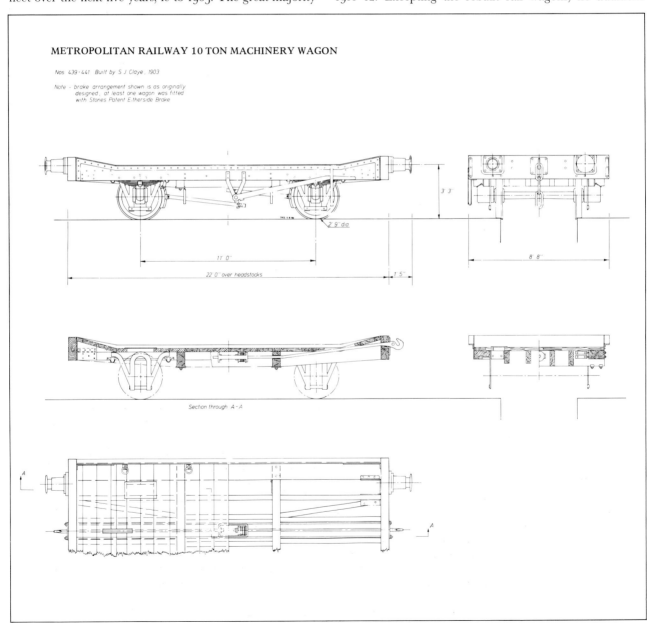

**METROPOLITAN RAILWAY 10 TON MACHINERY WAGON**

Nos 439-441  Built by S J Claye, 1903

Note - brake arrangement shown is as originally
   designed, at least one wagon was fitted
   with Stones Patent Eitherside Brake

3' 3"

2' 9" dia

11' 0"

8' 8"

22' 0" over headstocks

1' 5"

Section through A-A

A

A

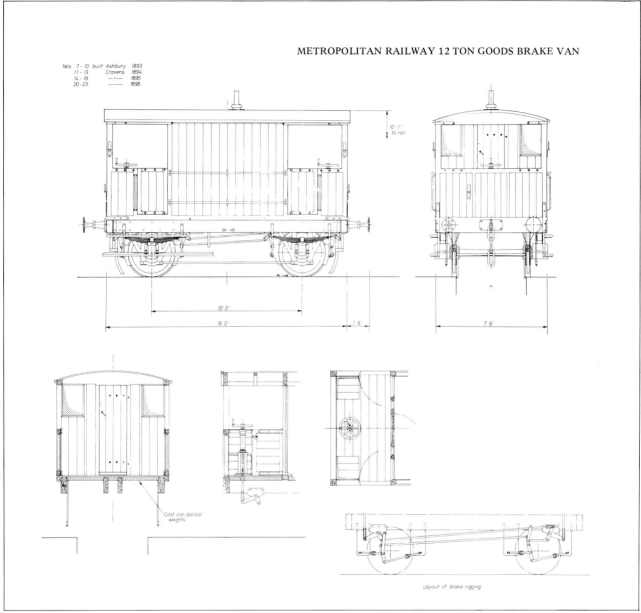

METROPOLITAN RAILWAY 12 TON GOODS BRAKE VAN

Nos 7 - 10 built Ashbury 1893
11 - 13   Cravens 1894
14 - 19   —"— 1895
20 - 23   —"— 1896

10' 11" to rail

10' 0"
16' 0"
1' 6"
7' 6"

Cast iron ballast weights

Layout of brake rigging

were made to the fleet after this until 1921, when the Met purchased six second-hand 20 ton goods brake vans from the War Department.

To cope with the expansion of its goods services through the 1890s, the Met had also acquired a further 17 Goods Brake Vans, all to a standard design derived from the original outside-framed 1860s vans, modified to have internal body framing and flush external planking. They were rated at only 10 tons, which, although probably adequate at the time of their construction, was not really enough in later years, particularly during the First World War, to control the heavier trains which were then being operated. This need appears to have been recognised by the Met in that, shortly after the war, Neasden proposed a design for a six-wheeled

20 ton van which, although obviously descended from the 1893 pattern 10 ton vans, represented a considerable advance in its design. This was particularly evident in the construction of the underframe, the greater part of which consisted of a series of large interlocking cast-iron sections, all bolted together as a block between the solebars, which were formed from back-to-back pairs of rolled steel channels. Clasp brakes were to be provided on all wheels.

Unfortunately, perhaps, nothing more came of this design, none being built, probably because at this time, large numbers of 20 ton brake vans were becoming available as surplus from the War Department, having been built specially for use in France during the war. These vans, the design of which was almost identical to that of the L&SWR 20T road

*B564 ex Met 12, one of the batch of 10T vans built by Cravens in 1894. The design for these vans goes back to at least 1870, after which they became the Met Standard type, remaining such until the arrival of the post-war 20T vans.* A. CRUIKSHANK COLLECTION

*B567, ex Met 15, from the 1895 batch of brake vans, showing the final stencilled version of the LT livery.*

*In 1921 the Met purchased six war surplus 20T Goods Brake Vans, built to a modified version of the LSWR design. Seen here, bearing both its new number and insignia, as well as the initials of its previous owners, is van No. 28.* A. CRUIKSHANK COLLECTION

van, suited the Metropolitan's purposes, as well as almost certainly being significantly cheaper than a new vehicle, as a result of which six were acquired in 1921. As road vans, they were fitted with side doors, opening into a small goods compartment, and as a consequence were somewhat draughty in service. It is not surprising that, within the first five years under Met ownership, these side doors were removed, being replaced with a plain boarded panel to match the remainder of the body. The standard LSWR pattern side lookouts, with which these vans had also been fitted, survived a little longer,

before being removed and the hole filled by a boarded panel in the original style.

These vans, which took over from the earlier 10 ton examples on the main Finchley Road–Aylesbury goods working, were evidently successful, for in 1926, a further three vans were acquired from the War Department, this time for a price little greater than 50% of the cost of the original vans.

It was not until 1896, five years after its initial development, that the Metropolitan's own revenue-earning wagon

*20-ton Goods Brake Van No. 27 was one of several purchased by the Metropolitan as war-surplus stock, having originally been built to a slightly modified LSWR Road Van design for the War Department. This one, photographed in 1929, had lost its side doors, the space having been planked and beaded to match the style of the rest of the body.*

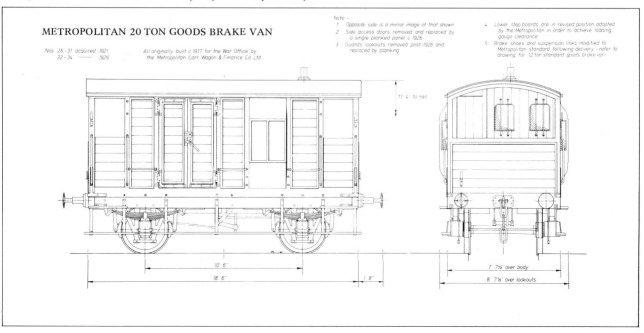

**METROPOLITAN 20 TON GOODS BRAKE VAN**

Nos 26–31 acquired 1921     All originally built c.1917 for the War Office by
32–34 ———— 1926     the Metropolitan Carr Wagon & Finance Co Ltd

Note -
1   Opposite side is a mirror image of that shown
2   Side access doors removed and replaced by a single planked panel c 1926
3   Guards lookouts removed post-1926 and replaced by planking
4   Lower step boards are in revised position adopted by the Metropolitan in order to achieve loading gauge clearance
5   Brake shoes and suspension links modified to Metropolitan standard following delivery - refer to drawing for 12 ton standard goods brake van

11' 4" to rail

10' 6"

18' 6"

1' 8"

7' 7½" over body

8' 7½" over lookouts

Taken at Watford (Met) some time in the late 1930s, this collection of redundant goods stock shows (from right to left) 10T Van 584, dating from 1914, 1896-built low open (dropside) 167, cattle wagons 6 & 10 and 376, built as a dropside wagon in 1902 and later converted to a 3-plank open.
MILE POST 92½

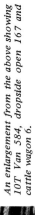

An enlargement from the above showing 10T Van 584, dropside open 167 and cattle wagon 6.

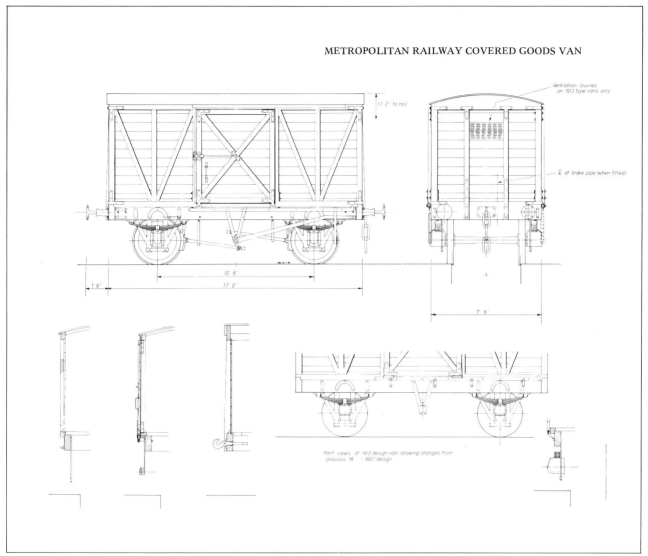

METROPOLITAN RAILWAY COVERED GOODS VAN

Ventilation louvres
on 1913 type vans only

11' 2" to rail

₵ of brake pipe (when fitted)

10' 6"

1' 6"

17' 0"

7' 6"

Part views of 1913 design van showing changes from
previous 18    1897 design

fleet consisted of anything other than open goods wagons. That year, however, the Met introduced six covered goods vans, built by Birmingham C&W to a Neasden design which clearly owed much to the contemporary Midland Railway van, although it differed in a number of respects, principally in length and in having doors which slid open toward the same end of the van. Growing traffic, assisted by the opening of Uxbridge station, whose goods yard directly served the warehouse of a sizeable grocery company, created a need for further covered vans, resulting in twelve more being supplied in 1903 by Ashbury and a further six in 1904 from Metropolitan C&W, bringing the total up to 38 vans, or roughly 10% of the total wagon fleet at the time. These vans were built to the same design as the earlier 1896 examples, apart from a small number of detail modifications. As with the rest of the Metropolitan's goods fleet, the stock of covered vans remained static after this time until 1913 when a further fourteen new goods vans were created by rebuilding

a like number of rail wagons which had by then become redundant following the completion of the initial programme to electrify the Metropolitan's suburban area.

Of these fourteen 'new' vans, six were created from the original single-bolster rail and timber wagons. Since these were considerably smaller than the standard goods van, reuse of the underframe as it stood would have resulted in a distinctly small van, which would in consequence have been of only limited value. Instead, it is likely that the rebuilding was partly an accountancy exercise, with, in practice, only the ironwork, as well as some of the timber underframe members, being retained.

The other eight vans were rebuilt from twin rail wagons by the expedient of building a new van body onto the original underframe, which was unaltered except for minor detail changes and the fitting of full buffing and drawgear at the inner ends of the frames, the two rail wagons having previously been equipped with a solid bar coupling and dead

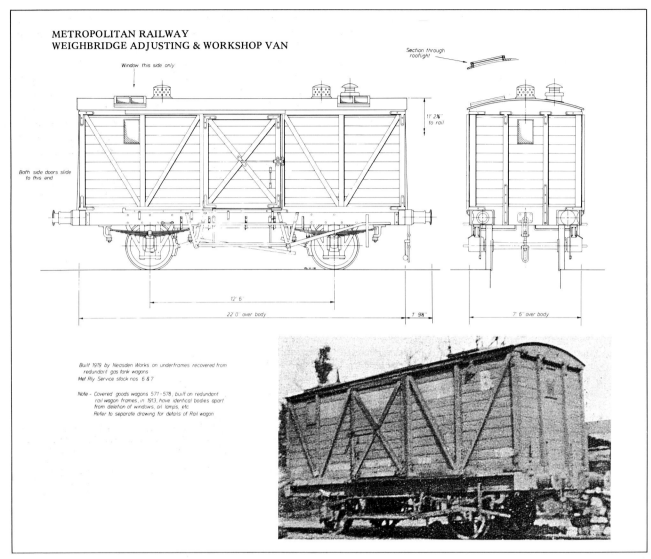

METROPOLITAN RAILWAY
WEIGHBRIDGE ADJUSTING & WORKSHOP VAN

*Section through roof light*

*Window this side only*

*11' 2⅜" to rail*

*Both side doors slide to this end*

*12' 6"*

*22' 0" over body*

*1' 9½"*

*7' 6" over body*

*Built 1919 by Neasden Works on underframes recovered from redundant gas tank wagons*
*Met Rly Service stock nos 6 & 7*

*Note - Covered goods wagons 571-578, built on redundant rail wagon frames, in 1913, have identical bodies apart from deletion of windows, oil lamps, etc*
*Refer to separate drawing for details of Rail wagon*

buffer. The Metropolitan's standard 17ft long van design had to be stretched to fit the 22ft length of these underframes, resulting in a very capacious vehicle, the design of which formed a precedent for two later conversions to provide workshop vans for Messrs Henry Pooley, who supplied and maintained the Metropolitan's weighbridges.

These two vans, which were constructed in 1919, utilised the underframes from a pair of gas tank wagons, most of which were by then redundant as a result of the earlier decisions taken by the company to adopt electric lighting in place of the gas system. As noted, these vans were, externally, very similar to the long goods vans described earlier. Internally, however, they were fitted out with full workshop facilities, as well as lockers below floor level for the carriage of other heavy lifting tackle and for the test weights used to calibrate each weighbridge installation. Both survived to be taken into LPTB stock, being allocated appropriately prefixed numbers in the LPTB engineering vehicles series. Both survived until 1943/1944, when they were sold out of service,

but not scrapped. One remains intact, being preserved, although not restored, at the Rutland Railway Museum, Cottesmore.

Although the size of its own goods stock fleet had stabilised by the end of the First World War, goods working continued to be a feature of the Metropolitan's operations for the remainder of its life, making a significant proportion of the company's income. The formation of the LPTB in 1933, however, marked a major change in attitudes; dominated as it was by the London Electric Railways group, it did not consider freight operations to be amongst its interests, preferring to concentrate on passenger train operation. Further, the management of these freight services required a level of manpower resourcing that was difficult to justify in relation to the revenue earned.

The Metropolitan's freight services continued under LPTB control for four years, until in 1937 agreement was reached with the LNER, with whom the Met shared a considerable proportion of its main-line mileage and stations.

This provided for the LNER to take over operation of all the freight services to and from Metropolitan stations, and to provide motive power for both these and the main-line trains beyond the limits of electric haulage. Most of the wagon fleet, as well as the larger steam locomotives, was transferred to the LNER, the LPTB retaining only a modest fleet of open wagons and some of the smaller locomotives in order to service the needs of Neasden power station and to carry ballast and spoil from track maintenance. With some exceptions, the low-sided wagons were reclassified as ballast wagons, whilst the high-sided wagons were used within Neasden yard to carry ash and boiler waste from the power station. A small number of low-sided wagons escaped from ballast duties by being converted to match wagons to allow tube-gauge vehicles to be hauled by surface locomotives.

Of those which had been designated as ballast wagons, comparatively few survived the war, partly through sheer age, many being 50 years old by then, and partly as a consequence of the LPTB's 1930s modernisation of the engineer's vehicle fleet. By the mid-1950s, the remainder of the ballast wagons had gone, whilst the conversion of Neasden power station to oil firing spelled the end for almost all of the power station wagons. Some of the match wagons and brake vans survived longer, although seeing little use before their demise in the late 1960s. The wagons transferred to the LNER fared little better, most having been scrapped either soon after acquisition or within five years of the end of the war.

Of the six hundred strong fleet, only three wagons now survive, two low-sided open wagons, which had latterly been match wagons, and one of the two weighing machine workshop vans.

*Met low-sided goods wagon 118, now as LT Ballast wagon BW159. Built in 1893 by Cravens and withdrawn in 1966, after 73 years of service.*
A. CRUIKSHANK
COLLECTION

*Another Met conversion, now a Match Truck after being a ballast wagon. The origin of this wagon is unknown; it appears to be a Met conversion of an open goods wagon, cut down, but various items of its detail design do not accord with Neasden's standards.*
A. CRUIKSHANK
COLLECTION

# APPENDIX I
# METROPOLITAN RAILWAY CARRIAGE NUMBERING

In the beginning, the only vehicles the Metropolitan owned, other than the locomotives, were the carriages, which were simply numbered in order of acquisition, irrespective of class or type. As the railway grew, other types of non-passenger vehicles were acquired, such as the milk vans, passenger brake vans, and horse-boxes, each of which was allocated a new number series starting from 1.

The arrival of the Jubilee stock in 1892 broke this pattern, being delivered in block-numbered sets, the vehicles in which were numbered in order of class preference, starting with the first class. A similar system was used for the next group of vehicles, the Bogie stock, differing only in that, as this stock was delivered several trains at a time, the carriages were numbered in class groups, i.e. of a group of four trains, all the first class vehicles were numbered in order, followed by all the second class carriages and so on. The Dreadnought stock followed the same pattern until the arrival of the trailer vehicles for the 1929 MW stock, where block numbering according to type was retained, but the principle of 'first class first' was abandoned.

As might have been expected, the new electric stock of 1904 was numbered into several new series, again according to class or type.

Thus there became new number ranges, all starting from 1 for the motor cars and for the first and third class trailer cars; a fourth, later, series covered the composite cars, which did not appear until the ten East London Railway cars were created. This was maintained, with one exception, until the last saloon stock vehicles, motor cars 198 and 199 and trailer car 106, were delivered. The one exception was the converted Bogie stock, where the vehicles retained their compartment stock numbers.

A strange situation developed with the main-line electric stock, which was of compartment type, in that the motor coaches were numbered sequentially from the saloon stock motor cars, whilst their trailer cars were numbered sequentially from the last Dreadnought vehicles, i.e. in the steam stock series. This anomaly only disappeared with the coming of the LPTB, who renumbered all the electric stock together in new blocks, still according to class or type, but left all the compartment stock, as it had by then become identified, under their old Metropolitan numbers, where they remained until their demise in 1961.

## ELECTRIC STOCK

### Key to abbreviations

| | |
|---|---|
| BTH | British Thompson Houston Co. — 10 wire control system |
| BWE | British Westinghouse Electric Co. — 9 wire 14V control system |
| BTH (2) or BWE (2) | Refers to vehicle wired to BTH or BWE system *both* sides. |
| BTH/BWE | Refers to vehicle wired with BTH on one side and BWE on the other. |
| \<BTH\> | GN&C stock only, wired with BTH control wiring on centre at roof level. Not compatible with other Met stock. |
| T | Trailer car |
| DT | Driving Trailer car |
| C | Composite |
| 1DT | First Class DT |
| CDT | Composite DT |
| B3 (B2) | Third (Second) Class Brake Carriage |
| C2 | First & Second Class Composite carriage |
| C3 | First & Third Class Composite carriage |

### Third Class Trailer Cars

| Number | Type | MU Train Line | Seats | LPTB Numbers/Remarks |
|---|---|---|---|---|
| 1–30 | 1904 T | BWE (2) | 48 | 9483–9512 in sequence. Car 23 scrapped before carrying allocated LT number. Car 29 equipped with BTH control line one side. |
| 31–33 | 1905 T | BTH/BWE | 48 | 9513–9515 in sequence. |
| 34 | 1905 T | BTH/BWE | 48 | 9210 |
| 35–36 | 1905 T | BTH/BWE | 48 | 9516–9517 in sequence. Car 35 rebuilt to 1919 3T, scrapped 1941 |
| 37 | 1905 DT | BTH/BWE | 48 | 9590 |
| 38 | 1905 DT | BTH/BWE | 48 | 9479. Converted by Met to 3T. |
| 39 | 1905 DT | BTH (2) | 48 | 6221 |
| 40 | 1905 DT | BTH/BWE | 48 | 6592 |
| 41 | 1905 DT | BTH/BWE | 48 | 6220 |
| 42 | 1905 DT | BTH/BWE | 48 | 6593 |
| 43 | 1905 DT | BTH/BWE | 48 | 6222 |
| 44 | 1905 DT | BTH/BWE | 48 | 9480. Converted by Met to 3T. |
| 45 | 1905 DT | BTH (2) | 48 | 6223 |
| 46 | 1905 DT | BTH (2) | 48 | 9481. Converted by Met to 3T. |
| 47 | 1905 DT | BTH/BWE | 48 | 6596 |
| 48 | 1905 DT | BTH/BWE | 48 | 9482. Converted by Met to 3T. |
| 49 | 1905 DT | BTH (2) | 48 | 6598 |
| 50 | 1905 DT | BTH (2) | 48 | 6224 |
| 51–59 | 1905 T | BTH/BWE | 48 | 9518–9526 in sequence. |
| 60 | 1905 T | BTH/BWE | 48 | 9211 |
| 61 | 1905 T | BTH/BWE | 48 | 9527 |
| 62 | 1905 T | BTH/BWE | 48 | 9212 |
| 63–64 | 1905 T | BTH/BWE | 48 | 9528–9529. |
| 65 | 1905 T | BTH/BWE | 48 | Converted 1912 to Composite Car 8. |
| 66 | 1905 T | BTH/BWE | 48 | 9530 |
| 67 | 1905 T | BTH/BWE | 48 | 9531. Rebuilt to 1919 3T. |
| 68 | 1905 T | BTH/BWE | 48 | 9532 |
| 69 | 1905 T | BTH/BWE | 48 | Converted 1912 to Composite Car 9. |
| 70 | 1905 T | BTH/BWE | 48 | 9533 |
| 71 | 1905 T | BTH/BWE | 48 | Converted 1912 to Composite Car 10. |
| 72–76 | 1905 T | BTH/BWE | 48 | 9534–9538 in sequence. |
| 77–79 | 1913 T | BTH/BWE | 48 | 9546–9548. Allocated to Circle Service. |
| 80–83 | 1913 T | BTH/BWE | 48 | 9542–9545 |
| 84–86 | 1913 T | BTH/BWE | 48 | 9539–9541 |
| 87–119 | 1921 T | BTH/BWE | 48 | 9549–9581. Allocated to Circle Service. |
| 120–159 | 1905 DT | BTH (2) | 48 | 6225–6264. Ex Hammersmith & City Joint stock. |
| 160–164 | 1902 DT | \<BTH\> | 58 | Ex GN & C, Wood body. 6901–6909 odd nos. only in sequence. |
| 165 | 1902 DT | \<BTH\> | 58 | Ex GN & C, Wood body. Allocated LT 6911 but never carried. |
| 166 | 1902 DT | \<BTH\> | 58 | Ex GN & C, Wood body. 6913. |
| 167 | 1902 DT | \<BTH\> | 58 | Ex GN & C, Wood body. Scrapped without being allocated LT number. |

| Number | Type | MU Train Line | Seats | LPTB Numbers/Remarks |
|---|---|---|---|---|
| 168 | 1902 DT | <BTH> | 58 | Ex GN & C, Wood body. 6915. |
| 169–171 | 1902 T | <BTH> | 58 | Ex GN & C, Wood body. 9950–9952. |
| 172 | 1902 DT | <BTH> | 58 | Ex GN & C, Wood body. 6902. |
| 173–174 | 1902 T | <BTH> | 58 | Ex GN & C, Wood body. 9953–9954. |
| 175–176 | 1902 T | <BTH> | 58 | Ex GN & C, Wood body. Not renumbered into LT Fleet. |
| 177–178 | 1902 DT | <BTH> | 58 | Ex GN & C, Wood body. 6917 & 6919. |
| 179–190 | 1902 T | <BTH> | 64 | Ex GN & C, Steel body. 9957–9968 in sequence; only 179, 183 & 189 actually renumbered. |
| 191 | 1904 T | BTH/West | 46 | 9582. Ex motor car 2. |
| 192 | 1904 T | BTH/West | 46 | 9583. Ex motor car 13. |
| 193 | 1905 T | BTH/West | 48 | 9584. Ex motor car 21. |
| 194 | 1905 T | BTH/West | 48 | 9585. Ex motor car 26. |
| 195 | 1904 T | BTH/West | 48 | 9586. Ex motor car 29. |
| 196 | 1905 T | BTH/West | 48 | 9587. Ex motor car 39. |
| 197 | 1905 T | BTH | 52 | 9588. Ex motor car 36. |
| 198 | 1905 T | BTH | 52 | 9589. Ex motor car 44. |
| 199 | 1904 T | BTH | 50 | 9590. Ex motor car 10. |
| 200 | 1904 T | BTH | 50 | 9591. Ex motor car 4. |
| 201 | 1905 T | BTH | 50 | 9592. Ex motor car 49 |
| 202 | 1905 T | BTH | 50 | 9593. Ex motor car 45. |
| 203 | 1904 T | BTH | 50 | 9594. Ex motor car 1. |
| 204 | 1905 T | BTH | 50 | 9595. Ex motor car 27. |
| 205 | 1904 T | BTH | 50 | 9596. Ex motor car 15. |
| 206 | 1904 T | BTH | 50 | 9597. Ex motor car 12. |
| 207 | 1905 T | BTH | 50 | 9598. Ex motor car 48. |
| 208 | 1905 T | BTH | 50 | 9599. Ex motor car 55. |
| | 1905 T | BTH | 48 | 9477. Converted by LPTB from 1T 9404 (ex Met 61). |
| | 1905 T | BTH | 48 | 9478. Converted by LPTB from 1T 9407 (ex Met 65). |

## Composite Cars

| Number | Type | MU Train Line | LPTB Numbers/Remarks |
|---|---|---|---|
| 1 | [1912] CDT | BTH/BWE | 6580. Ex 1T 29. |
| 2 | [1912] CDT | BTH/BWE | 6581. Ex 1T 33. |
| 3 | [1912] CDT | BTH/BWE | 6582. Ex 1T 50. |
| 4 | [1912] CDT | BTH/BWE | 6853. Ex 1T 71. |
| 5 | [1912] CDT | BTH (2) | 6212. Ex 1T 72. |
| 6 | [1912] CDT | BTH (2) | 6211. Ex 1T 73. |
| 7 | [1912] CDT | BTH/BWE | 6584. Ex 1T 74. |
| 8 | [1912] CDT | BTH/BWE | 6585. Ex 3T 65. Later 1T 6580? |
| 9 | [1912] CDT | BTH/BWE | 6586. Ex 3T 69. |
| 10 | [1912] CDT | BTH/BWE | 6587. Ex 3T 71. |
| 11–50 | 1905 CT | BTH (2) | 9221–9259. Ex H&C Joint Stock. |
| 50 | 1905 CT | BTH (2) | 9220. Ex H&C Joint Stock. |

## 1st Class Trailer Cars

| Number | Type | MU Train Line | Seats | LPTB Numbers/Remarks |
|---|---|---|---|---|
| 1–20 | 1904 DT | BTH/BWE * | 24/24 | 6500–6519. *1–3 & 5 BWE (2). |
| 21 | 1905 DT | BTH/BWE | 24/24 | 6520 |
| 22 | 1905 DT | BTH/BWE | 24/24 | Converted 1910 to coach 425. |
| 23–25 | 1905 DT | BTH/BWE | 24/24 | 6521–6523 |
| 26 | 1905 DT | BTH/BWE | 24/24 | Converted 1910 to coach 428. |
| 27 | 1905 DT | BTH/BWE | 24/14 | 6524 |
| 28 | 1905 DT | BTH/BWE | 24/24 | 6501 |
| 29 | 1905 DT | BTH/BWE | 24/24 | Converted 1912 to Comp 1. |
| 30 | 1905 DT | BTH/BWE | 24/24 | Converted 1910 to coach 423. |
| 31–32 | 1905 DT | BTH/BWE | 24/24 | 6525–6526. |
| 33 | 1905 DT | BTH/BWE | 24/24 | Converted 1912 to Comp 2. |
| 34 | 1905 DT | BTH/BWE | 24/24 | Converted 1910 to coach 420. |
| 35–37 | 1905 DT | BTH/BWE | 24/24 | 6527–6529. |
| 38 | 1905 DT | BTH/BWE | 24/24 | Converted 1910 to coach 419. |
| 39–40 | 1905 DT | BTH/BWE | 24/24 | 6530–6531. |
| 41 | 1905 DT | BTH/BWE | 24/24 | Converted 1910 to coach 426. |

| Number | Type | MU Train Line | Seats | LPTB Numbers/Remarks |
|---|---|---|---|---|
| 42 | 1905 DT | BTH/BWE | 24/24 | Converted 1910 to coach 427. |
| 43 | 1905 DT | BTH/BWE | 24/24 | 6532 |
| 44 | 1905 DT | BTH/BWE | 24/24 | Converted 1910 to coach 422. |
| 45 | 1905 DT | BTH/BWE | 24/24 | Converted 1910 to coach 421. |
| 46 | 1905 DT | BTH/BWE | 24/24 | 6533 |
| 47 | 1905 DT | BTH/BWE | 24/24 | 6537. Allocated to Circle Service. |
| 48 | 1905 DT | BTH/BWE | 24/24 | Converted 1910 to coach 424. |
| 49 | 1905 DT | BTH/BWE | 24/24 | 6538. Allocated to Circle Service. |
| 50 | 1905 DT | BTH/BWE | 24/24 | Converted 1912 to Comp 3. |
| 51 | 1905 DT | BTH/BWE | 24/24 | 6536 Allocated to Circle Service. |
| 52 | 1905 DT | BTH/BWE | 24/24 | 6534 |
| 53 | 1905 DT | BTH/BWE | 24/24 | 6535. Rebuilt to 1919 1DT. |
| 54 | 1905 DT | BTH/BWE | 24/24 | 6554 |
| 55 | 1905 DT | BTH/BWE | 24/24 | 6555. Rebuilt to 1919 1DT. |
| 56 | 1905 DT | BTH/BWE | 24/24 | 6556 |
| 57 | 1905 T | BTH/BWE | 24/24 | 6562. Converted 1935 by LPTB to DT. |
| 58 | 1905 T | BTH/BWE | 24/24 | 9401 |
| 59 | 1905 T | BTH/BWE | 24/24 | 6558. Converted 1935 by LPTB to DT. |
| 60 | 1905 T | BTH/BWE | 24/24 | 6561. Converted 1935 by LPTB to DT. |
| 61 | 1905 T | BTH/BWE | 24/24 | 9477. Converted to 3T. |
| 62 | 1905 T | BTH/BWE | 24/24 | 9200 |
| 63–64 | 1905 T | BWE (2) | 24/24 | Scrapped before renumbering. |
| 65 | 1905 T | BTH/BWE | 24/24 | 9478. Converted to 3T. |
| 66 | 1905 T | BWE (2) | 24/24 | Destroyed by fire. |
| 67 | 1905 DT | BTH/BWE | 24/24 | 9201 |
| 68 | 1905 T | BWE (2) | 24/24 | Scrapped before renumbering. |
| 69 | 1905 T | BTH/BWE | 24/24 | 9203 |
| 70 | 1905 T | BWE (2) | 24/24 | 6559. Converted 1935 by LPTB to DT. |
| 71–74 | 1905 T | BWE (2) | 24/24 | Converted by Met to Composite cars 4–7. |
| 75 | 1905 T | BTH/BWE | 24/24 | Scrapped before renumbering. |
| 76 | 1905 DT | BTH (2) | 24/24 | 6203. Demoted to 1T by removal of driving equipment. |
| 77 | 1912 DT | BTH/BWE | 24/24 | 6542. Allocated to Circle Service. |
| 78 | 1912 DT | BTH/BWE | 24/24 | 9410. Demoted to 1T by removal of driving equipment. |
| 79–86 | 1912 DT | BTH/BWE | 24/24 | 6543–6550. Allocated to Circle Service. |
| 87–89 | 1921 DT | BTH/BWE | 20/24 | 6551–6553. Allocated to Circle Service. |
| 90–92 | 1921 DT | BTH/BWE | 20/24 | 6539–6541. Allocated to Circle Service. |
| 93–105 | 1902/6 T | <BTH> | 28/26 | 9900–9912. Ex-GN&C Stock. Cars 94, 96, 97, 101, 102 & 105 scrapped without carrying allocated numbers. |
| 106 | 1921 DT | BTH (2) | 20/25 | 6557. Built 1924 for British Empire Exhibition, Wembley. Allocated to E.London Line service. |
| | 1906 DT | BTH/BWE | 24/24 | 6560. Converted by LPTB from Composite car 6585 (ex Met 8). |

## Motor Coaches

| Number | Type | MU Train Line | Seats | LPTB Numbers/Remarks |
|---|---|---|---|---|
| 1 | 1904 | BWE (2) | 40 | Converted by Met to 3T 203. |
| 2 | 1904 | BWE (2) | 40 | Converted by Met to 3T 191. |
| 3 | 1904 | BWE (2) | 40 | Scrapped by Met. |
| 4 | 1904 | BWE (2) | 40 | Converted by Met to 3T 200. |
| 5–9 | 1904 | BWE (2) | 40 | Scrapped by Met. |
| 10 | 1904 | BWE (2) | 40 | Converted by Met to 3T 199. |
| 11 | 1904 | BWE (2) | 40 | Scrapped by Met. |
| 12 | 1904 | BWE (2) | 40 | Converted by Met to 3T 206. |
| 13 | 1904 | BWE (2) | 40 | Converted by Met to 3T 192. |
| 14 | 1904 | BWE (2) | 40 | Scrapped by Met. |

| Number | Type | MU Train Line | Seats | LPTB Numbers/Remarks |
|---|---|---|---|---|
| 15 | 1904 | BWE (2) | 40 | Converted by Met to 3T 205. |
| 16–17 | 1904 | BWE (2) | 40 | Scrapped by Met. |
| 18 | 1905 | BWE (2) | 38 | Scrapped by Met. |
| 19–20 | 1904 | BWE (2) | 40 | Scrapped by Met. |
| 21 | 1905 | BWE (2) | 38 | Converted by Met to 3T 193. |
| 22–25 | 1905 | BWE (2) | 38 | Scrapped by Met. |
| 26 | 1905 | BWE (2) | 38 | Converted by Met to 3T 194. |
| 27 | 1905 | BWE (2) | 38 | Converted by Met to 3T 204. |
| 28 | 1905 | BWE (2) | 38 | Scrapped by Met. |
| 29 | 1905 | BWE (2) | 38 | Converted by Met to 3T 196. |
| 30 | 1905 | BWE (2) | 38 | 2500. Loaned to GN&C, thence to LPTB. |
| 31 | 1905 | BWE (2) | 38 | 2502. Loaned to GN&C, thence to LPTB. |
| 32 | 1905 | BWE (2) | 38 | 2501. Loaned to GN&C, thence to LPTB. |
| 33 | 1905 | BWE (2) | 38 | 2504. Loaned to GN&C, thence to LPTB. |
| 34 | 1905 | BWE (2) | 38 | 2503. Loaned to GN&C, thence to LPTB. |
| 35 | 1905 | BWE (2) | 38 | 2505. Loaned to GN&C, thence to LPTB. |
| 36 | 1905 | BWE (2) | 38 | Converted by Met to 1919 3T 197. |
| 37 | 1905 | BWE (2) | 38 | Scrapped by Met. |
| 38 | 1905 | BWE (2) | 38 | 2525 |
| 39 | 1905 | BWE (2) | 38 | Converted by Met to 3T 196. |
| 40–43 | 1905 | BWE (2) | 38 | Scrapped by Met. |
| 44 | 1905 | BWE (2) | 38 | Converted by Met to 1919 3T 198 |
| 45 | 1905 | BWE (2) | 38 | Converted by Met to 3T 202. |
| 46 | 1905 | BWE (2) | | Rebuilt by Met as Composite M/C 46, later LPTB 2768. |
| 47 | 1905 | BWE (2) | 38 | Scrapped by Met. |
| 48 | 1905 | BWE (2) | 38 | Converted by Met to 3T 207. |
| 49 | 1905 | BWE (2) | 38 | Converted by Met to 3T 201. |
| 50–54 | 1905 | BWE (2) | 38 | Scrapped by Met. |
| 55 | 1905 | BWE (2) | 38 | Converted by Met to 3T 208. |
| 56 | 1905 | BWE (2) | 38 | Scrapped by Met. |
| 57–62 | 1905 | BTH (2) | 38 | 2540–2545 |
| 63–68 | 1905 | BTH (2) | 38 | 2553–2558. Car 64 (2554) scrapped before carrying allocated LPTB number. |
| 69 | 1905 | BTH (2) | 38 | Rebuilt by Met as Composite M/C 69, later LPTB 2769. |
| 70 | 1905 | BTH (2) | 38 | 2559 |
| 71 | 1905 | BTH (2) | 38 | 2200 |
| 72 | 1905 | BTH (2) | 38 | 2537 |
| 73 | 1905 | BTH (2) | 38 | 2201 |
| 74 | 1905 | BTH (2) | 38 | 2203 |
| 75 | 1905 | BTH (2) | 38 | 2538 |
| 76 | 1905 | BTH (2) | 38 | 2205 |
| 77 | 1905 | BTH (2) | 38 | 2560 |
| 78 | 1905 | BTH (2) | 38 | 2539 |
| 79 | 1905 | BTH (2) | 38 | 2207 |
| 80 | 1905 | BTH (2) | 38 | 2202 |
| 81 | 1905 | BTH (2) | 38 | 2204 |
| 82 | 1905 | BTH (2) | 38 | 2206 |
| 83–92 | 1913 | BTH (2) | 46 | 2587–2596. Allocated for Circle Service. |
| 93–98 | 1913 | BWE (2) | 46 | 2581–2586. Allocated for Circle Service. Cars 96–98 reduced to motors driving end only. |
| 99–105 | 1913 | BWE (2) | 38 | 2546–2552 |
| 106–107 | 1921 | BWE (2) | 40 | 2561–2562. Allocated for Circle Service. Both cars reduced to motors driving end only. |
| 108–115 | 1921 | BWE (2) | 40 | 2573–2580. Allocated for Circle Service. All cars reduced to motors driving end only. |
| 116–125 | 1921 | BWE (2) | 40 | 2563–2572. Allocated for Circle Service. |
| 126–165 | 1905 | BTH (2) | 38 | 2208–2247. Ex H&C Joint stock. Car 161 scrapped before carrying allocated LPTB number. |

| Number | Type | MU Train Line | Seats | LPTB Numbers/Remarks |
|---|---|---|---|---|
| 166 | 1906 | \<BTH\> | 60 | 2901. Ex GN&C steel car. |
| 167 | 1902 | \<BTH\> | 54 | 2900. Ex GN&C wood car. |
| 168–169 | 1902/6 | \<BTH\> | 60,54 | [2902–2903]. Ex GN&C steel/wood car. Scrapped without carrying allocated LPTB numbers. |
| 170–181 | 1902 | \<BTH\> | 54 | 2904–2926, even numbers. |
| 182–183 | 1902 | \<BTH\> | 54 | 2905–2907, odd numbers. |
| 184–185 | 1902 | \<BTH\> | 54 | 2928–2930, even numbers. |
| 186–188 | 1902 | \<BTH\> | 54 | 2909–2913, odd numbers. |
| 189–191 | 1902 | \<BTH\> | 54 | 2932–2936, even numbers. |
| 192–197 | 1902 | \<BTH\> | 60 | 2915–2921, odd numbers only. |
| 198–199 | 1924 | BTH (T) | 33 | 2598–2599 |
| 200–205 | 1927 MW | BTH (T) | 60 | 2700–2705 |
| 206–211 | 1927 MV | BTH (T) | 60 | 2706–2711 |
| 212–241 | 1929 MW | BTH (T) | 60 | 2712–2741. 232–241 equipped with roller bearings. |
| 242–259 | 1931 MW | BTH (T) | 60 | 2742–2759. Equipped with roller bearings. |
| 376 | Bogie | BTH (2) | 30 | 2764. Converted 1906 by Met from coach 376. |
| 384 | Bogie | BWE (2) | 30 | 2760. Converted 1908 by Met from coach 384. |
| 387 | Bogie | BWE (2) | 30 | 2761. Converted 1908 by Met from coach 387. |
| 388 | Bogie | BTH (2) | 30 | 2765. Converted 1906 by Met from coach 388. |
| 397–398 | Bogie | BTH (2) | 30 | 2766–2767. Converted 1906 by Met from coaches 397–398. |
| 417–418 | Bogie | BWE (2) | 30 | 2762–2763. Converted 1908 by Met from coaches 417–418. |

# COMPARTMENT STOCK

## Eight-wheel stock

| Numbers | Class | Year | Builder |
|---|---|---|---|
| 1–34 | M | 1863 | Ashbury |
| 35–40 | I | 1864 | Oldbury |
| 41–60 | M | 1865 | Oldbury |
| 61–72 | 1 | 1866 | Oldbury |
| 73–82 | 3 | 1866 | Oldbury |
| 83–86 | 2 | ? | ? |
| 87–90 | I | ? | ? |
| 91–92 | C2 | ? | ? |
| 93–142 | M | | ? |

## Twin-carriage stock

| Numbers | Class | Year | Builder |
|---|---|---|---|
| 143–144 | C2 | 1869 | Oldbury? Prototype Twin set. |
| 145–148 | 3 | 1869 | Oldbury |
| 149–157 | 2 | | |
| 158–168 | I | | |

## Eight-wheeled stock

| Numbers | Class | Year | Builder |
|---|---|---|---|
| 169–171 | I | 1870 | Ashbury |
| 172–174 | 2 | ? | ? |
| 175–177 | C2 | ? | ? |
| 178–180 | C3 | ? | ? |
| 181–185 | 2 | 1879 | Ashbury |
| 186–195 | 3 | ? | ? |
| 196–201 | 3 | 1880 | Ashbury |
| 202–204 | I | ? | ? |
| 205–207 | 2 | ? | ? |
| 208–210 | C | ? | ? |
| 211–216 | 3 | 1881 | Ashbury |
| 217–236 | 3 | 1883 | Brown Marshall |
| 237–238 | 2 | ? | ? |
| 239–240 | I | ? | ? |
| 241 | C | ? | ? |
| 242–244 | C | 1884 | Cravens |
| 245–260 | 3 | ? | ? |
| 261–276 | 3 | 1884 | Gloucester |
| 277–284 | I | 1884 | Cravens |
| 285–301 | 2 | 1884 | Brown Marshall |

## Eight-wheel stock retained post 1900 for emergency and excursion duties

### Steam sets

| SB/3 | 3 | 1 | Compo | 3 | LB/3 |
|---|---|---|---|---|---|
| 300 | 223 | 280 | 209 | 217 | 249 |
| 236 | 294 | 240 | 208 | 220 | 226 |
| 295 | 194 | 239 | 210 | 187 | 268 |
| 213* | 292 | 279 | 278 | 285 | 273 |
| 269 | 301 | 283 | 264 | 237 | 252 |

*Long brake 3rd

### Electric sets

| LB/3 | 3 | 1 | 1 | 3 | LB/3 |
|---|---|---|---|---|---|
| 199 | 298 | 282 | 277 | 289 | 214 |
| 266 | 288 | 274 | 204 | 287 | 263 |
| 261 | 271 | 203 | 202 | 270 | 251 |

## The Jubilee Stock

| Numbers | Class | Year | Remarks |
|---|---|---|---|
| 302–303 | 1 | 1887 | |
| 304 | B2 | 1887 | 9-car Set No 1 |
| 305 | 2 | 1887 | |
| 306–309 | 3 | 1887 | |
| 310 | B3 | 1887 | |
| 311–312 | 1 | 1887 | |
| 313 | B2 | 1887 | 9-car Set No 2 |
| 314 | 2 | 1887 | |
| 315–318 | 3 | 1887 | |
| 319 | B3 | 1887 | |
| 320–321 | 1 | 1887 | |
| 322 | B2 | 1887 | 9-car Set No 3 |
| 323 | 2 | 1887 | |
| 324–327 | 3 | 1887 | |
| 328 | B3 | 1887 | |
| 329–330 | 1 | 1892 | |
| 331–332 | B2 | 1892 | 4-car Sets 1 & 2 |
| 333–334 | 3 | 1892 | |
| 335–336 | B3 | 1892 | |
| 337–338 | 1 | 1892 | |
| 339–340 | B2 | 1892 | 4-car Sets 3 & 4 |
| 341–342 | 3 | 1892 | |
| 343–344 | B3 | 1892 | |
| 345–346 | 1 | 1892 | |
| 347–348 | B2 | 1892 | 4-car Sets 5 & 6 |
| 349–350 | 3 | 1892 | |
| 351–352 | B3 | 1892 | |
| 353–354 | 1 | 1892 | |
| 355–356 | B2 | 1892 | 4-car Sets 7 & 8 |
| 357–358 | B3 | 1892 | |
| 359–360 | B3 | 1892 | |

## Bogie Stock

| Numbers | Class | LT Renumbering | Remarks |
|---|---|---|---|
| 361 | 1 | 9700 | Converted 1906 for electric working. |
| 362 | 1 | | Destroyed in collision at Baker Street, pre-1933. |
| 363 | 1 | 9706 | Converted 1924 for electric working. |
| 364 | 1 | 9701 | Converted 1905 for electric working. |
| 365 | C | 9746 | Converted 1905 for electric working. |
| 366–367 | C[1] | 9707–9708 | Converted 1921 for electric working. |
| 368 | C[1] | 9702 | Converted 1906 for electric working. |
| 369 | 2(3) | 9748 | Converted 1906 for electric working. |
| 370–371 | 2(3) | 9758–9759 | Converted 1921 for electric working. |
| 372 | 3[3] | 9749 | Converted 1905 for electric working. |
| 373 | B2[3] | 9750 | Converted 1907 for electric working. |
| 374–375 | B2[3] | 9763–9764 | Converted 1921 for electric working. |

| Numbers | Class | LT Renumbering | Remarks |
|---|---|---|---|
| 376 | B2 | 2764 | Converted 1906 to Motor coach 376. |
| 377 | 3 | 9751 | Converted 1906 for electric working. |
| 378 | 3[DT3] | 6700 | Converted 1921 for electric working. Later converted to DT3. |
| 379 | 3 | 9760 | Converted 1921 for electric working. |
| 380 | 3 | 9752 | Converted 1905 for electric working. |
| 381 | B3[3] | 9753 | Converted 1907 for electric working. |
| 382–383 | B3[3] | 9765–9766 | Converted 1921 for electric working. |
| 384 | B3 | 2760 | Converted 1908 to Motor coach 384. |
| 385–386 | B3[3] | 9767–9768 | Converted 1921 for electric working. |
| 387 | B3 | 2761 | Converted 1908 to Motor coach 387. |
| 388 | B3 | 2765 | Converted 1906 to Motor coach 388. |
| 389 | B3[3] | 9769 | Converted 1921 for electric working. |
| 390 | 3[DT3] | 6701 | Converted 1921 for electric working. Later converted to DT3. |
| 391 | 3 | 9761 | Converted 1921 for electric working. |
| 392–393 | 3 | 9754–9755 | Converted 1906 for electric working. |
| 394 | 3[DT3] | 6702 | Converted 1921 for electric working. Later converted to DT3. |
| 395–396 | B2[3] | 9770–9771 | Converted 1921 for electric working. |
| 397–398 | B2 | | Converted 1906 to Motor coaches 397–398. |
| 399 | B2[3] | 9772 | Converted 1921 for electric working. |
| 400–401 | 2[3][DT3] | 6703–6704 | Converted 1921 for electric working. Later converted to DT3. |
| 402–403 | 2[3] | 9756–9757 | Converted 1906 for electric working. |
| 404 | 2[3][DT3] | 6705 | Converted 1921 for electric working. Later converted to DT3. |
| 405–406 | 1 | 9709–9710 | Converted 1921 for electric working. |
| 407–408 | 1 | 9703–9704 | Converted 1906 for electric working. |
| 409 | 1 | 9711 | Converted 1921 for electric working. |
| 410–411 | C[1] | 9712–9713 | Converted 1921 for electric working. |
| 412 | C[1] | 9705 | Converted 1906 for electric working. |
| 413 | C | | Scrapped by Met Rly. |
| 414 | C[1] | 9714 | Converted 1921 for electric working. |
| 415 | 1 | 9715 | Converted 1921 for electric working. |
| 416 | 3 | 9762 | Converted 1924 for electric working. |
| 417–418 | B3 | 2762–2763 | Converted 1908 to Motor coaches 417–418. |

## Dreadnought & Derived Stocks

| Numbers | Class | Year | LT Renumbering | Remarks |
|---|---|---|---|---|
| 419–422 | 1 | 1910 | | New bodies on underframes from 1905 Trailer cars. |
| 423–424 | 3 | 1910 | | New bodies on underframes from 1905 Trailer cars. |
| 425–428 | B3 | 1910 | | New bodies on underframes from 1905 Trailer cars. |
| 429–436 | 1 | 1912 | | |
| 437–440 | 3 | 1912 | | |
| 441–448 | B3 | 1912 | | |
| 449–459 | 1 | 1920 | | |
| 460–462 | 1 | 1920 | 9716–9718 | Wired to run in MV stock trains. |
| 463–475 | 3 | 1920 | | |
| 476 | 3 | 1920 | | Wired to run in MV stock trains. |
| 477–482 | B3 | 1920 | 6706–6711 | Wired to run in MV stock trains. Converted to DT3. |
| 483–485 | B3 | 1920 | | |
| 486–490 | B3 | 1920 | | |
| 491–496 | B3* | 1923 | | |
| 497–499 | 3 | 1923 | | Wired to run in MV stock trains. |
| 500–501 | 3 | 1923 | 9774–9775 | Wired to run in MV stock trains. |
| 502–504 | 1 | 1923 | | |
| 505–507 | 1 | 1923 | 9719–9331 | |
| 508–510 | C | 1923 | | Wired to run in MV stock trains. |
| 511–520 | 1 | 1929 | 9722–9731 | 1929 MW Stock. |
| 521–525 | 3 | 1929 | 9776–9780 | 1929 MW Stock. |
| 526–535 | DT3 | 1929 | 6712–6721 | 1929 MW Stock. |
| 536–549 | DT3 | 1931 | 6722–6735 | 1931 MW Stock |
| 550–568 | 3 | 1931 | 9781–9799 | 1931 MW Stock. |
| 569–582 | 1 | 1931 | 9732–9745 | 1931 MW Stock. |

# APPENDIX 2
# LPTB RENUMBERING OF METROPOLITAN RAILWAY ELECTRIC STOCK

## Key to abbreviations

| | |
|---|---|
| T | Trailer car |
| DT | Driving Trailer car |
| C | Composite |
| 1DT | First Class DT |
| CDT | Composite DT |
| B3 (B2) | Third (Second) Class Brake Carriage |
| C2 | First & Second Class Composite carriage |
| C3 | First & Third Class Composite carriage |
| Bogie | Bogie Stock |
| D19** | Dreadnought Stock |

## MOTOR COACHES

| LPTB Number | Met Number | Type | Remarks |
|---|---|---|---|
| 2200 | 71 | 1905 | |
| 2201 | 73 | 1905 | |
| 2202 | 80 | 1905 | |
| 2203 | 74 | 1905 | |
| 2204 | 81 | 1905 | |
| 2205 | 76 | 1905 | |
| 2206 | 82 | 1905 | |
| 2207 | 79 | 1905 | |
| 2208–2247 | 126–165 | 1905 | Ex H&C Joint stock. Car 161 scrapped before carrying allocated LPTB number. |
| 2500 | 30 | 1905 | Loaned to GN&C, thence to LPTB. |
| 2501 | 32 | 1905 | Loaned to GN&C, thence to LPTB. |
| 2502 | 31 | 1905 | Loaned to GN&C, thence to LPTB. |
| 2503 | 34 | 1905 | Loaned to GN&C, thence to LPTB. |
| 2504 | 33 | 1905 | Loaned to GN&C, thence to LPTB. |
| 2505 | 35 | 1905 | Loaned to GN&C, thence to LPTB. |
| 2525 | 38 | 1905 | |
| 2537 | 72 | 1905 | |
| 2538 | 75 | 1905 | |
| 2539 | 78 | 1905 | |
| 2540–2545 | 57–62 | 1905 | |
| 2546–2552 | 99–105 | 1913 | |
| 2553 | 63 | 1905 | |
| 2554 | 64 | 1905 | Car scrapped by LPTB without carrying allocated number. |
| 2555–2558 | 65–68 | 1905 | |
| 2559 | 70 | 1905 | |
| 2560 | 77 | 1905 | |
| 2561–2562 | 106–107 | 1921 | |
| 2563–2572 | 116–125 | 1921 | Allocated for Circle Service. |
| 2573–2580 | 108–115 | 1921 | |
| 2581–2586 | 93–98 | 1913 | Allocated for Circle Service. Cars 96–98 reduced to motors at driving end only. |
| 2587–2596 | 83–92 | 1913 | Allocated for Circle Service. |
| 2598–2599 | 198–199 | 1924 | |
| 2700–2705 | 200–205 | 1927MW | |
| 2706–2711 | 206–211 | 1927MV | |
| 2712–2741 | 212–241 | 1929MW | 232–241 equipped with roller bearings. |

| LPTB Number | Met Number | Type | Remarks |
|---|---|---|---|
| 2742–2759 | 242–259 | 1931MW | Equipped with roller bearings. |
| 2760 | 384 | Bogie | |
| 2761 | 387 | Bogie | |
| 2762–2763 | 417–418 | Bogie | |
| 2764 | 376 | Bogie | |
| 2765 | 388 | Bogie | |
| 2766–2767 | 397–398 | Bogie | |
| 2768 | 46 | 1905 | Rebuilt by Met as Composite M/C 46. |
| 2769 | 69 | 1905 | Rebuilt by Met as Composite M/C 69. |
| 2900 | 167 | 1902 | Ex GN&C wood car. |
| 2901 | 166 | 1906 | Ex GN&C steel car. |
| 2902–2903 | 168–169 | 1902/6 | Ex GN&C steel/wood car. Scrapped without carrying allocated LPTB numbers. |
| 2904 | 170 | 1902 | Ex GN&C. |
| 2905 | 182 | 1902 | Ex GN&C. |
| 2906 | 171 | 1902 | Ex GN&C. |
| 2907 | 183 | 1902 | Ex GN&C. |
| 2908 | 172 | 1902 | Ex GN&C. |
| 2909 | 186 | 1902 | Ex GN&C. |
| 2910 | 173 | 1902 | Ex GN&C. |
| 2911 | 187 | 1902 | Ex GN&C. |
| 2912 | 174 | 1902 | Ex GN&C. |
| 2913 | 188 | 1902 | Ex GN&C. |
| 2914 | 175 | 1902 | Ex GN&C. |
| 2915 | 194 | 1902 | Ex GN&C. |
| 2916 | 176 | 1902 | Ex GN&C. |
| 2917 | 195 | 1902 | Ex GN&C. |
| 2918 | 177 | 1902 | Ex GN&C. |
| 2919 | 196 | 1902 | Ex GN&C. |
| 2920 | 178 | 1902 | Ex GN&C. |
| 2921 | 197 | 1902 | Ex GN&C. |
| 2922 | 179 | 1902 | Ex GN&C. |
| 2924 | 180 | 1902 | Ex GN&C. |
| 2926 | 181 | 1902 | Ex GN&C. |
| 2928 | 184 | 1902 | Ex GN&C. |
| 2930 | 185 | 1902 | Ex GN&C. |
| 2932 | 189 | 1902 | Ex GN&C. |
| 2934 | 190 | 1902 | Ex GN&C. |
| 2936 | 191 | 1902 | Ex GN&C. |

## TRAILER COACHES

| LPTB Number | Met Number | Type | Remarks |
|---|---|---|---|
| 6211 | 6 | [1912]CDT | Ex 1T 73. |
| 6212 | 5 | [1912]CDT | Ex 1T 72. |
| 6220 | 41 | 1905 3DT | |
| 6221 | 39 | 1905 3DT | |
| 6222 | 43 | 1905 3DT | |
| 6223 | 45 | 1905 3DT | |
| 6224 | 50 | 1905 3DT | |
| 6225–6264 | 120–159 | 1905 3DT | Ex Hammersmith & City Joint stock. |
| 6500–6519 | 1–20 | 1904 1DT | |
| 6520 | 21 | 1905 1DT | |
| 6521–6523 | 23–25 | 1905 1DT | |
| 6524 | 27 | 1905 1DT | |
| 6525–6526 | 31–32 | 1905 1DT | |

| LPTB Number | Met Number | Type | Remarks |
|---|---|---|---|
| 6527–6529 | 35–37 | 1905 1DT | |
| 6530–6531 | 39–40 | 1905 1DT | |
| 6532 | 43 | 1905 1DT | |
| 6533 | 46 | 1905 1DT | |
| 6534 | 52 | 1905 1DT | |
| 6535 | 53 | 1905 1DT | Rebuilt to 1919 1DT. |
| 6536 | 51 | 1905 1DT | Allocated to Circle Service. |
| 6537 | 47 | 1905 1DT | Allocated to Circle Service. |
| 6538 | 49 | 1905 1DT | Allocated to Circle Service. |
| 6539–6541 | 90–92 | 1921 1DT | Allocated to Circle Service. |
| 6542 | 77 | 1912 1DT | Allocated to Circle Service. |
| 6543–6550 | 79–86 | 1912 1DT | Allocated to Circle Service. |
| 6551–6553 | 87–89 | 1921 1DT | Allocated to Circle Service. |
| 6554 | 54 | 1905 1DT | |
| 6555 | 55 | 1905 1DT | Rebuilt to 1919 1DT. |
| 6556 | 56 | 1905 1DT | |
| 6557 | 106 | 1921 1DT | Built 1924 for British Empire Exhibition, Wembley. Allocated to E.London Line service. |
| 6558 | 59 | 1905 DT | Converted 1935 by LPTB from 1T. |
| 6559 | 70 | 1905 1T | Converted 1935 by LPTB to 1DT. |
| 6560 | | 1906 1DT | Converted by LPTB from Composite car 6585 (ex Met 8). |
| 6561 | 60 | 1905 1T | Converted 1935 by LPTB to DT. |
| 6562 | 57 | 1905 1T | Converted 1935 by LPTB to DT. |
| 6580–6583 | 1–4 | [1912] CDT | Ex 1T 29. |
| 6584 | 7 | [1912] CDT | Ex 1T 74. |
| 6585 | 8 | [1912] CDT | Ex 3T 65. Later 1T 6580? |
| 6586 | 9 | [1912] CDT | Ex 3T 69. |
| 6587 | 10 | [1912] CDT | Ex 3T 71. |
| 6590 | 37 | 1905 3DT | |
| 6592 | 40 | 1905 3DT | |
| 6593 | 42 | 1905 3DT | |
| 6596 | 47 | 1905 3DT | |
| 6598 | 49 | 1905 3DT | |
| 6700 | 378 | Bogie 3[DT3] | Converted 1921. Later converted to DT3. |
| 6701 | 390 | Bogie 3[DT3] | Converted 1921. Later converted to DT3. |
| 6702 | 394 | Bogie 3[DT3] | Converted 1921. Later converted to DT3. |
| 6703–6704 | 400–401 | Bogie 2[3][DT3] | Converted 1921. Later converted to DT3. |
| 6705 | 404 | Bogie 2[3][DT3] | Converted 1921. Later converted to DT3. |
| 6706–6711 | 477–482 | D1920 B3[DT3] | Wired to run in MV stock, then converted to DT3. |
| 6712–6721 | 526–535 | 1929MW DT3 | |
| 6722–6735 | 536–549 | 1931MW DT3 | |
| 6901 | 160 | 1902 3DT | Ex GN & C, wood body. |
| 6902 | 172 | 1902 3DT | Ex GN & C, wood body. |
| 6903 | 161 | 1902 3DT | Ex GN & C, wood body. |
| 6905 | 162 | 1902 3DT | Ex GN & C, wood body. |
| 6907 | 163 | 1902 3DT | Ex GN & C, wood body. |
| 6909 | 164 | 1902 3DT | Ex GN & C, wood body. |
| 6911 | 165 | 1902 3DT | Ex GN & C, wood body. Car scrapped by LPTB without carrying allocated number. |
| 6913 | 166 | 1902 3DT | Ex GN & C, wood body. |
| 6915 | 168 | 1902 3DT | Ex GN & C, wood body. |
| 6917 | 177 | 1902 3DT | Ex GN & C, wood body. |
| 6919 | 178 | 1902 3DT | Ex GN & C, wood body. |
| 9200 | 62 | 1905 1T | |
| 9201 | 67 | 1905 1DT | |
| 9203 | 69 | 1905 1DT | |
| 9210 | 34 | 1905 3T | |
| 9211 | 60 | 1905 3T | |
| 9212 | 62 | 1905 3T | |
| 9220 | 50 | 1905 CT | Ex H&C Joint Stock. |
| 9221–9259 | 11–50 | 1905 CT | Ex H&C Joint Stock. |
| 9401 | 58 | 1905 1T | |
| 9410 | 78 | 1912 1DT | Demoted to 1T by removal of driving equipment. |
| 9477 | [61] | 1905 3T | Converted by LPTB from 1T 9404 (ex Met 61). |
| 9478 | [65] | 1905 3T | Converted by LPTB from 1T 9407 (ex Met 65). |
| 9479 | 38 | 1905 3DT | Converted by Met to 3T. |
| 9480 | 44 | 1905 3DT | Converted by Met to 3T. |
| 9481 | 46 | 1905 3DT | Converted by Met to 3T. |
| 9482 | 48 | 1905 3DT | Converted by Met to 3T. |
| 9483–9512 | 1–30 | 1904 3T | |
| 9513–9515 | 31–33 | 1905 3T | |
| 9516–9517 | 35–36 | 1905 3T | |
| 9518–9526 | 51–59 | 1905 3T | |
| 9527 | 61 | 1905 3T | |
| 9528–9529 | 63–64 | 1905 3T | |
| 9530 | 66 | 1905 3T | |
| 9531 | 67 | 1905 3T | Rebuilt to 1919 3T. |
| 9532 | 68 | 1905 3T | |
| 9533 | 70 | 1905 3T | |
| 9534–9538 | 72–76 | 1905 3T | |
| 9539–9541 | 84–86 | 1913 3T | |
| 9542–9545 | 80–83 | 1913 3T | |
| 9546–9548 | 77–79 | 1913 3T | Allocated to Circle Service. |
| 9549–9581 | 87–119 | 1921 3T | Allocated to Circle Service. |
| 9582–9599 | 191–208 | 1904 3T | Ex motor cars. |
| 9700 | 361 | Bogie 1 | Converted 1906. |
| 9701 | 364 | Bogie 1 | Converted 1905. |
| 9702 | 368 | Bogie C[1] | Converted 1906. |
| 9703–9704 | 407–408 | Bogie 1 | Converted 1906. |
| 9705 | 412 | Bogie C[1] | Converted 1906. |
| 9706 | 363 | Bogie 1 | Converted 1924. |
| 9707–9708 | 366–367 | Bogie C[1] | Converted 1921. |
| 9709–9710 | 405–406 | Bogie 1 | Converted 1921. |
| 9711 | 409 | Bogie 1 | Converted 1921. |
| 9712–9713 | 410–411 | Bogie C[1] | Converted 1921. |
| 9714 | 414 | Bogie C[1] | Converted 1921. |
| 9715 | 415 | Bogie 1 | Converted 1921. |
| 9716–9718 | 460–462 | D1920 1 | Wired to run in MV stock trains. |
| 9719–9721 | 505–507 | D1923 1 | |
| 9722–9731 | 511–520 | 1929MW 1 | |
| 9732–9745 | 569–582 | 1931MW 1 | |
| 9746 | 365 | Bogie C | Converted 1905. |
| 9748 | 369 | Bogie 2 (3) | Converted 1906. |
| 9749 | 372 | Bogie 3 [3] | Converted 1905. |
| 9750 | 373 | Bogie B2 [3] | Converted 1907. |
| 9751 | 377 | Bogie 3 | Converted 1906. |
| 9752 | 380 | Bogie 3 | Converted 1905. |
| 9753 | 381 | Bogie B3[3] | Converted 1907. |
| 9754–9755 | 392–393 | Bogie 3 | Converted 1906. |
| 9756–9757 | 402–403 | Bogie 2[3] | Converted 1906. |
| 9758–9759 | 370–371 | Bogie 2(3) | Converted 1921. |
| 9760 | 379 | Bogie 3 | Converted 1921. |
| 9761 | 391 | Bogie 3 | Converted 1921. |
| 9762 | 416 | Bogie 3 | Converted 1924. |
| 9763–9764 | 374–375 | Bogie B2[3] | Converted 1921. |
| 9765–9766 | 382–383 | Bogie B3[3] | Converted 1921. |
| 9767–9768 | 385–386 | Bogie B3[3] | Converted 1921. |
| 9769 | 389 | Bogie B3[3] | Converted 1921. |
| 9770–9771 | 395–396 | Bogie B2[3] | Converted 1921. |
| 9772 | 399 | Bogie B2[3] | Converted 1921. |
| 9774–9775 | 500–501 | D1920 3 | Wired to run in MV stock trains. |

| LPTB Number | Met Number | Type | Remarks |
|---|---|---|---|
| 9776–9780 | 521–525 | 1929 MW 3 | |
| 9781–9799 | 550–568 | 1931 MW 3 | |
| 9900 | 93 | 1902/6 1T | Ex-GN&C Stock. |
| 9901 | 94 | 1902/6 1T | Ex-GN&C Stock. Car scrapped by LPTB without carrying allocated number. |
| 9902 | 95 | 1902/6 1T | Ex-GN&C Stock. |
| 9903–9904 | 96–97 | 1902/6 1T | Ex-GN&C Stock. Cars scrapped by LPTB without carrying allocated number. |
| 9905–9907 | 98–100 | 1902/6 1T | Ex-GN&C Stock. |
| 9908–9909 | 101–102 | 1902/6 1T | Ex-GN&C Stock. Cars scrapped by LPTB without carrying allocated number. |
| 9910–9911 | 103–104 | 1902/6 1T | Ex-GN&C Stock. |
| 9912 | 105 | 1902/6 1T | Ex-GN&C Stock. Car scrapped by LPTB without carrying allocated number. |
| 9950–9952 | 169–171 | 1902 3T | Ex GN & C, wood body. |
| 9953–9954 | 173–174 | 1902 3T | Ex GN & C, wood body. |
| 9957 | 179 | 1902 3T | Ex GN & C, steel body. |
| 9958–9960 | 180–182 | 1902 3T | Ex GN & C, steel body. Car scrapped by LPTB without carrying allocated number. |
| 9961 | 183 | 1902 3T | Ex GN & C, steel body. |
| 9962–9966 | 184–188 | 1902 3T | Ex GN & C, steel body. Car scrapped by LPTB without carrying allocated number. |
| 9967 | 189 | 1902 3T | Ex GN & C, steel body. |
| 9968 | 190 | 1902 3T | Ex GN & C, steel body. Car scrapped by LPTB without carrying allocated number. |

## METROPOLITAN RAILWAY GOODS AND NON-PASSENGER STOCK

| Met No | Type | LPTB/LNER No | Built | Builder/Remarks | Scrapped |
|---|---|---|---|---|---|
| 1 | Ballast | BW41 | 1866 | | 7. 6.39 |
| 2 | Ballast | BW42 | 1866 | | 30. 5.40 |
| 3 | Ballast | MW500 | 1866 | Conv. to Match wagon by Met. | 15.10.43 |
| 4 | Ballast | BW43 | 1866 | | 1. 8.39 |
| 5 | Ballast | J680 | 1866 | Conv. to Jib carrier by Met. | 1. 5.47 |
| 6 | Ballast | BW44 | 1869 | | 7. 6.39 |
| 7 | Ballast | BW45 | 1869 | | 7. 6.39 |
| 8 | Ballast | BW46 | 1869 | | 1. 8.39 |
| 9 | Ballast | BW47 | 1869 | | 31. 5.40 |
| 10 | Ballast | BW48 | 1869 | | 7. 6.39 |
| 11 | Ballast | BW49 | 1878 | Ashbury | 1. 8.30 |
| 12 | Ballast | BW50 | 1878 | Ashbury | 28. 5.42 |
| 13 | Ballast | BW51 | 1878 | Ashbury | 28. 5.42 |
| 14 | Ballast | BW52 | 1878 | Ashbury | 1. 8.39 |
| 15 | Ballast | BW53 | 1878 | Ashbury | 7. 6.39 |
| 16 | Ballast | BW54 | 1880 | Ashbury | 31. 5.40 |
| 17 | Ballast | BW55 | 1880 | Ashbury | 28. 5.42 |
| 18 | Ballast | BW56 | 1880 | Ashbury | 14. 7.39 |
| 19 | Ballast | BW57 | 1880 | Ashbury | 13. 9.54 |
| 20 | Ballast | BW58 | 1880 | Ashbury | 18.11.49 |
| 21 | Ballast | BW59 | 1881 | Ashbury | 14. 7.39 |
| 22 | Ballast | BW60 | 1881 | Ashbury | 7. 6.39 |
| 23 | Ballast | BW61 | 1881 | Ashbury | 28. 5.42 |
| 24 | Ballast | BW62 | 1881 | Ashbury | 27. 1.53 |
| 25 | Ballast | BW63 | 1881 | Ashbury | 7. 6.39 |
| 26 | Ballast | BW64 | 1881 | | 6. 8.55 |
| 27 | Ballast | BW65 | 1881 | | 7. 6.39 |
| 28 | Ballast | BW66 | 1881 | | 14. 7.39 |
| 29 | Ballast | BW67 | 1881 | | 7. 6.39 |
| 30 | Ballast | BW68 | 1881 | | 4. 8.49 |
| 31 | Ballast | MW501 | 1882 | to Match wagon by Met. | 1. 5.43 |

| Met No | Type | LPTB/LNER No | Built | Builder/Remarks | Scrapped |
|---|---|---|---|---|---|
| 32 | Ballast | MW502 | 1882 | to Match wagon by Met. | 1. 5.43 |
| 33 | Ballast | BW69 | 1882 | | 13. 9.54 |
| 34 | Ballast | BW70 | 1882 | | 30. 4.47 |
| 35 | Ballast | BW71 | 1882 | | 7. 6.39 |
| 36 | Ballast | BW72 | 1882 | | 7. 6.39 |
| 37 | Ballast | BW73 | 1882 | | 14. 7.39 |
| 38 | Ballast | BW74 | 1882 | | 25.10.43 |
| 39 | Ballast | BW75 | 1882 | | 7. 6.39 |
| 40 | Ballast | BW76 | 1882 | | 13. 1.53 |
| 41 | Ballast | BW77 | 1882 | | 30. 4.47 |
| 42 | Ballast | J681 | 1882 | to Crane runner by Met. | |
| 43 | Ballast | BW78 | 1882 | | 28. 5.42 |
| 44 | Ballast | BW79 | 1882 | | 31. 5.40 |
| 45 | Ballast | BW80 | 1882 | | 7. 6.39 |
| 46 | Ballast | BW81 | 1882 | | 8. 9.55 |
| 47 | Ballast | BW82 | 1882 | | 7. 6.39 |
| 48 | Ballast | BW83 | 1882 | | 14. 7.39 |
| 49 | Ballast | BW84 | 1882 | | 13. 9.54 |
| 50 | Ballast | J682 | 1886 | to Crane runner J682 ?.?.?; scr ? | |
| 51 | Low open goods | 63400 | 1891 | Cravens; Reb. as Open goods to runner for M&GN crane 577 7.12.1940 | 58 |
| 52 | Low open goods | 634001 | 1891 | Reb. as Open goods | 23.10.43 |
| 53 | Low open goods | | 1891 | | |
| 54 | Low open goods | BW128 | 1891 | | 6. 4.62 |
| 55 | Low open goods | 634002 | 1891 | Reb. as Open goods | 9. 3.46 |
| 56 | Low open goods | 634003 | 1891 | Reb. as Open goods | 29. 6.46 |
| 57 | Low open goods | | | Reb. as Open goods | pre.33 |
| 58 | Low open goods | 634004 | 1891 | Reb. as Open goods | 25. 9.43 |
| 59 | Low open goods | BW235 | 1891 | | 23. 8.55 |
| 60 | Low open goods | BW125 | 1891 | | 26.10.56 |
| 61 | Low open goods | BW244 | 1891 | | 24. 1.66 |
| 62 | Low open goods | BW239 | 1891 | | 24. 1.49 |
| 63 | Low open goods | 634005 | 1891 | Reb. as Open goods | 5. 9.42 |
| 64 | Low open goods | 634006 | 1891 | Reb. as Open goods | 12.11.49 |
| 65 | Low open goods | BW30 | 1891 | | |
| 66 | Low open goods | 634007 | 1891 | Reb. as Open goods | 9. 1.43 |
| 67 | Low open goods | 634008 | 1891 | Reb. as Open goods | 6. 8.49 |
| 68 | Low open goods | 634009 | 1891 | Reb. as Open goods | 14. 8.43 |
| 69 | Low open goods | BW242 | 1891 | | 24. 1.66 |
| 70 | Low open goods | 634010 | 1891 | Reb. as Open goods | 8. 1.38 |
| 71 | Low open goods | 634011 | 1891 | Reb. as Open goods | 11. 2.50 |
| 72 | Low open goods | 634012 | 1891 | Reb. as Open goods | 16. 3.46 |
| 73 | Low open goods | 634013 | 1891 | Reb. as Open goods to Crane runner 962204 2.12.44. | 11.53 |
| 74 | Low open goods | | 1891 | | pre 33 |
| 75 | Low open goods | BW130 | 1891 | | 24. 1.66 |
| 76 | Low open goods | 634014 | 1891 | Reb. as Open goods | 29.10.38 |
| 77 | Low open goods | BW152 | 1891 | | 6. 8.55 |
| 78 | Low open goods | 634015 | 1891 | Reb. as Open goods | 9.11.46 |
| 79 | Low open goods | 634016 | 1891 | Reb. as Open goods | 8. 6.40 |
| 80 | Low open goods | BW16 | 1891 | | 6. 8.55 |
| 81 | Low open goods | BW38 | 1891 | | |
| 82 | Low open goods | BW6 | 1891 | | |
| 83 | Low open goods | BW19 | 1891 | | 23. 8.55 |
| 84 | Low open goods | 634017 | 1891 | Reb. as Open goods | 1. 4.44 |
| 85 | Low open goods | BW9 | 1891 | | 23. 8.55 |
| 86 | Low open goods | BW230 | 1891 | | 6. 8.55 |
| 87 | Low open goods | BW21 | 1891 | | |
| 88 | Low open goods | BW1 | 1891 | | 1. 1.53 |
| 89 | Low open goods | BW31 | 1891 | | 23. 8.55 |
| 90 | Low open goods | 634018 | 1891 | Reb. as Open goods | 13.11.43 |
| 91 | Low open goods | BW28 | 1891 | | 9.12.52 |
| 92 | Low open goods | BW197 | 1891 | | 6. 8.55 |
| 93 | Low open goods | BW24 | 1891 | | |
| 94 | Low open goods | BW126 | 1891 | | 6. 4.62 |
| 95 | Low open goods | 634019 | 1891 | Reb. as Open goods; to shops internal use Ex 0415 29.11.38 | |

| Met No | Type | LPTB/LNER No | Built | Builder/Remarks | Scrapped |
|---|---|---|---|---|---|
| 96 | Low open goods | BW2 | 1891 | | |
| 97 | Low open goods | 634020 | 1891 | Reb. as Open goods | 3.52 |
| 98 | Low open goods | BW180 | 1891 | | 6. 4.62 |
| 99 | Low open goods | BW240 | 1891 | | 6. 8.55 |
| 100 | Low open goods | 634021 | 1891 | Reb. as Open goods | 29. 5.43 |
| 101 | Low open goods | 634022 | 1893 | Cravens. Reb. as Open goods | 6. 9.41 |
| 102 | Low open goods | BW139 | 1893 | Reb. as Open goods | 26. 1.46 |
| 103 | Low open goods | 634023 | 1893 | Reb. as Open goods | 30.11.40 |
| 104 | Low open goods | 634024 | 1893 | Reb. as Open goods | 28. 2.48 |
| 105 | Low open goods | 634025 | 1893 | Reb. as Open goods | |
| 106 | Low open goods | BW243 | 1893 | | 23. 8.55 |
| 107 | Low open goods | BW191 | 1893 | | 19. 9.55 |
| 108 | Low open goods | 634026 | 1893 | Reb. as Open goods | 6. 9.41 |
| 109 | Low open goods | 634027 | 1893 | Reb. as Open goods | 8. 1.38 |
| 110 | Low open goods | BW248 | 1893 | Reb. as Tunnel Line Cleaning wagon TLC2 8.6.48 | |
| 111 | Low open goods | 634028 | 1893 | Reb. as Open goods | 21. 7.45 |
| 112 | Low open goods | BW175 | 1893 | | 24. 1.66 |
| 113 | Low open goods | BW15 | 1893 | | |
| 114 | Low open goods | | 1893 | | |
| 115 | Low open goods | BW3 | | | |
| 116 | Low open goods | BW209 | 1893 | | 19. 5.53 |
| 117 | Low open goods | 634029 | 1893 | Reb. as Open goods; w/drawn 2.8.41; to MoS 23.8.41 | |
| 118 | Low open goods | BW159 | 1893 | | 24. 1.66 |
| 119 | Low open goods | BW172 | 1893 | | 13. 8.51 |
| 120 | Low open goods | 634030 | 1893 | Reb. as Open goods | 8. 1.38 |
| 121 | Low open goods | BW147 | 1893 | | 6. 4.62 |
| 122 | Low open goods | BW148 | 1893 | | 1. 1.53 |
| 123 | Low open goods | BW164 | 1893 | | 1. 7.62 |
| 124 | Low open goods | BW179 | 1893 | | 26.10.56 |
| 125 | Low open goods | BW11 | 1893 | | |
| 126 | Low open goods | SL931 | 1893 | Reb. as Open goods | 14. 3.68 |
| 127 | Low open goods | SL940 | 1893 | Reb. as Open goods | 6. 4.62 |
| 128 | Low open goods | SL920 | 1893 | Reb. as Open goods | 6. 8.55 |
| 129 | Low open goods | SL914 | 1893 | Reb. as Open goods | 6. 4.62 |
| 130 | Open goods | A957 | 1893 | Cravens | 14. 3.68 |
| 131 | Open goods | A956 | 1893 | | 19.11.68 |
| 132 | Open goods | SL911 | 1893 | | 6. 8.55 |
| 133 | Open goods | BW252 | 1896 | | 1. 6.53 |
| 134 | Open goods | BW253 | 1896 | | 20.11.52 |
| 135 | Open goods | A944 | 1896 | 19.11.68 | |
| 136 | Open goods | A958 | 1896 | 19.11.68 | |
| 137 | Open goods | BW254 | 1896 | | 23. 8.55 |
| 138 | Open goods | A950 | 1896 | 19.11.68 | |
| 139 | Open goods | SL939 | 1896 | | 6. 4.62 |
| 140 | Open goods | SL925 | 1896 | | 6. 8.55 |
| 141 | Open goods | A954 | 1896 | 19.11.68 | |
| 142 | Open goods | A959 | 1896 | 19.11.68 | |
| 143 | Open goods | A943 | 1896 | 19.11.68 | |
| 144 | Open goods | A949 | 1896 | 14. 3.68 | |
| 145 | Open goods | SL909 | 1896 | | 6. 4.62 |
| 146 | Open goods | SL917 | 1896 | 19.11.68 | |
| 147 | Open goods | SL969 | 1896 | | 6. 4.62 |
| 148 | Open goods | SL924 | 1896 | | 6. 4.62 |
| 149 | Open goods | | 1896 | | |
| 150 | Open goods | SL932 | 1896 | | 6. 4.62 |
| 151 | Open goods | BW255 | 1896 | Reb. to Low Open goods 1904 | 1. 5.70 |
| 152 | Open goods | BW256 | 1896 | | 6. 8.55 |
| 153 | Open goods | SL905 | 1896 | Ren. SL929 | 23. 3.55 |
| 154 | Open goods | BW257 | 1896 | | 8. 1.48 |
| 155 | Open goods | SL961 | 1896 | | 16.12.69 |
| 156 | Low open goods | BW12 | 1893 | Ashbury. to MW518 10.1.38 | |
| 157 | Low open goods | BW25 | 1893 | | |
| 158 | Low open goods | BW169 | 1893 | | 26.10.56 |
| 159 | Low open goods | 634031 | 1893 | Reb. as Open goods | 21. 1.50 |
| 160 | Low open goods | 634032 | 1893 | Reb. as Open goods; t/f 24.2.40 to int. user Ex 0359 9.3.40 | |

| Met No | Type | LPTB/LNER No | Built | Builder/Remarks | Scrapped |
|---|---|---|---|---|---|
| 161 | Low open goods | 634033 | 1893 | Reb. as Open goods | 4. 3.39 |
| 162 | Low open goods | BW142 | 1893 | | 6. 8.55 |
| 163 | Low open goods | 634034 | 1893 | Reb. as Open goods | 26. 1.46 |
| 164 | Low open goods | BW161 | 1893 | | 7. 7.53 |
| 165 | Low open goods | BW127 | 1893 | | 6. 4.62 |
| 166 | Low open goods | 634035 | 1896 | | 5.12.42 |
| 167 | Low open goods | 634036 | 1896 | | 8. 1.38 |
| 168 | Low open goods | 634037 | 1896 | | 30. 3.46 |
| 169 | Low open goods | 634038 | 1896 | w/d 31.10.42. t/f to MoS Bicester | 13. 3.43 |
| 170 | Low open goods | 634039 | 1896 | t/f to service stock DE634039 8.10.49 | 4.55 |
| 171 | Low open goods | 634040 | 1896 | | 13.11.43 |
| 172 | Low open goods | 634041 | 1896 | t/f to MoS 2.8.41 | |
| 173 | Low open goods | 634042 | 1896 | | 29. 5.43 |
| 174 | Low open goods | BW29 | 1896 | | |
| 175 | Low open goods | BW14 | 1896 | | |
| 176 | Low open goods | BW215 | 1896 | | 19. 9.55 |
| 177 | Low open goods | 634043 | 1896 | | 21. 9.46 |
| 178 | Low open goods | 634044 | 1896 | | 16. 3.46 |
| 179 | Low open goods | BW182 | 1896 | to Match wagon MW532 10.1.38 | |
| 180 | Low open goods | BW220 | 1896 | | 6. 8.55 |
| 181 | Low open goods | 634045 | 1896 | t/f to Int. User Ex???? 26.11.38 | |
| 182 | Low open goods | 634046 | 1896 | | 22.12.45 |
| 183 | Low open goods | 634047 | 1896 | | 28. 9.40 |
| 184 | Low open goods | | 1896 | to Match wagon by Met.; to MW505; BW263 7.3.41 | |
| 185 | Low open goods | BW228 | 1896 | to MW511 10.1.38 | 28.10.52 |
| 186 | Low open goods | BW210 | 1896 | | 15. 9.55 |
| 187 | Low open goods | 634048 | 1896 | | 15.11.41 |
| 188 | Low open goods | 634049 | 1896 | | 11. 5.46 |
| 189 | Low open goods | BW13 | 1896 | | |
| 190 | Low open goods | 634050 | 1896 | | |
| 191 | Low open goods | 634051 | 1896 | | 17. 8.46 |
| 192 | Low open goods | 634052 | 1896 | | 8. 1.38 |
| 193 | Low open goods | BW32 | 1896 | | |
| 194 | Low open goods | 634053 | 1896 | | 15. 2.47 |
| 195 | Low open goods | 634054 | 1896 | t/f to Int. User Ex 0360 6.4.40 | |
| 196 | Low open goods | 634055 | 1896 | | 5. 8.39 |
| 197 | Low open goods | BW247 | 1896 | | 12. 7.50 |
| 198 | Low open goods | 634056 | 1896 | | 25. 6.38 |
| 199 | Low open goods | | 1896 | | |
| 200 | Low open goods | 634057 | 1896 | | 28. 1.50 |
| 201 | Low open goods | BW216 | 1896 | | 23. 8.55 |
| 202 | Low open goods | BW196 | 1896 | | 19. 5.53 |
| 203 | Low open goods | BW234 | 1896 | | 25. 8.53 |
| 204 | Low open goods | 634058 | 1896 | | 4. 3.44 |
| 205 | Low open goods | BW8 | 1896 | | |
| 206 | Covered goods | 634186 | 1896 | Birmingham RCW | 20. 6.42 |
| 207 | Covered goods | 634187 | 1896 | | 1. 6.46 |
| 208 | Covered goods | 634188 | 1896 | | 30. 6.45 |
| 209 | Covered goods | 634189 | 1896 | | 7.10.44 |
| 210 | Covered goods | 634190 | 1896 | | 4. 1.47 |
| 211 | Covered goods | 634191 | 1896 | Sold 29.6.40 | |
| 212 | Low open goods | 634059 | 1897 | Reb. as Open goods. Ashbury | 31. 5.47 |
| 213 | Low open goods | 634060 | 1897 | Reb. as Open goods | 6. 1.45 |
| 214 | Low open goods | 634061 | 1897 | Reb. as Open goods | 19.10.46 |
| 215 | Low open goods | BW185 | 1897 | to MW515 10.1.38 | 16.12.69 |
| 216 | Low open goods | BW35 | 1897 | | |
| 217 | Low open goods | BW112 | 1897 | | 13. 4.49 |
| 218 | Low open goods | BW109 | 1897 | | 6. 4.62 |
| 219 | Low open goods | BW115 | 1897 | | 27. 1.53 |
| 220 | Low open goods | BW213 | 1897 | | 1. 5.70 |
| 221 | Low open goods | BW119 | 1897 | | 5.12.49 |
| 222 | Low open goods | 634062 | 1897 | Reb. as Open goods | 7. 9.46 |
| 223 | Low open goods | BW184 | 1897 | to MW512 10.1.38 | 20. 7.50 |
| 224 | Low open goods | 634063 | 1897 | Reb. as Open goods | 12. 4.47 |
| 225 | Low open goods | 634064 | 1897 | Reb. as Open goods | 9.10.43 |
| 226 | Low open goods | 634065 | 1897 | Reb. as Open goods | 14. 5.38 |

| Met No | Type | LPTB/ LNER No | Built | Builder/Remarks | Scrapped | Met No | Type | LPTB/ LNER No | Built | Builder/Remarks | Scrapped |
|---|---|---|---|---|---|---|---|---|---|---|---|
| 227 | Low open goods | 634192 | 1897 | Reb. to Covered goods 1914 | 4.11.44 | 289 | Low open goods | 634093 | 1897 | Reb. as Open goods. Sold 10.10.42 to ? | |
| 228 | Low open goods | BW246 | 1897 | to MW528 10.1.38 | 8. 7.48 | 290 | Low open goods | 634094 | 1897 | Reb. as Open goods | 17.10.42 |
| 229 | Low open goods | 634066 | 1897 | Reb. as Open goods | 2.11.46 | 291 | Low open goods | BW5 | 1897 | | |
| 230 | Low open goods | 634067 | 1897 | Reb. as Open goods | 27. 6.42 | 292 | Low open goods | 634095 | 1897 | Reb. as Open goods | 19. 8.39 |
| 231 | Low open goods | BW222 | 1897 | | 1. 4.59 | 293 | Low open goods | BW203 | 1897 | to MW531 10.1.38 | |
| 232 | Low open goods | BW110 | 1897 | | 1. 4.59 | 294 | Low open goods | 634196 | 1897 | Reb. Covered goods 1914 | 10. 1.48 |
| 233 | Low open goods | 634068 | 1897 | Reb. as Open goods | 8. 7.39 | | | | | | |
| 234 | Low open goods | BW4 | 1897 | | | 295 | Low open goods | 634096 | 1897 | Reb. as Open goods | 6. 5.44 |
| 235 | Low open goods | BW200 | 1897 | | 4. 7.50 | 296 | Low open goods | 634097 | 1897 | Reb. as Open goods | 12. 6.48 |
| 236 | Low open goods | 634069 | 1897 | Reb. as Open goods | 6.12.47 | 297 | Low open goods | 634098 | 1897 | Reb. as Open goods | 15. 1.38 |
| 237 | Low open goods | 634070 | 1897 | Reb. as Open goods | 11. 5.46 | 298 | Low open goods | BW17 | 1897 | | |
| 238 | Low open goods | 634071 | 1897 | Reb. as Open goods | 20.11.43 | 299 | Low open goods | BW36 | 1897 | | |
| 239 | Low open goods | BW136 | 1897 | | 1. 4.59 | 300 | Low open goods | 634099 | 1897 | Reb. as Open goods | 6. 3.43 |
| 240 | Low open goods | BW236 | 1897 | | 1. 6.53 | | | | | | |
| 241 | Low open goods | BW238 | 1897 | | 6. 4.62 | 301 | Low open goods | 634100 | 1897 | Ashbury. Reb as Open goods | 30. 7.38 |
| 242 | Low open goods | BW124 | 1897 | | 29. 6.48 | | | | | | |
| 243 | Low open goods | 634072 | 1897 | Reb. as Open goods | 23. 3.46 | 302 | Low open goods | 634101 | 1897 | Reb. as Open goods | 6. 4.46 |
| 244 | Low open goods | BW206 | 1897 | | 9.12.52 | 303 | Low open goods | BW155 | 1897 | | 30. 7.62 |
| 245 | Low open goods | BW40 | 1897 | | | 304 | Low open goods | 634102 | 1897 | | 18. 3.44 |
| 246 | Low open goods | BW129 | 1897 | to MW521 10.1.38 | 11. 7.58 | 305 | Low open goods | BW154 | 1897 | | 1. 4.59 |
| 247 | Low open goods | BW165 | 1897 | | 8. 2.51 | 306 | Low open goods | BW214 | 1897 | | 1. 5.70 |
| 248 | Low open goods | BW6 | 1897 | | | 307 | Low open goods | BW23 | 1897 | | |
| 249 | Low open goods | BW250 | 1897 | Destroyed 11.4.41 by enemy action | | 308 | Low open goods | BW231 | 1897 | to MW517 10.1.38 | |
| 250 | Low open goods | BW193 | 1897 | to MW540 27.11.48 | | 309 | Low open goods | BW181 | 1897 | to MW534 10.1.38 | 4.11.52 |
| 251 | Low open goods | BW18 | | | | 310 | Low open goods | 634197 | 1897 | Reb. Covered goods 1914 | 20. 9.47 |
| 252 | Low open goods | 634073 | 1897 | Reb. as Open goods | 21. 7.45 | | | | | | |
| 253 | Low open goods | 634074 | 1897 | Reb. as Open goods. t/f to MoS 13.2.43 | | 311 | Low open goods | 634103 | 1897 | | 13. 4.46 |
| 254 | Low open goods | BW217 | 1897 | | 7. 7.53 | 312 | Low open goods | BW85 | 1900 | Purchased s/h from W. Jones for P. Way | 26.10.56 |
| 255 | Low open goods | 634075 | 1897 | Reb. as Open goods | 15. 1.38 | 313 | Low open goods | BW86 | 1900 | | 1. 5.70 |
| 256 | Low open goods | 634076 | 1897 | Reb. as Open goods | 27.11.43 | 314 | Low open goods | BW104 | 1900 | Reb. 1913 | 24. 1.66 |
| 257 | Low open goods | 634077 | 1897 | Reb. as Open goods. t/f to MoS 31.5.41 | | 315 | Low open goods | BW87 | 1900 | | 26.10.56 |
| 258 | Low open goods | 634078 | 1897 | Reb. as Open goods | 23.12.39 | 316 | Low open goods | BW88 | 1900 | | 20. 4.54 |
| 259 | Low open goods | 634079 | 1897 | Reb. as Open goods. Conv. to Guards truck 962220 19.11.38 | | 317 | Low open goods | BW105 | 1900 | Reb. 1913. to MW514 10.1.38 | 8.11.60 |
| 260 | Low open goods | BW188 | 1897 | | 12. 7.50 | 318 | Low open goods | BW89 | 1900 | to MW525 10.1.38 | 18. 6.48 |
| 261 | Low open goods | 634080 | 1897 | Reb. as Open goods | 17.12.38 | 319 | Low open goods | BW90 | 1900 | | 31. 5.40 |
| 262 | Low open goods | BW212 | 1897 | | 2. 7.52 | 320 | Low open goods | BW91 | 1900 | | 7.10.47 |
| 263 | Low open goods | BW170 | 1897 | | 26.10.56 | 321 | Low open goods | BW92 | 1900 | | 7. 7.53 |
| 264 | Low open goods | BW237 | 1897 | | 5. 1.49 | 322 | Low open goods | BW93 | 1900 | 24.1.66 | |
| 265 | Low open goods | 634081 | 1897 | Reb. as Open goods. to Intl. User Ex 0436 29.11.38 | | 323 | Low open goods | BW94 | 1900 | Destroyed 11.4.41 by enemy action | |
| 266 | Low open goods | 634082 | 1897 | Reb. as Open goods | 2. 5.42 | 324 | Low open goods | BW95 | 1900 | | 6. 8.55 |
| 267 | Low open goods | 634083 | 1897 | Reb. as Open goods | 27. 7.46 | 325 | Low open goods | BW106 | 1900 | Reb. 1913 | 26.10.56 |
| 268 | Low open goods | 634084 | 1897 | Reb. as Open goods | 8.11.44 | 326 | Low open goods | BW96 | 1900 | | 24. 1.66 |
| 269 | Low open goods | BW195 | 1897 | to Open BD704 22.2.46. BW251 | 19. 7.65 | 327 | Low open goods | BW97 | 1900 | | 6. 5.48 |
| 270 | Low open goods | 634085 | 1897 | Reb. as Open goods | 10.50? | 328 | Low open goods | BW98 | 1900 | | 23. 8.55 |
| 271 | Low open goods | 634193 | 1897 | Reb. Covered goods 1914 | 4. 3.48 | 329 | Low open goods | BW99 | 1900 | | 13. 9.54 |
| 272 | Low open goods | 634194 | 1897 | Reb. Covered goods 1914. Body sold 9.4.49 | | 330 | Low open goods | BW100 | 1900 | to MW535 10.1.38, BW265 1.1.44 | |
| 273 | Low open goods | 634086 | 1897 | Reb. as Open goods | 29. 3.47 | 331 | Low open goods | BW101 | 1900 | | 4. 5.50 |
| 274 | Low open goods | BW221 | 1897 | | 6. 4.62 | 332 | Low open goods | BW102 | 1900 | | 14. 7.39 |
| 275 | Low open goods | 634087 | 1897 | Reb. as Open goods | 14. 8.43 | 333 | Low open goods | BW103 | 1900 | | 23. 8.55 |
| 276 | Low open goods | 634088 | 1897 | Reb. as Open goods | 23.11.40 | 334 | Low open goods | 634104 | 1900 | Reb. as Open goods | 14. 8.43 |
| 277 | Low open goods | BW162 | 1897 | to MW516 10.1.38 | 4. 8.55 | 335 | Low open goods | | 1900 | | |
| 278 | Low open goods | BW223 | 1897 | | 6. 8.55 | 336 | Low open goods | 634105 | 1900 | | 9. 7.49 |
| 279 | Low open goods | 634089 | 1897 | Reb. as Open goods | 27. 8.38 | 337 | Low open goods | | 1900 | | |
| 280 | Low open goods | 634195 | 1897 | Reb. Covered goods 1914 | 13. 3.48 | 338 | Low open goods | 634106 | 1900 | Reb. as Open goods | 29. 6.40 |
| 281 | Low open goods | BW173 | 1897 | | 1. 5.70 | 339 | Low open goods | BW22 | 1900 | | |
| 282 | Low open goods | 634090 | 1897 | Reb. as Open goods | 15. 1.38 | 340 | Low open goods | 634107 | 1900 | Reb. as Open goods | 29.10.38 |
| 283 | Low open goods | 624091 | 1897 | Reb. as Open goods | 13. 8.38 | 341 | Low open goods | BW151 | 1900 | | 7. 7.53 |
| 284 | Low open goods | BW245 | 1897 | | | 342 | Low open goods | BW241 | 1900 | | 24. 1.66 |
| 285 | Low open goods | BW163 | 1897 | to MW526 10.1.38 | 8.11.60 | 343 | Low open goods | | 1900 | | |
| 286 | Low open goods | BW144 | 1897 | | 10. 2.50 | 344 | Low open goods | BW208 | 1900 | Destroyed 11.4.41 by enemy action | |
| 287 | Low open goods | 634092 | 1897 | Reb. as Open goods | 29. 7.44 | 345 | Low open goods | 634108 | 1900 | Reb. as Open goods | 28. 1.50 |
| 288 | Low open goods | BW121 | 1897 | | 26.10.56 | 346 | Low open goods | 634109 | 1900 | Reb. as Open goods | 29. 5.48 |
| | | | | | | 347 | Low open goods | 634110 | 1900 | Reb. as Open goods | 27. 2.43 |
| | | | | | | 348 | Low open goods | 634111 | 1900 | Reb. as Open goods | 24. 3.45 |
| | | | | | | 349 | Low open goods | 634112 | 1900 | Reb. as Open goods | 23.10.43 |
| | | | | | | 350 | Low open goods | BW205 | 1900 | to MW539 10.1.38 | 16.12.69 |
| | | | | | | 351 | Low open goods | BW204 | 1900 | to MW510 10.1.38 ren. MW543 | |

| Met No | Type | LPTB/LNER No | Built | Builder/Remarks | Scrapped |
|---|---|---|---|---|---|
| 352 | Low open goods | BW187 | 1900 | to MW527 10.1.38 | |
| 353 | Low open goods | 634113 | 1900 | | 12. 6.48 |
| 354 | Low open goods | 634114 | 1900 | | 12. 6.43 |
| 355 | Low open goods | BW123 | 1900 | to MW541 27.11.48 | |
| 356 | Low open goods | 634115 | 1900 | | 19. 8.39 |
| 357 | Low open goods | 634116 | 1900 | to MoS 6.5.43 | |
| 358 | Low open goods | A951 | 1902 | Reb. as Open goods | 19.11.68 |
| 359 | Low open goods | 634117 | 1900 | | 5. 1.46 |
| 360 | Low open goods | BW134 | 1900 | | 12. 3.48 |
| 361 | Low open goods | BW118 | 1900 | | 11. 2.52 |
| 362 | Low open goods | SL915 | 1902 | Reb. as Open goods | 6. 8.55 |
| 363 | Low open goods | BW174 | 1900 | | 23. 8.55 |
| 364 | Low open goods | 634118 | 1900 | | 23.12.39 |
| 365 | Low open goods | BW258 | 1900 | Reb. as Open goods | 6. 4.62 |
| 366 | Low open goods | SL908 | 1902 | Reb. as Open goods | 6. 4.62 |
| 367 | Low open goods | BW192 | 1900 | to MW520 10.1.38 | 4. 7.50 |
| 368 | Low open goods | SL904 | 1902 | Reb. as Open goods | 6. 4.62 |
| 369 | Low open goods | 634119 | 1900 | | 5. 2.38 |
| 370 | Low open goods | 634120 | 1900 | Reb. as Open goods | 6. 8.55 |
| 371 | Low open goods | 634120 | 1900 | to Intl. Use Immingham 010376 | |
| 372 | Low open goods | 634121 | 1900 | | |
| 373 | Low open goods | 634122 | 1900 | Sold 22.12.45 | |
| 374 | Low open goods | 634123 | 1900 | | 13. 3.48 |
| 375 | Low open goods | BW27 | 1900 | | |
| 376 | Low open goods | SL919 | 1902 | Reb. as Open goods | 27. 2.64 |
| 377 | Low open goods | SL926 | 1902 | Reb. as Open goods | 27. 2.64 |
| 378 | Low open goods | A952 | 1902 | Reb. as Open goods | 19.11.68 |
| 379 | Low open goods | 634124 | 1902 | | 5. 8.39 |
| 380 | Low open goods | BW183 | 1900 | | 26.10.56 |
| 381 | Low open goods | BW146 | 1900 | | 24. 1.66 |
| 382 | Low open goods | BW120 | 1900 | | 26.10.56 |
| 383 | Low open goods | BW114 | 1900 | | 6. 8.47 |
| 384 | Low open goods | 634125 | 1900 | | 2.56 |
| 385 | Low open goods | SL913 | 1902 | Reb. as Open goods | 4. 4.52 |
| 386 | Low open goods | BW259 | 1902 | Orig. 1896? | 1. 5.70 |
| 387 | Low open goods | 634126 | 1900 | Reb. as Open goods | 28. 8.43 |
| 388 | Low open goods | SL912 | 1902 | Reb. as Open goods | 27. 2.64 |
| 389 | Low open goods | BW229 | 1902 | Harrison & Camm | 20. 7.50 |
| 390 | Low open goods | 634129 | 1902 | | 15. 7.39 |
| 391 | Low open goods | 634127 | 1902 | | 23.11.46 |
| 392 | Low open goods | BW220 | 1902 | | 6. 8.55 |
| 393 | Low open goods | 634128 | 1902 | to MoS Derby 12.10.40 | |
| 394 | Low open goods | | 1902 | | |
| 395 | Low open goods | BW131 | 1902 | 1.5.70 | |
| 396 | Low open goods | BW160 | 1902 | | 6. 4.62 |
| 397 | Low open goods | BW150 | 1902 | | 16.12.52 |
| 398 | Low open goods | SC631 | 1902 | Stores wagon SC631 | 11. 7.58 |
| 399 | Low open goods | BW116 | 1902 | | 6. 4.62 |
| 400 | Low open goods | BW219 | 1902 | to MW529 10.1.38 | 16.12.69 |
| 401 | Low open goods | BW207 | 1902 | | 28. 1.48 |
| 402 | Low open goods | BW133 | 1902 | | 1. 6.53 |
| 403 | Low open goods | BW218 | 1902 | | 26.10.58 |
| 404 | Low open goods | 634130 | 1902 | to Crane runner 962215 22.4.44 | 9.59 |
| 405 | Low open goods | 634131 | 1902 | to Intl. Use Immingham 010224 10.11.45 | |
| 406 | Low open goods | BW158 | 1902 | to MW538 6.3.48 | 8.11.60 |
| 407 | Low open goods | BW226 | 1902 | | 13. 1.53 |
| 408 | Low open goods | BW117 | 1902 | | 1. 7.62 |
| 409 | Low open goods | 634132 | 1902 | | 13. 9.41 |
| 410 | Low open goods | BW227 | 1902 | | 13. 1.53 |
| 411 | Low open goods | 634133 | 1902 | | 1. 8.42 |
| 412 | Low open goods | BW113 | 1902 | | 24. 1.66 |
| 413 | Low open goods | 634134 | 1902 | | 18. 8.45 |
| 414 | Low open goods | 634135 | 1902 | | 24. 9.38 |
| 415 | Low open goods | 634136 | 1902 | | 18.12.48 |
| 416 | Low open goods | BW137 | 1902 | to MW537 21.3.46 | 16.12.69 |
| 417 | Low open goods | BW211 | 1902 | | 6. 8.55 |
| 418 | Low open goods | 634137 | 1902 | to MoS 29.3.41 | |
| 419 | Open goods | SL923 | 1902 | Harrison & Camm | 6. 8.55 |
| 420 | Open goods | SL963 | 1902 | Destroyed by enemy action 29.9.40 | |
| 421 | Open goods | SL922 | 1902 | | 6. 8.55 |
| 422 | Open goods | SL928 | 1902 | | 6. 8.55 |
| 423 | Open goods | SL929 | 1902 | ren. SL905 | 19.11.68 |
| 424 | Open goods | SL962 | 1902 | | 6. 8.55 |
| 425 | Open goods | SL916 | 1902 | | 6. 4.62 |
| 426 | Open goods | A942 | 1902 | | 14. 3.68 |
| 427 | Open goods | SL901 | 1904 | ren. SL921 | |
| 428 | Open goods | SL964 | 1902 | | 6. 8.55 |
| 429 | Open goods | SL910 | 1904 | | 6. 8.55 |
| 430 | Open goods | SL906 | 1904 | | 6. 8.55 |
| 431 | Open goods | SL970 | 1904 | | 6. 8.55 |
| 432 | Open goods | BW260 | 1904 | | 19. 9.55 |
| 433 | Open goods | A960 | 1904 | | 14. 3.68 |
| 434 | Open goods | SL921 | 1904 | ren. SL901 | 19.11.68 |
| 435 | Open goods | SL935 | 1904 | | 27. 2.64 |
| 436 | Open goods | SL902 | 1904 | | 6. 8.55 |
| 437 | Open goods | SL907 | 1904 | | 6. 8.55 |
| 438 | Open goods | A948 | 1904 | | 19.11.68 |
| 439 | Machinery | 634249 | 1903 | S J Claye | 21.10.39 |
| 440 | Machinery | 634250 | 1903 | | 8. 1.38 |
| 441 | Machinery | 634251 | 1903 | | 19. 8.39 |
| 442 | Covered goods | 634198 | 1903 | Ashbury | 20. 2.43 |
| 443 | Covered goods | 634199 | 1903 | | 18. 9.43 |
| 444 | Covered goods | 634200 | 1903 | | 30. 4.38 |
| 445 | Covered goods | 634201 | 1903 | | 27. 9.47 |
| 446 | Covered goods | 634202 | 1903 | t/f Goods Manager, Loughborough, 31.1.42 | |
| 447 | Covered goods | 634203 | 1903 | Scrapped following enemy action | 8. 3.41 |
| 448 | Covered goods | 634204 | 1903 | Scrapped following e/a at Norwich Thorpe | 10.42 |
| 449 | Covered goods | 634205 | 1903 | | 15.11.41 |
| 450 | Covered goods | 634206 | 1903 | | 22. 8.46 |
| 451 | Covered goods | 634207 | 1903 | Sold 15.5.48 | |
| 452 | Covered goods | 634208 | 1903 | | 9.10.43 |
| 453 | Covered goods | 634209 | 1903 | Sold 21.9.46 | |
| 454 | Low open goods | BW168 | 1904 | Metropolitan C&W. to MW536 10.1.38. BW266 1.1.44 | |
| 455 | Low open goods | 634138 | 1904 | Reb. as Open goods. Sold 17.8.46 | |
| 456 | Low open goods | BW186 | 1904 | | 7.10.53 |
| 457 | Low open goods | BW177 | 1904 | to MW530 10.1.38 | 21.10.52 |
| 458 | Low open goods | 634139 | 1904 | Reb. as Open goods | 15.10.38 |
| 459 | Low open goods | 634140 | 1904 | Reb. as Open goods | 23. 2.46 |
| 460 | Low open goods | 634141 | 1904 | Reb. as Open goods | 23. 1.43 |
| 461 | Low open goods | BW140 | 1904 | | 10.12.47 |
| 462 | Low open goods | BW149 | 1904 | to MW509 10.1.38 | 7. 5.48 |
| 463 | Low open goods | 634142 | 1904 | Reb. as Open goods | 12. 6.48 |
| 464 | Low open goods | 634143 | 1904 | Reb. as Open goods | 30. 9.39 |
| 465 | Low open goods | BW171 | 1904 | | 15. 9.55 |
| 466 | Low open goods | MW506 | 1904 | To Match wagon by Met. to BW264 7.3.41 | |
| 467 | Low open goods | 634144 | 1904 | Reb. as Open goods | 26.10.46 |
| 468 | Low open goods | 634145 | 1904 | Reb. as Open goods | 5. 2.38 |
| 489 | Low open goods | BW202 | 1904 | | 26.10.56 |
| 470 | Low open goods | 634146 | 1904 | Reb. as Open goods | 30. 3.46 |
| 471 | Low open goods | BW189 | 1904 | | 11.12.52 |
| 472 | Low open goods | BW157 | 1904 | to MW533 10.1.38 | 21.10.52 |
| 473 | Low open goods | BW156 | 1904 | | 26.10.56 |
| 474 | Low open goods | 634147 | 1904 | Reb. as Open goods. to MoS 15.2.41 | |
| 475 | Low open goods | BW225 | 1904 | | 3. 2.48 |
| 476 | Low open goods | BW132 | 1904 | | 6. 4.62 |
| 477 | Low open goods | BW176 | 1904 | | 16.12.52 |
| 478 | Low open goods | BW26 | 1904 | | |
| 479 | Low open goods | BW135 | 1904 | | 26.10.56 |
| 480 | Low open goods | 634148 | 1904 | Reb. as Open goods | 27. 8.38 |
| 481 | Low open goods | 634149 | 1904 | Reb. as Open goods | 17.12.38 |
| 482 | Low open goods | 634150 | 1904 | Reb. as Open goods | 2. 9.39 |
| 483 | Low open goods | 634151 | 1904 | Reb. as Open goods | 10. 2.45 |
| 484 | Low open goods | BW20 | 1904 | | |
| 485 | Low open goods | 634152 | 1904 | Reb. as Open goods | 17. 7.43 |
| 486 | Low open goods | 634153 | 1904 | Reb. as Open goods. to MoS 30.8.41 | |

| Met No | Type | LPTB/LNER No | Built | Builder/Remarks | Scrapped |
|---|---|---|---|---|---|
| 487 | Low open goods | 634154 | 1904 | Reb. as Open goods | 29.11.47 |
| 488 | Low open goods | 634155 | 1904 | Reb. as Open goods | 8. 1.38 |
| 489 | Low open goods | BW166 | 1904 | | 5.11.47 |
| 490 | Low open goods | BW108 | 1904 | to TLC1 8.6.48 | |
| 491 | Low open goods | BW201 | 1904 | to MW519 10.1.38 | 4. 8.55 |
| 492 | Low open goods | BW34 | 1904 | | |
| 493 | Low open goods | 634156 | 1904 | Reb. as Open goods | 24. 4.48 |
| 494 | Low open goods | 634157 | 1904 | Reb. as Open goods | 28. 5.38 |
| 495 | Low open goods | 634158 | 1904 | Reb. as Open goods | 22. 7.39 |
| 496 | Low open goods | BW190 | 1904 | | 23. 8.55 |
| 497 | Low open goods | BW167 | 1904 | | 1. 7.62 |
| 498 | Low open goods | 634159 | 1904 | Reb. as Open goods | 1. 1.44 |
| 499 | Low open goods | 634160 | 1904 | Reb. as Open goods. Sold 17.11.45 | |
| 500 | Low open goods | 634161 | 1904 | Reb. as Open goods | 21. 8.43 |
| 501 | Low open goods | BW143 | 1904 | | 6. 4.62 |
| 502 | Low open goods | 634162 | 1904 | Reb. as Open goods | 7.10.44 |
| 503 | Low open goods | 634163 | 1904 | Reb. as Open goods. to Intl. Use Lowestoft Ex 0356 27.1.140 | |
| 504 | Low open goods | 634164 | 1904 | Reb. as Open goods. to Intl. Use Ex 0442 17.1.42 | |
| 505 | Low open goods | | 1904 | Reb. as Open goods | |
| 506 | Low open goods | 634165 | 1904 | Reb. as Open goods | 4. 6.38 |
| 507 | Low open goods | 634166 | 1904 | Reb. as Open goods | 1. 8.42 |
| 508 | Low open goods | 634167 | 1904 | Reb. as Open goods | 8. 1.38 |
| 509 | Low open goods | BW39 | 1904 | | |
| 510 | Low open goods | 634168 | 1904 | Reb. as Open goods | 4. 5.46 |
| 511 | Low open goods | 634169 | 1904 | Reb. as Open goods | 18. 1.47 |
| 512 | Low open goods | 634170 | 1904 | Reb. as Open goods | 21. 1.39 |
| 513 | Low open goods | BW233 | 1904 | | 23. 9.49 |
| 514 | Low open goods | 634171 | 1904 | Reb. as Open goods | 4. 2.39 |
| 515 | Low open goods | BW37 | 1904 | | |
| 516 | Low open goods | BW198 | 1904 | | 24. 1.66 |
| 517 | Low open goods | 634172 | 1904 | Reb. as Open goods | 13. 4.46 |
| 518 | Low open goods | 634173 | 1904 | Reb. as Open goods | 30.10.48 |
| 519 | Low open goods | 634174 | 1904 | Reb. as Open goods. to Intl. Use Ex 0361 6.4.40 | |
| 520 | Low open goods | BW138 | 1904 | | 8. 8.55 |
| 521 | Low open goods | 634175 | 1904 | | 21. 1.39 |
| 522 | Low open goods | BW33 | 1904 | | |
| 523 | Low open goods | 634176 | 1904 | Reb. as Open goods? to Crane runner 962224 1.8.42 | 11.56 |
| 524 | Low open goods | BW199 | 1904 | | 24. 1.66 |
| 525 | Low open goods | 634177 | 1904 | Reb. as Open goods | 29. 4.44 |
| 526 | Low open goods | BW232 | 1904 | | 6. 4.62 |
| 527 | Low open goods | 634178 | 1904 | Reb. as Open goods | 9. 3.46 |
| 528 | Low open goods | 634179 | 1904 | Reb. as Open goods. to MoS 23.11.40 | |
| 529 | Low open goods | 634180 | 1904 | Reb. as Open goods | 9.10.48 |
| 530 | Low open goods | | 1904 | Reb. as Open goods | |
| 531 | Low open goods | 634181 | 1904 | Reb. as Open goods. to Int. Use Immingham 010332 8.12.45 | |
| 532 | Low open goods | BW194 | 1904 | | 9. 9.55 |
| 533 | Low open goods | 634182 | 1904 | Reb. as Open goods | 3. 6.39 |
| 534 | Open goods | BW261 | 1904 | Metropolitan RCW | 6. 4.62 |
| 535 | Open goods | A941 | 1904 | | 19.11.68 |
| 536 | Open goods | A947 | 1904 | | 19.11.68 |
| 537 | Open goods | SL930 | 1904 | | |
| 538 | Open goods | SL965 | 1904 | | 27. 2.64 |
| 539 | Open goods | SL936 | 1904 | | 14. 3.68 |
| 540 | Open goods | SL918 | 1904 | | 16.10.50 |
| 541 | Open goods | SL933 | 1904 | | 27. 2.64 |
| 542 | Open goods | A945 | 1911 | | |
| 543 | Open goods | A955 | 1912 | | 19.11.68 |
| 544 | Open goods | A953 | 1912 | | 19.11.68 |
| 545 | Open goods | SL934 | 1912 | | 27. 2.64 |
| 546 | Open goods | SL946 | 1912 | | 14. 3.68 |
| 547 | Open goods | SL967 | 1912 | | 27. 2.64 |
| 548 | Open goods | SL903 | 1912 | | 27. 2.64 |
| 549 | Open goods | SL927 | 1912 | | 27. 2.64 |
| 550 | Open goods | SL966 | 1912 | | 19.11.68 |
| 551 | Open goods | SL930 | 1902 | | 19.11.68 |
| 552 | Open goods | SL968 | 1912 | | 27. 2.64 |
| 553 | Open goods | BW262 | 1912 | orig. 1896? | 1. 5.70 |
| 554 | Covered goods | 634210 | 1904 | Metropolitan C&W | 28. 1.50 |
| 555 | Covered goods | 634211 | 1904 | | |
| 556 | Covered goods | 634212 | 1904 | | 11.51 |
| 557 | Covered goods | 634213 | 1904 | | 4. 9.43 |
| 558 | Covered goods | 634214 | 1904 | | 8.12.45 |
| 559 | Covered goods | 634215 | 1904 | | 23.10.48 |
| 560 | Low open goods | BW122 | 1904 | | 1. 7.62 |
| 561 | Low open goods | BW153 | 1904 | | 24. 1.66 |
| 562 | Low open goods | 634183 | 1904 | | 4.11.39 |
| 563 | Low open goods | BW111 | 1904 | | 8. 8.55 |
| 564 | Low open goods | BW141 | 1904 | | 24. 1.66 |
| 565 | Low open goods | BW145 | 1904 | | 24. 1.66 |
| 566 | Low open goods | BW10 | 1904 | | |
| 567 | Low open goods | BW249 | 1904 | | 1. 5.70 |
| 568 | Low open goods | 634184 | 1904 | | 14.10.44 |
| 569 | Low open goods | 634185 | 1904 | | 17. 8.46 |
| 570 | Low open goods | BW107 | 1904 | | 6. 4.62 |
| 571 | Covered goods | 634216 | 1913 | Reb. by Met. from 22ft Rail wagons | 4. 1.47 |
| 572 | Covered goods | 634217 | 1913 | | 31. 8.46 |
| 573 | Covered goods | 634218 | 1913 | | 10.50 |
| 574 | Covered goods | 634219 | 1913 | | 7. 2.48 |
| 575 | Covered goods | 634220 | 1914 | w/d 4.7.42 for Home Guard Use, Shenfield Sold 18.1.47 | |
| 576 | Covered goods | 634221 | 1914 | | |
| 577 | Covered goods | 634222 | 1914 | | 8.54 |
| 578 | Covered goods | 634223 | 1914 | | 1.52 |
| 579 | Covered goods | 634224 | 1914 | Reb. by Met from Short Timber Wagons | 8. 9.45 |
| 580 | Covered goods | 634225 | 1914 | | 31. 7.48 |
| 581 | Covered goods | 634226 | 1914 | | 26. 2.49 |
| 582 | Covered goods | 634227 | 1914 | | 17.12.55 |
| 583 | Covered goods | 634228 | 1914 | | 2. 2.46 |
| 584 | Covered goods | 634229 | 1914 | Sold to Dist. Loco S'int'd't, Gidea Park 5.7.41 | |

## BRAKE VAN SERIES

| Met No | Type | LPTB/LNER No | Built | Builder/Remarks | Scrapped |
|---|---|---|---|---|---|
| 1 | 10T Goods | B561 | 1868 | | 1. 7.62 |
| 2 | | | 1869 | | |
| 3 | | | 1870 | Sold to Bute Works Supply Co. 7.07 | |
| 4 | | B551 | 1872 | | 29. 5.50 |
| 5 | | B552 | 1888 | | 3.11.69 |
| 6 | | | 1890 | Sold to Bute Works Supply Co. 7.07 | |
| 7 | 10T Goods | 634252 | 1893 | Ashbury | 22.12.45 |
| 8 | | B562 | | | |
| 9 | | | | | |
| 10 | | | | | |
| 11 | 10T Goods | 634253 | 1894 | Cravens. t/f to Engrs. use 16.4.38 | |
| 12 | | B564 | | | 3.11.69 |
| 13 | | B565 | | | 1. 7.62 |
| 14 | 10T Goods | B563 | 1895 | Cravens | 28. 3.61 |
| 15 | | B567 | | | 14. 3.68 |
| 16 | | B566 | | | 14. 3.68 |
| 17 | | B569 | | | 28. 3.61 |
| 18 | | 634254 | | t/f to Engrs. use 16.4.38 | 5.58 |

| Met No | Type | LPTB/LNER No | Built | Builder/Remarks | Scrapped |
|---|---|---|---|---|---|
| 19 | | 634255 | | t/f to Engrs. use 16.4.38 | 2.61 |
| 20 | 10T Goods | B572 | 1896 | Cravens | 14. 3.68 |
| 21 | | B573 | | | 28. 3.61 |
| 22 | | B574 | | | 10. 1.52 |
| 23 | | B575 | | | 3.11.69 |
| 24 | 10T Ballast | B553 | 1914 | Reb. from 22ft Rail wagons | 3.11.69 |
| 25 | | B554 | | | 3.11.69 |
| 26 | 20T Goods | 634256 | 1921 | LSWR design ex-WD surplus 1918 | 4.10.47 |
| 27 | | 634257 | | | |
| 28 | | 634258 | | to Stores Wagon at Ipswich 8.5.48 | 13.12.47 |
| 29 | | 634259 | | Sold 6.50 | |
| 30 | | 634260 | | | 29. 9.45 |
| 31 | | 634261 | | | 22.10.49 |
| 32 | | 634262 | 1926 | Met? Modified copy of WD design | 30.11.46 |
| 33 | | 634263 | | | 27. 5.50 |
| 34 | | 634264 | | | 23. 8.47 |

## RAIL & TIMBER WAGONS
### (Twin single bolster)

Original series (conjectural)

| Met Nos. | Type |
|---|---|
| 1–6 | 14'6" Timber |
| 7–14 | 22' Rail Reb. as Covered goods (long) |
| 15–20 | 22' Rail Reb. as Cattle wagon |
| 21–22 | 22' Rail Reb. as Ballast Brake Van |
| 23–26 | 22' Rail Transferred to LNER |
| 27–28 | 22' Rail Transferred to LPTB as RW450 A & B |

## RENUMBERED SERIES

| Met No. | LPTB/LNER No. | Scrapped |
|---|---|---|
| 1 | to RW450A | to Crane runner J686 |
| 2 | 634245 | 8.10.49 |
| 3 | to RW450B | to Crane runner J687 |
| 4 | 634246 | 12.8.39 |
| 5 | 634247 | 23.4.48 |
| 6 | 634248 | 8.12.45 |

## CATTLE TRUCK SERIES

| Met No. | LNER No. | Built | Builder/Remarks | Scrapped |
|---|---|---|---|---|
| 1 | | | | |
| 2 | 634230 | 1894 | Cravens | 18. 6.49 |
| 3 | | | | 10. 5.47 |
| 4 | 634232 | | | 7. 9.46 |
| 5 | 634233 | | | 11. 1.47 |
| 6 | 634234 | | | 18.12.48 |
| 7 | 634235 | 1902 | S J Claye | 17. 5.41 |
| 8 | 634236 | | | 23.12.39 |
| 9 | 634237 | | | 7. 2.42 |
| 10 | 634238 | | | 15.11.41 |
| 11 | | | | .21 |
| 12 | 634239 | 1912 | Reb. from 22ft Rail wagons | 8. 4.44 |
| 13 | 634240 | | | 9.54 |
| 14 | 634241 | | | 17. 4.48 |
| 15 | 634242 | | | 8. 2.47 |
| 16 | 634243 | | | 11. 5.46 |
| 17 | 634244 | | | 24.12.38 |
| 18 | | | | .21 |

## PASSENGER BRAKE VANS

| Met No. | Built | LPTB No. | Scrapped |
|---|---|---|---|
| 1 | 1899 | | 2.36 |
| 2 | 1899 | | 2.36 |
| 3 | 1900 | | 2.36 |
| 4 | 1901 | | 2.36 |
| 5 | 1901 | B576 | 29.11.39 |
| 6 | 1901 | B577 | 4. 7.58 |

## MILK VANS

| Met No. | Built | LPTB No. | Builder | Scrapped |
|---|---|---|---|---|
| 1 | 1896 | | Birmingham C&W | 12. 2.36 |
| 2 | 1896 | | | 9. 4.36 |
| 3 | 1896 | BDV700 | | |
| 4 | 1897 | | | 7. 2.36 |
| 5 | 1903 | BDV701 | Met Rly | 21. 6.44 |
| 6 | 1903 | SC632 | | 11. 7.58 |

## CARRIAGE TRUCK SERIES

| Met No. | Type | Built | Builder | Scrapped |
|---|---|---|---|---|
| 1 | Open CT | 1896 | Birmingham C&W | .29 |
| 2 | Open CT | 1896 | Birmingham C&W | .29 |
| 3 | Covered CT | 1903 | Ashbury. Reb. by LPTB as 7T Flat F126 | 15. 6.40 |
| 4 | Covered CT | 1903 | Ashbury | .29 |

## HORSE-BOXES

| Met No. | Built | Builder | Scrapped |
|---|---|---|---|
| 1 | 1892 | Met Rly, Neasden | 1.38 |
| 2 | 1892 | Met Rly, Neasden | 1.38 |
| 3 | 1892 | Met Rly, Neasden | 1.38 |
| 4 | 1898 | Met Rly, Neasden | 1.38 |
| 5 | 1898 | Met Rly, Neasden | 1.38 |
| 6 | 1898 | Met Rly, Neasden | 1.38 |
| 7 | 1898 | Met Rly, Neasden | 1.38 |
| 8 | 1904 | G R Turner | c.25 |
| 9 | 1904 | G R Turner | Sold 1914 to Brecon & Merthyr Rly. Scrapped by GWR | c.25 |
| 10 | 1904 | G R Turner | 1.38 |

## SERVICE STOCK FLEET

| | | | | |
|---|---|---|---|---|
| 1 | 1899 | BDV702 | 4-wheel Tool Van for Breakdown train | |
| 2 | 1910 | BDV703 | 8-wheel Tool Van for Breakdown train | |
| 3 | | BDV704 | Low side open for Breakdown train | |
| 4 | | | | |
| 5 | | | | |
| 6 | 1919 | TV750 | Weighing m/c workshop van | 12. 1.43 |
| 7 | 1919 | TV751 | Weighing m/c workshop van | 5. 6.44 |
| 8 | | MW507 | Match wagon | |
| 9 | | MW508 | Match wagon | |
| 10 | | | | |
| 11 | | | | |
| 12 | | CE740 | Coal elevator wagon | 5. 3.42 |
| 13 | | CE741 | Coal elevator wagon | 5. 3.42 |
| 14 | 1919 | J683 | Jib wagon for 30T Breakdown Crane | 1. 6.65 |

## ACKNOWLEDGEMENTS

I would like to acknowledge the valuable and enthusiastic help given me by the late Alan Cruikshank, both for allowing me access to his photographic collection and for reviewing the text, as well as the efforts of Ken Benest, without whose notes on the earlier rolling stock I would not have got started, and the late Robin Greenaway, for access to the LURS photographic archives. Lastly, and by no means least, to Paul Karau and his colleagues at Wild Swan for giving me the inspirational support to carry through what seemed to be a never-ending task.

*As time progressed, the ex War Department Goods Brakes were progressively modified by Neasden, the final version being seen here, on 13th December 1947, minus lookouts and side doors.*
ALAN CRUIKSHANK COLLECTION